Exam Ref 70-346 Managing Office 365 Identities and Requirements

Orin Thomas

PUBLISHED BY
Microsoft Press
A Division of Microsoft Corporation
One Microsoft Way
Redmond, Washington 98052-6399

Library of Congress Control Number: 2015936024
ISBN: 978-1-5093-0066-2

Printed and bound in the United States of America.

Second Printing

Microsoft Press books are available through booksellers and distributors worldwide. If you need support related to this book, email Microsoft Press Book Support at mspinput@microsoft.com. Please tell us what you think of this book at http://aka.ms/tellpress.

This book is provided "as-is" and expresses the author's views and opinions. The views, opinions and information expressed in this book, including URL and other Internet Web site references, may change without notice.

Some examples depicted herein are provided for illustration only and are fictitious. No real association or connection is intended or should be inferred.

Microsoft and the trademarks listed at http://www.microsoft.com on the "Trademarks" Web page are trademarks of the Microsoft group of companies. All other marks are property of their respective owners.

Acquisitions Editor: Karen Szall
Developmental Editor: Karen Szall
Editorial Production: Troy Mott, Ellie Volckhausen
Technical Reviewers: Mike Toot; Technical Review services provided by Content Master, a member of CM Group, Ltd.
Copyeditor: Eryn Leavens and Christopher Friedman
Indexer: Julie Grady
Cover: Twist Creative • Seattle

Contents

What do you think of this book? We want to hear from you!

Microsoft is interested in hearing your feedback so we can continually improve our books and learning resources for you. To participate in a brief online survey, please visit:

www.microsoft.com/learning/booksurvey/

What do you think of this book? We want to hear from you!

Microsoft is interested in hearing your feedback so we can continually improve our
books and learning resources for you. To participate in a brief online survey, please visit:

www.microsoft.com/learning/booksurvey/

Introduction

The 70-346 exam deals with advanced topics that require candidates to have an excellent working knowledge of both Office 365 and Windows Server. Some of the exam comprises topics that even experienced Office 365 and Windows Server administrators may rarely encounter, unless they are consultants who deploy new Office 365 tenancies on a regular basis. To be successful in taking this exam, candidates not only need to understand how to deploy and manage Office 365, they need to understand how to integrate Office 365 with an on-premises Active Directory environment.

Candidates for this exam are Information Technology (IT) Professionals who want to validate their advanced Office 365 and Windows Server management skills, configuration skills, and knowledge. To pass this exam, candidates require a strong understanding of how to provision Office 365, plan and implement networking and security in Office 365, manage cloud identities, configure and manage identity synchronization between on-premises and cloud Active Directory instances, implement and manage federated identities, as well as have the ability to monitor and troubleshoot Office 365 availability and usage. To pass, candidates require a thorough theoretical understanding as well as meaningful practical experience implementing the technologies involved.

This book covers every exam objective, but it does not cover every exam question. Only the Microsoft exam team has access to the exam questions themselves and Microsoft regularly adds new questions to the exam, making it impossible to cover specific questions. You should consider this book a supplement to your relevant real-world experience and other study materials. If you encounter a topic in this book that you do not feel completely comfortable with, use the links you'll find in text to find more information and take the time to research and study the topic. Great information is available on TechNet, through MVA courses, and in blogs and forums.

Microsoft certifications

Microsoft certifications distinguish you by proving your command of a broad set of skills and experience with current Microsoft products and technologies. The exams and corresponding certifications are developed to validate your mastery of critical competencies as you design and develop, or implement and support, solutions with Microsoft products and technologies both on-premises and in the cloud. Certification brings a variety of benefits to the individual and to employers and organizations.

MORE INFO   ALL MICROSOFT CERTIFICATIONS

For information about Microsoft certifications, including a full list of available certifications, go to *http://www.microsoft.com/learning/en/us/certification/cert-default.aspx*.

Free ebooks from Microsoft Press

From technical overviews to in-depth information on special topics, the free ebooks from Microsoft Press cover a wide range of topics. These ebooks are available in PDF, EPUB, and Mobi for Kindle formats, ready for you to download at:

http://aka.ms/mspressfree

Check back often to see what is new!

Errata, updates, & book support

We've made every effort to ensure the accuracy of this book and its companion content. You can access updates to this book—in the form of a list of submitted errata and their related corrections—at:

http://aka.ms/ER346/errata

If you discover an error that is not already listed, please submit it to us at the same page.

If you need additional support, email Microsoft Press Book Support at *mspinput@microsoft.com*.

Please note that product support for Microsoft software and hardware is not offered through the previous addresses. For help with Microsoft software or hardware, go to *http://support.microsoft.com*.

We want to hear from you

At Microsoft Press, your satisfaction is our top priority, and your feedback our most valuable asset. Please tell us what you think of this book at:

http://aka.ms/tellpress

The survey is short, and we read every one of your comments and ideas. Thanks in advance for your input!

Stay in touch

Let's keep the conversation going! We're on Twitter: *http://twitter.com/MicrosoftPress*.

Preparing for the exam

Microsoft certification exams are a great way to build your resume and let the world know about your level of expertise. Certification exams validate your on-the-job experience and product knowledge. Although there is no substitute for on-the-job experience, preparation through study and hands-on practice can help you prepare for the exam. We recommend that you augment your exam preparation plan by using a combination of available study materials and courses. For example, you might use the Exam ref and another study guide for your "at home" preparation, and take a Microsoft Official Curriculum course for the classroom experience. Choose the combination that you think works best for you.

Note that this Exam Ref is based on publicly available information about the exam and the author's experience. To safeguard the integrity of the exam, authors do not have access to the live exam.

CHAPTER 1

Provision Office 365

Setting up an Office 365 tenancy is straightforward as long as you have a good understanding of what you need to have ready before you provision the tenancy, and what steps you need to take immediately after you provision the tenancy so that you can start seamlessly moving workloads into the cloud.

> **IMPORTANT**
> **Have you read page xv?**
> It contains valuable information regarding the skills you need to pass the exam.

Objectives in this chapter:

- Objective 1.1: Provision tenants
- Objective 1.2: Add and configure custom domains
- Objective 1.3: Plan a pilot

Objective 1.1: Provision tenants

This objective deals with the basic process of setting up an Office 365 tenancy. To master this objective you'll need to understand some of the prerequisites, such as what you'll need to think about before signing up for an Office 365 subscription, what an Office 365 tenant name is, what the different administrator roles are, and what to manage regarding tenant subscriptions and licensing.

> **This objective covers the following topics:**
> - Set up an Office 365 trial
> - Configure the tenant name
> - Tenant region
> - Administrator roles
> - Manage tenant subscriptions and licensing

Setting up an Office 365 trial

To set up an Office 365 trial, you need to have access to the following things:

- **An email account that will be associated with the trial** You should sign up for a brand-new email account that you will use only with the trial. To ensure that the email account remains secure, you should also configure this account to use two-factor authentication. Outlook.com email accounts support two-factor authentication, including text-messages and time-based codes generated by apps that are downloadable from each mobile operating system vendor's app store. You should avoid associating a subscription, even a trial subscription, with a personal email account because trial subscriptions can eventually become ongoing corporate subscriptions.

- **A mobile device that can receive SMS messages** This device will be used to verify your identity.

Once you have the prerequisite elements to set up an Office 365 enterprise trial, perform the following steps:

1. Navigate to *https://products.office.com/en-us/business/office-365-enterprise-e3-business-software* and click Free Trial.

2. On the Welcome page, shown in Figure 1-1 (be aware that Office 365 screens are liable to change as the product evolves), provide the following information and click Next:

   - **Region** Note that you will be unable to change the region associated with the subscription after signup. This should be the geographical region in which the organization for which you are creating the subscription is based. For example, if you were in Hobart, in the state of Tasmania, Australia, you would choose Australia.

   - **First name** Input your first name.

   - **Last name** Input your last name.

   - **Business email address** Input the email address to be associated with the subscription. This should not be a personal account, but should be a secure account created expressly for the purpose of being associated with the subscription. This account will be used if you need to recover the tenancy's global administrator account password. Because the global administrator is able to take any action, you want to ensure that the account that the recovery password can be sent to is secure and is only accessible to authorized people.

   - **Business phone number** Input the phone number to be associated with the subscription.

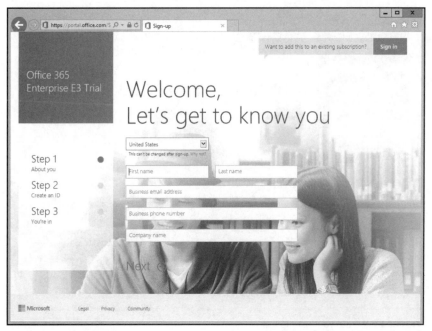

FIGURE 1-1 Welcome page

3. On the Create Your User ID page, shown in Figure 1-2, specify the following and click Next:

- **User name**   This will be the username of the global administrator account. For an organization, the name for this account should not be a standard user name, but should be appropriate for an account that will have the highest level of permissions.

- **Company name**   This will be your organization's onmicrosoft.com name. You'll be able to configure Office 365 to use a more traditional domain name at a later point in time.

- **Password**   The password must be 8-16 characters, combine upper case and lower case letters, numbers, and the following symbols: ! @ # $ % ^ & * - _ = [ ] | \ : ' , . ? / ` ~ " ( ) ;.

FIGURE 1-2 Create your user ID

4. On the Prove You're Not A Robot page, shown in Figure 1-3, provide a mobile phone number where you can receive a text message and click Text Me. The important takeaway from this page is that the secret to humanity defeating the eventual robot uprising is that robots are unable to read text messages.

FIGURE 1-3 Prove you are not a robot

5. When you receive the text message, enter the verification code and then click Create My Account on the page shown in Figure 1-4.

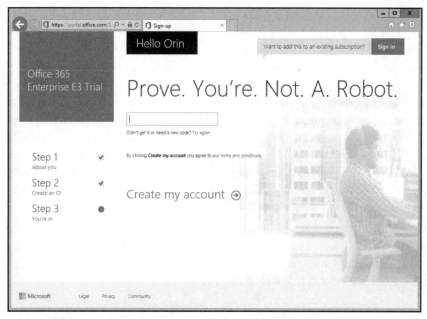

FIGURE 1-4 Enter the verification code

6. On the Save This Info page, shown in Figure 1-5, review the information, which will include your Office 365 ID and the Office 365 sign-in page.

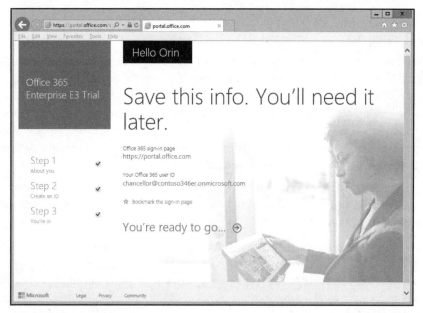

FIGURE 1-5 Trial ready

Configure the tenant name

When you set up your Office 365 subscription, you specify a tenant name in the form of *name*.onmicrosoft.com where *name* is the name you want to assign to your organization's tenancy. This name has to be unique and no two organizations can share the same tenant name. The tenant name cannot be changed after you configure your Office 365 subscription.

You can assign a domain name that you own to the tenant so that you don't have to use the tenant name on a regular basis. For example, you might sign up to an Office 365 subscription with the tenant name contoso.onmicrosoft.com. Any accounts you create will use the contoso.onmicrosoft.com email suffix for their Office 365 mailboxes. However, once you've set up Office 365, you can assign a custom domain name and have the custom domain name used as the primary email suffix. For example, assuming that you owned the domain name contoso.com, you could configure your tenancy to use the custom domain name contoso.com with the contoso.onmicrosoft.com tenancy. You'll learn more about using custom domains later in this chapter.

While you can configure a custom domain name to be the default domain name and use the custom domain name exclusively when performing Office 365 related tasks, you won't be able to remove the tenant name. The tenant name chosen at setup remains with the subscription over the course of the subscription's existence.

> **MORE INFO ONMICROSOFT.COM DOMAIN**
>
> You can learn more about initial onmicrosoft.com domains at *https://support.office. com/en-za/article/About-your-initial-onmicrosoftcom-domain-in-Office-365-b9fc3018- 8844-43f3-8db1-1b3a8e9cfd5a*.

Tenant region

Tenant region determines which Office 365 services will be available to the subscription, the taxes that will be applied as a part of the subscription charges, the billing currency for the subscription, and the Microsoft datacenter that will host the resources allocated to the subscription. For example, selecting United States for a region will mean that your organization's Office 365 tenancy is allocated resources in a United States datacenter. Selecting New Zealand currently means that your organization's Office 365 will be allocated resources in a datacenter in Australia as this is currently the closest Microsoft datacenter to New Zealand.

Unlike other Office 365 settings, you cannot change the tenant region once you have selected it. The only way to alter a tenant region is to cancel your existing subscription and to create a new subscription.

> **MORE INFO ABOUT OFFICE 365 REGIONS**
>
> You can learn more about Office 365 regions at *https://support.office.microsoft.com/en-US/ article/Change-your-organizations-address-technical-contact-email-and-other-information- a36e5a52-4df2-479e-bb97-9e67b8483e10*.

Administrator roles

There are five Office 365 management roles. The Office 365 roles are as follows:

- **Global administrator**   Office 365 users assigned this role have access to all administrative features. Users assigned this role are the only users able to assign other admin roles. More than one Office 365 user account can be assigned the global admin role. The first tenancy account created when you sign up for Office 365 is automatically assigned the global admin role. This role has the most rights of any available role.

- **Billing administrator**   Office 365 users assigned this role are able to make purchases, manage subscriptions, manage support tickets, and monitor service health.

- **Password administrator**   Office 365 users assigned the password admin role are able to reset the passwords of most Office 365 user accounts, except those assigned the global admin, service admin, or billing roles. Users assigned the password admin role can reset the passwords of other users assigned the password admin role.

- **Service administrator**   Office 365 users assigned the service admin role are able to manage service requests and monitor service health.

- **User management administrator**   When assigned this role, users can reset passwords and monitor service health. They can also manage user accounts, user groups, and service requests. Users assigned this role are unable to delete accounts assigned the global admin role; create other admin roles; or reset passwords for users assigned the billing, global, or service admin roles.

To assign a user the global admin role, perform the following steps:

1. In the Office 365 Admin Center, select the Active Users node under the Users node as shown in Figure 1-6.

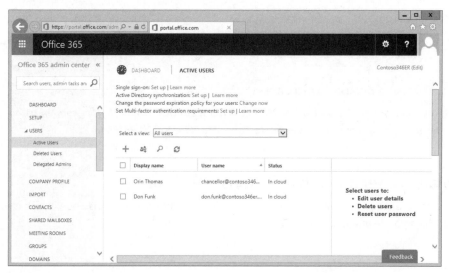

FIGURE 1-6 Active Users

2. In the Active Users node, select the user that you want to assign global admin privileges to and then click Edit.

3. On the user properties page, click Settings.

4. On the Settings page, select Yes under Assign Role and then select the Global Administrator role as shown in Figure 1-7 and provide an email address where password reset information can be sent. Ensure that this account is secure and protected by two-factor authentication. Click Save to apply the changes.

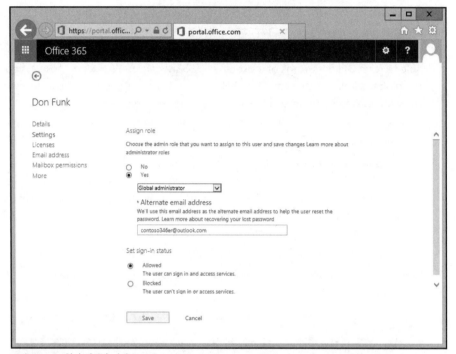

FIGURE 1-7 Global Administrator

MORE INFO **ADMINISTRATOR ROLES**

You can learn more about Office 365 Permissions at *https://support.office.com/en-us/article/Assigning-admin-roles-eac4d046-1afd-4f1a-85fc-8219c79e1504*.

Manage tenant subscriptions and licenses

You can manage Office 365 tenant subscriptions from the Subscriptions node, which is under the Billing node and is shown in Figure 1-8.

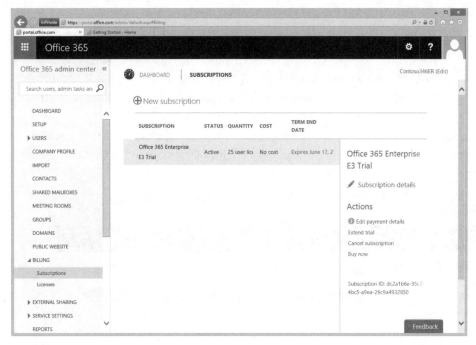

FIGURE 1-8 Subscriptions

When you are signed up to an Office 365 subscription that is not a trial subscription, you'll also be able to view a node named Bills. You can use this node to review invoices by date. Organizations can pay for Office 365 by credit card or invoice. If you want to change the payment method at a later point in time, you will need to call Office 365 support as altering the payment method cannot be performed through the Office 365 Admin Center.

> **MORE INFO TENANT SUBSCRIPTIONS AND LICENSES**
>
> You can learn more about tenant subscriptions and licenses at *https://support.office.com/ en-us/article/Billing-in-Office-365-for-business-e28093-Admin-Help-ea7bf1b2-1c2f-477f- a813-313e3ce0d896*.

Assigning licenses

Office 365 users require licenses to use Outlook, SharePoint Online, Skype for Business (formerly Lync Online), and other services. Users who have been assigned the global admin- istrator or user management administrator roles can assign licenses to users when creating new Office 365 user accounts or can assign licenses to accounts that are created through directory synchronization or federation.

When a license is assigned to a user, the following occurs:

- An Exchange Online mailbox is created for the user.

- Edit permissions for the default SharePoint Online team site are assigned to the user.

- The user will have access to Skype for Business features associated with the license.

- For Office 365 ProPlus, the user will be able to download and install Microsoft Office on up to five computers running Windows or Mac OS X.

You can view the number of valid licenses and the number of those licenses that have been assigned on the Licenses node, which is underneath the Billing node in the Office 365 Admin Center. This node is shown in Figure 1-9.

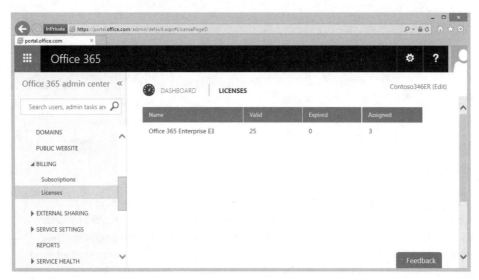

FIGURE 1-9 Licenses

You can assign a license to a user by editing the properties of the user. To do this, select the user's account in the Office 365 Admin Center and then click Edit. On the Licenses tab of the user's properties, you can assign a license by selecting the check box next to each license type. You can also remove a license by clearing the check box. Figure 1-10 shows the Licenses tab of the properties of an Office 365 user.

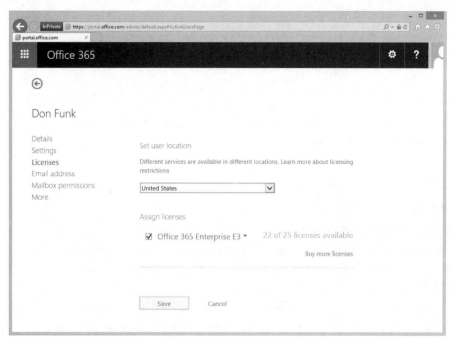

FIGURE 1-10 User license

> **MORE INFO ASSIGNING LICENSES**
>
> You can learn more about assigning licenses at *https://support.office.com/en-us/article/ Assign-or-unassign-licenses-for-Office-365-for-business-997596b5-4173-4627-b915- 36abac6786dc.*

Resolving license conflicts

License conflicts occur when you have assigned more licenses than you have purchased. Methods that you can use to resolve this problem include:

- **Purchasing more licenses**   This resolves the issue by ensuring that the number of licenses being consumed matches the number of licenses that have been purchased.
- **Removing licenses from existing users**   You can resolve license conflicts by removing licenses from existing users so that the number of licenses being consumed matches the number of licenses that has been purchased.
- **Deleting users**   In many cases, license conflicts occur because users who are no longer associated with the organization are still consuming licenses. Deleting these users from Office 365 will release the licenses assigned to these users.

EXAM TIP

Remember that the account used to configure the Office 365 subscription will automatically be assigned the global administrator role.

Thought experiment

Office 365 setup at Fabrikam

In this thought experiment, apply what you've learned about this objective. You can find the answers to these questions in the "Answers" section at the end of the chapter.

You have been asked to provide some advice to Fabrikam, a small manufacturing business that migrated to Office 365. Fabrikam needs your advice because the person responsible for Fabrikam's IT recently left the company. During the process, they handed over the credentials of all their Office 365 accounts to the CEO.

The CEO also reports to you that there have been license problems. The company initially purchased a 50-license subscription. Since then, 10 new users have been employed to replace 10 people who left the company over the last few months. The employees who departed still have Office 365 accounts.

With this information in mind, answer the following questions:

1. Describe the nature of at least one user account that will have global administrator rights for Fabrikam's Office 365 subscription.

2. What methods can be used to resolve the license conflicts?

Objective summary

- The tenant name is the name that precedes the onmicrosoft.com name for the Office 365 tenancy. This name must be unique.

- While the tenant name can be used as the organization's email domain, you can also configure the tenancy to use a custom email domain for this purpose.

- You will need to have a device that can receive SMS messages to prove that you are not a robot during the Office 365 setup process.

- The first account setup for the tenancy will be assigned the global administrator role.

- Users assigned the global administrator role have access to all administrative features.

- Users assigned the billing administrator role are able to make purchases, manage subscriptions, manage support tickets, and monitor service health.
- Users assigned the password administrator role are able to reset the passwords of most Office 365 user accounts (except those assigned the global admin, service admin, or billing roles).
- Users assigned the service administrator role are able to manage service requests and monitor service health.
- Users assigned the user management admin are able to reset passwords; monitor service health; and manage user accounts, user groups, and service requests.
- You can assign and remove licenses by editing an Office 365 user's properties.
- Deleting a user removes all licenses assigned to that user.

Objective review

Answer the following questions to test your knowledge of the information in this objective. You can find the answers to these questions and explanations of why each answer choice is correct or incorrect in the "Answers" section at the end of the chapter.

1. Which of the following cannot be changed after you deploy an Office 365 tenancy? (Choose two.)
   A. Tenant name
   B. Tenant region
   C. Global administrator
   D. Billing administrator

2. Which of the following Office 365 user roles has the ability to change the password of users who are members of the global administrator role?
   A. Global administrator
   B. Password administrator
   C. User management administrator
   D. Service administrator

3. Which role should you assign to help desk staff who should be able to reset the passwords of non-privileged Office 365 users without assigning any unnecessary privileges?
   A. Global administrator
   B. Service administrator
   C. Password administrator
   D. User management administrator

4. Which role should you assign to staff who you want to be able to create non-privileged Office 365 users without assigning any unnecessary privileges?

A. Global administrator

B. Service administrator

C. Password administrator

D. User management administrator

Objective 1.2: Add and configure custom domains

This objective deals with configuring Office 365 to use a custom domain name, such as contoso.com, that your organization owns rather than an Office 365 tenant name, like contoso.onmicrosoft.com. To master this objective you'll need to understand the steps that you need to take to configure Office 365 to use a domain name that your organization has registered.

This objective covers the following topics:

- Specify domain name
- Confirm ownership
- Specify domain purpose
- Move ownership of DNS to Office 365

Specify domain name

The first step in configuring Office 365 to use a custom domain name is to add the name of the custom domain name to Office 365. To add a custom domain to Office 365, perform the following steps:

1. In the Office 365 Admin Center, click Domains as shown in Figure 1-11.

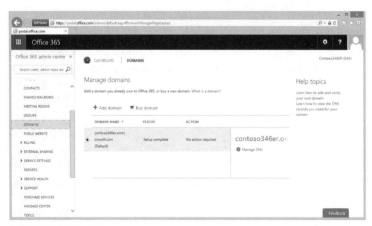

FIGURE 1-11 Domains

2. If your organization already has a domain, click Add A Domain. The alternative is to buy a domain through Office 365 and GoDaddy. The advantage of buying through GoDaddy is that you can have the entire process of assigning a custom domain to Office 365 occur automatically. If your organization's domain is already hosted elsewhere, you'll instead have to confirm ownership by configuring special TXT records.

3. On the What You Need To Know About Domains And DNS page, shown in Figure 1-12, click Let's Get Started.

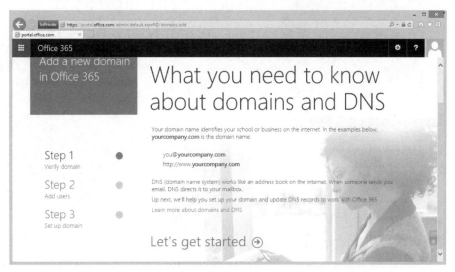

FIGURE 1-12 Add a new domain in Office 365

Confirm ownership

You can only use a custom domain name with Office 365 if your organization owns the domain name. Microsoft requires that you perform a series of DNS configuration changes to the domain name that will prove that your organization controls and has ownership of the domain.

To confirm ownership of your organization's domain, perform the following steps:

1. After clicking Let's Get Started as detailed in the previous section, on the Which Domain Do You Want To Use page, type the name of the domain as shown in Figure 1-13 and click Next.

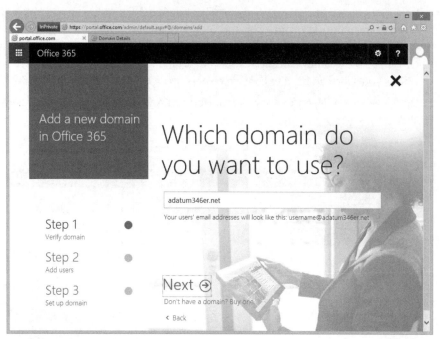

FIGURE 1-13 Choose a domain

2. If your account is registered through GoDaddy, you can sign in to GoDaddy to have Office 365 automatically configure the domain for you. Otherwise, click Use A TXT Record to verify that you own this domain.

3. Add the listed TXT record to your domain using the appropriate set of DNS tools. Figure 1-14 shows that the TXT record @ with a value of MS=ms94665460 with a time to live (TTL) of 3600 should be added to the domain. The value of this TXT record will be different each time you run the wizard.

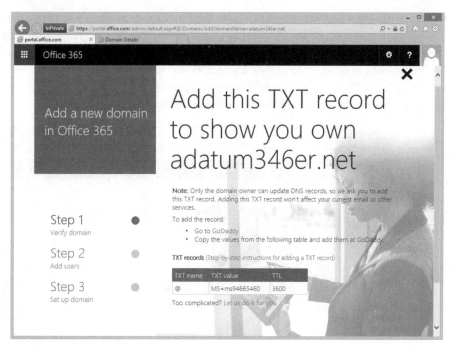

FIGURE 1-14 TXT records

4. Figure 1-15 shows the Add Zone Record dialog box in the GoDaddy DNS manager.

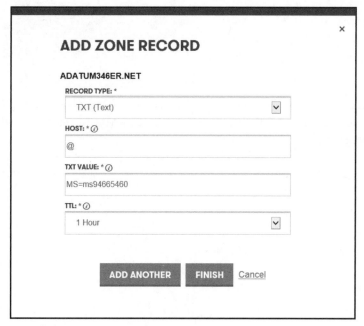

FIGURE 1-15 Add Zone record

5. Once you have added the record in your DNS manager, you'll need to click Okay, I've Added The Record. Office 365 will then attempt to verify that the record has been correctly added by performing a DNS query. Depending on DNS propagation delays, this might not occur immediately. Some DNS providers warn that it can take up to 48 hours for a DNS record to successfully propagate. When propagation is successful, you'll see the successful verification message shown in Figure 1-16.

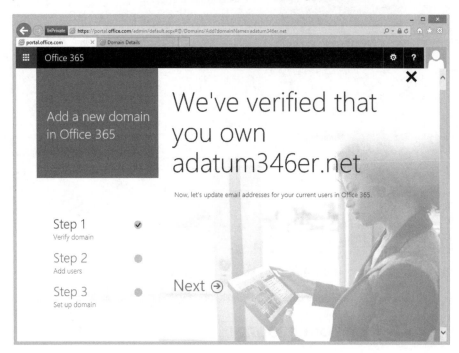

FIGURE 1-16 Custom domain verification

6. If you click Next, you'll have the option of updating user accounts to use the new name rather than the existing name as shown in Figure 1-17. Click Skip This Step to avoid updating these users.

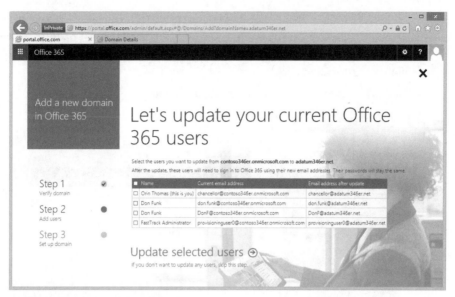

FIGURE 1-17 Update current Office 365 users

7. The next page is the Add New Users dialog box shown in Figure 1-18. You can click Skip This Step to bypass this page.

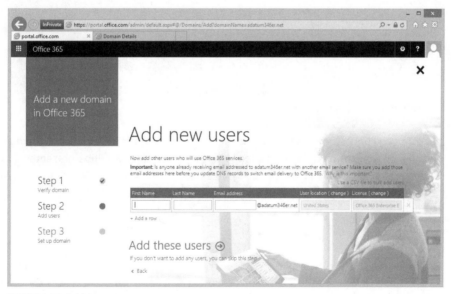

FIGURE 1-18 Add new users

8. On the Get Ready To Update DNS Records To Work With Office 365 page, click Next.

9. On the Which Services Do You Want To Use With adatum346er.net page, shown in Figure 1-19, specify whether you want to use the following services with the newly configured custom domain:

   ■ Outlook on the web for email, calendar, and contacts.

   ■ Skype for Business for instant messaging and online meetings.

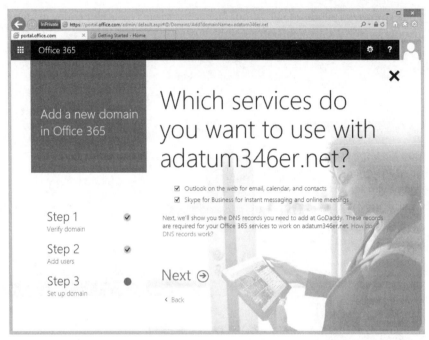

FIGURE 1-19 Domain services

10. You can choose not to set up these records by clearing the check boxes them at this step and performing this task later. When you click Next you'll be presented with the You're All Set Up page, shown in Figure 1-20.

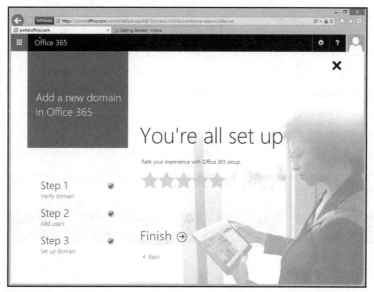

FIGURE 1-20 All set up

11. Once you click Finish, the custom domain will be listed in the list of domains as shown in Figure 1-21.

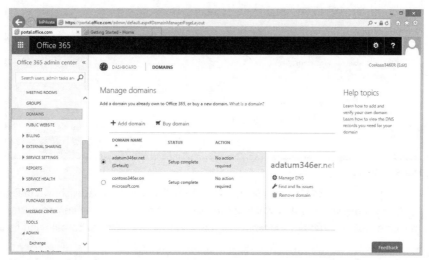

FIGURE 1-21 Domains

MORE INFO **VERIFYING THE DOMAIN NAME**

You can learn more about verifying the domain name at *https://support.office.com/en-in/ article/Verify-your-domain-in-Office-365-6383f56d-3d09-4dcb-9b41-b5f5a5efd611.*

Specify domain purpose

By configuring a custom domain's purpose, you can choose how it will be used with Office 365. For example, you might want to use one custom domain as an email suffix, and another custom domain for use with Skype for Business.

To configure domain purpose, perform the following steps:

1. In the Office 365 Admin Center, click Domains. Select the domain for which you want to configure and then click Manage DNS.

2. On the Manage DNS page, shown in Figure 1-22, click Change Domain Purpose.

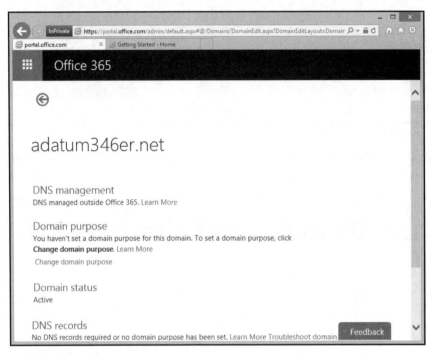

FIGURE 1-22 Domain purpose

3. On the Which Services Do You Want To Use With The Domain page, shown in Figure 1-23, select the services that you want to use with the custom domain name. These are the same options that are available when configuring the custom domain and include:

   - Outlook on the web for email, calendar, and contacts.
   - Skype for Business for instant messaging and online meetings.

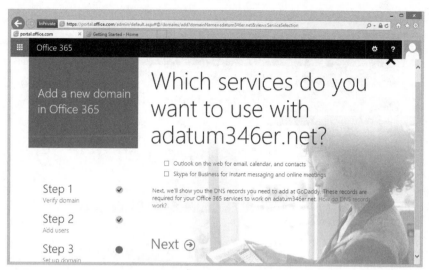

FIGURE 1-23 Which services do you want to use

4. Select the services that you want to configure for Office 365. When you click Next, you can either choose to have the DNS records added by Office 365 or you can click Add These Records Yourself.

5. If you click Add These Records Yourself, the wizard will provide you with the list of records that you need to add to support the selected services as shown in Figure 1-24.

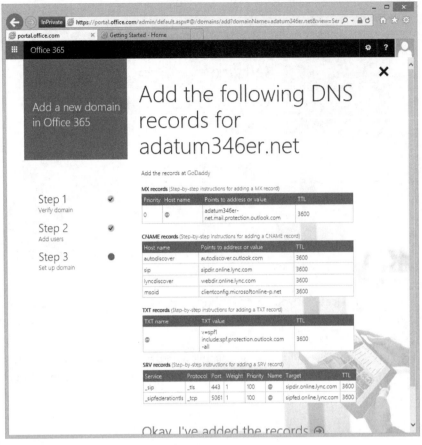

FIGURE 1-24 Add the following records

These records are listed in tables 1-1, 1-2, 1-3, and 1-4.

TABLE 1-1: MX records

Priority	Host name	Points to address or value	TTL
0	@	adatum346er-net.mail.protection.outlook.com	3600

TABLE 1-2: CNAME records

Host name	Points to address or value	TTL
Autodiscover	autodiscover.outlook.com	3600
Sip	sipdir.online.lync.com	3600
Lyncdiscover	webdir.online.lync.com	3600
msoid	clientconfig.microsoftonline-p.net	3600

TABLE 1-3: TXT records

TXT name	TXT value	TTL
@	v=spf1 include:spf.protection.outlook.com -all	3600

TABLE 1-4: SRV records

Service	Protocol	Port	Weight	Priority	Name	Target	TTL
_sip	_tls	443	1	100	@	sipdir.online.lync.com	3600
_sipfederationtls	_tcp	5061	1	100	@	sipfed.online.lync.com	3600

> **MORE INFO** **DOMAIN PURPOSE**
>
> You can learn more about configuring domain purpose at *https://support.office.com/en-ie/*
> *article/What-is-the-selecting-services-page-in-the-Office-365-domains-setup-wizard-*
> *17f4aa9b-5ece-4af8-8be4-a5e8ff8367f2.*

Move ownership of DNS to Office 365

You can change the name servers that host your custom domain from the original registrar to Office 365. The method that you use to do this depends on the domain registrar that currently hosts the records that point to the name servers associated with the custom domain.

You can only move ownership of DNS to Office 365 if you have gone through the process of confirming that your organization owns the domain through the configuration of the appropriate TXT records.

To move the domain ownership to Office 365, you need to configure the following settings:

- Primary name server: ns1.bdm.microsoftonline.com
- Secondary name server: ns2.bdm.microsoftonline.com

> **MORE INFO** **CHANGE NAMESERVER TO OFFICE 365**
>
> You can learn more about changing nameservers at *https://support.office.com/en-gb/ar-*
> *ticle/Change-nameservers-to-Office-365-a46bec33-2c78-4f45-a96c-b64b2a5bae22.*

EXAM TIP

Remember what type of DNS record you have to manually configure to confirm ownership of a custom domain.

> ## *Thought experiment*
> ### Custom domain at Fabrikam
>
> In this thought experiment, apply what you've learned about this objective. You can find the answers to these questions in the "Answers" section at the end of the chapter.
>
> Fabrikam has signed up for an Office 365 subscription and is currently using the tenant name Fabrikam.onmicrosoft.com. Fabrikam wants to assign their custom domain, Fabrikam.com, to Office 365 and to have Microsoft DNS servers host this zone. With this information in mind, answer the following questions:
>
> 1. What kind of DNS record must be added to confirm ownership of the Fabrikam.com DNS zone?
>
> 2. Which DNS records must be modified to have Microsoft DNS servers host the Fabrikam.com DNS zone?

Objective summary

- Before you can use a custom domain with Office 365, you need to prove that your organization has ownership of the domain.
- You prove to Microsoft that your organization has ownership of a domain by configuring a custom TXT record.
- You can configure MX records for your custom domain to allow mail to be routed to Office 365.
- You can configure CNAME and SRV records to configure the custom domain name to work with Skype for Business (formerly known as Lync).

Objective review

Answer the following questions to test your knowledge of the information in this objective. You can find the answers to these questions and explanations of why each answer choice is correct or incorrect in the "Answers" section at the end of the chapter.

1. You are in the process of moving ownership of the Adatum.com DNS zone from your current ISP to Office 365. Which of the following names should be configured as nameservers as a part of this process?

   A. Ns1.contoso.com, ns2.contoso.com

   B. Ns1.bdm.microsoftonline.com, ns2.bdm.microsoftonline.com

   C. Ns1.office365.com, ns2.office365.com

   D. Mx1.contoso.com, mx2.contoso.com

2. Which record type must you configure to route email from a custom domain to Office 365 once domain ownership has been confirmed?

   A. MX

   B. TXT

   C. NS

   D. SRV

3. Which DNS record types do you need to configure to use Skype for Business with your confirmed custom DNS zone? (Choose two.)

   A. SRV

   B. CNAME

   C. MX

   D. TXT

4. What type of record do you need to configure in your custom DNS zone to allow Office 365 to confirm that your organization owns this zone?

   A. TXT

   B. SRV

   C. CNAME

   D. AAAA

Objective 1.3: Plan a pilot

This objective deals with planning an Office 365 pilot project. To master this objective you'll need to understand the steps involved in planning a successful Office 365 pilot project, including determining a cohort of pilot users, determining which workloads should not be migrated to Office 365, leveraging the Office 365 on-ramp tool, having a test plan, and configuring email accounts for pilot users.

> **This objective covers the following topics:**
> - Designate pilot users
> - Identify workloads that don't require migration
> - Run the Office 365 on-ramp readiness tool
> - Create a test plan or use case
> - Connect existing email accounts for pilot users
> - Service descriptions

Designate pilot users

When selecting users for the Office 365 pilot, you need to ensure that you select a variety of users that represents the organization in its entirety. Part of the reason for the pilot is to identify potential pitfalls. For example, you want to figure out that there's a particular on-premises requirement for a group of workers in the accounting department before you migrate their workloads to Office 365. Figuring this out beforehand is much better than having to work out how to roll the accounting users back on-premises after the rest of the organization has migrated to Office 365.

The first step in selecting users for a pilot program is to determine how many users you want to include in the pilot program. Successful pilot programs often attempt to use a minimum of 5% of the potential group to be migrated. This 5% of pilot users should meet the following general criteria:

- **Full-time employees of the organization**   Full-time employees will be working with the new technology during normal work hours. Part-time employees may be more sporadic in their interaction with the technology and may be less able to provide useful feedback across the pilot period.

- **Representative of the organization**   Pilot users need to be from different parts of the organization. They need to have a mix of age, experience, and seniority.

- **Have been with the organization a minimum of six months**   This ensures that the pilot users are familiar with normal organizational procedures.

- **Already trained on the software that they will be using**   For example, if the pilot program involves moving to online mailboxes, pilot users should already be familiar with Outlook. If the pilot program means moving to an online version of SharePoint that the pilot users are already familiar with the on-premises deployment of SharePoint.

- **Willingness to provide feedback**   One of the most important aspects of a pilot program is hearing what works and what does not. Pilot users who don't provide both positive and negative feedback aren't providing you with the information necessary to allow you to determine if a full implementation of Office 365 for your organization will be successful.

Identify workloads that don't require migration

When planning an Office 365 pilot, an important thing to realize is that not all workloads need to be migrated to Office 365. Implementing Office 365 is not an all-or-nothing proposition. While it's possible to have all user accounts, Exchange mailboxes, Skype for Business infrastructure, and SharePoint sites hosted in Office 365, it's also possible to configure a hybrid deployment where these services are both on-premises and in the cloud. For example, you could have a deployment where only a fraction of your organization's user accounts are native to Office 365, some mailboxes are hosted on-premises, and some are hosted in Office 365 cloud. Your organization's SharePoint deployment could even be spread across servers in your local datacenter and others in Microsoft datacenters.

As part of your pilot, you should identify which workloads you don't need to migrate to Office 365. The factors that influence this decision will vary depending on your organization. Factors also vary depending on your region. Most countries/regions don't have local Microsoft datacenters, which might mean that moving workloads to Office 365 means moving workloads across national/regional borders. For some workload types, this may not present a problem; for other workload types, such as for workloads that deal with confidential medical data, it may not be possible to migrate the workloads across borders without contravening local legislation.

> **MORE INFO** **HYBRID DEPLOYMENTS**
>
> You can learn more about hybrid deployments at *https://support.office.com/en-us/article/Office-365-integration-with-on-premises-environments-263faf8d-aa21-428b-aed3-2021837a4b65*.

Run the Office 365 on-ramp readiness tool

The Office 365 on-ramp readiness tool allows you to run a set of tests to identify troubleshooting and configuration problems with Office 365. You access the tool either by navigating to *https://onramp.office365.com/* or by clicking Check Your Office 365 Configuration With Office 365 Health, Readiness, And Connectivity Checks from the Tools section of the Office 365 Admin Center as shown in Figure 1-25.

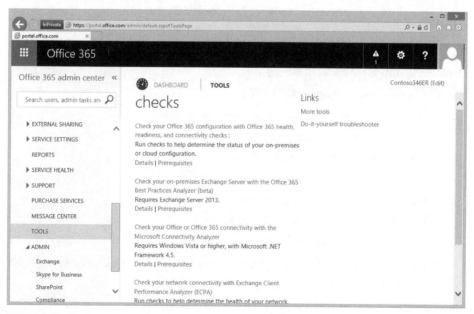

FIGURE 1-25 Checks

Running the tool involves performing the following steps:

1. On the Advanced Setup page, shown in Figure 1-26, you can elect either to make your own selections or to have an app run a check to discover what's installed in your organization's on-premises environment.

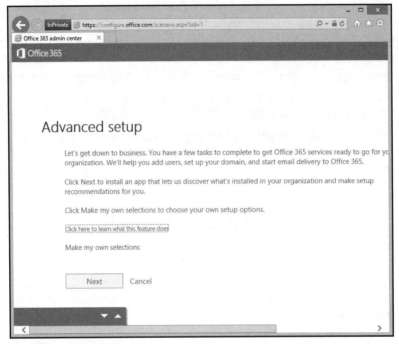

FIGURE 1-26 Advanced Setup

2. If you choose the Make My Own Selections option, you'll be presented with the following options show in in Figure 1-27:

   - Create new user accounts in Office 365
   - Sync users and passwords from an on-premises directory
   - Authenticate users with single sign-on
   - Use the free onmicrosoft.com domain
   - Add or buy your own domain
   - Add a domain you already use on-premises
   - Migrate from a system that supports IMAP
   - No migration or users will move their own email
   - Cutover migration from Exchange 2003, Exchange Server 2007, or Exchange Server 2010
   - Staged migration from Exchange 2003 or Exchange 2007
   - Hybrid environment with Exchange Server 2007 or later

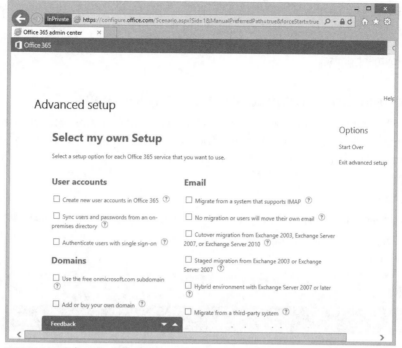

FIGURE 1-27 Select My Own Setup

Depending on your selections, you'll be provided with advice and tools about how to perform each step of the Office 365 deployment process. Much of the advice provided by the on-ramp readiness tool mirrors what is provided in the links to Office 365 documentation in this Exam Ref.

> **MORE INFO OFFICE 365 ON-RAMP READINESS TOOL**
>
> You can learn more about the Office 365 on-ramp readiness tool at *https://configure.office. com/SharedPages/WhatThisApplicationDoes.aspx*.

Create a test plan or use case

Creating a test plan or use case involves developing a formal process to describe how the pilot will proceed and how the results of the pilot will be assessed. The test plan should involve the following general phases:

- Deploying the Office 365 tenancy that will be used for the pilot
- Create user accounts for pilot users
- Configure active use of email for pilot users
- Deploy Office 365 ProPlus software
- Enable pilot user access to Office 365 services
- Solicit pilot user feedback about the experience

Each organization's plans will be slightly different. You need to ensure that pilot user feedback is recorded so that you can use it when evaluating how decisions made in the planning phase stack up against real-world outcomes, allowing you to make adjustments to the deployment phase.

Connect existing email accounts for pilot users

It is possible to migrate the email accounts of a small number of users from your on-premises environment to Office 365 while keeping the majority of your existing mailboxes in the on-premises mail solution. The method for doing this is termed simple domain sharing for SMTP email addresses as shown in Figure 1-28.

For example:

- Your organization has provisioned the contoso.microsoftonline.com Office 365 tenancy.
- Your organization has its own on-premises mail solution. It uses the contoso.com email suffix.

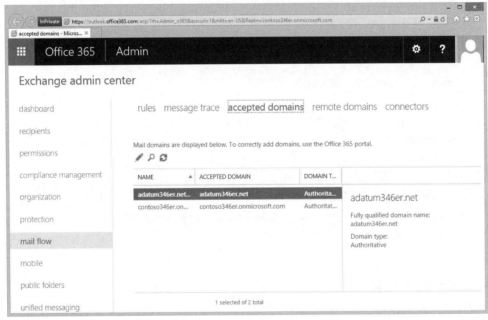

FIGURE 1-28 Mail flow

- You set the domain as an Internal Relay domain as shown in Figure 1-29.

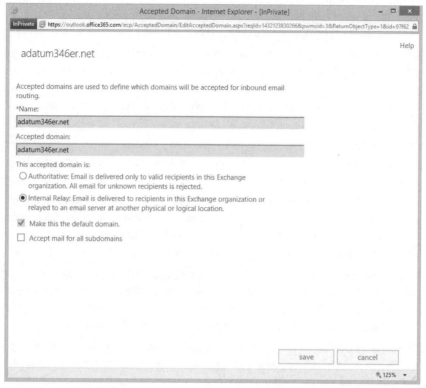

FIGURE 1-29 Internal Relay

- Configure the on-premises mail solution to configure mail forwarding of each pilot user account to the contoso.microsoftonline.com mail domain. For example, the on-premises mailbox for the don.funk@contoso.com email account should forward all incoming email to don.funk@contoso.microsoftonline.com.

- Configure each pilot user's account in Office 365 to use the on-premises DNS zone mail domain. For example, Don Funk's Office 365 user account should be configured with a reply-to address of don.funk@contoso.com.

- You can migrate the contents of pilot users' on-premises mailboxes using Exchange Admin Center.

MORE INFO **PILOT OFFICE 365 EMAIL**

You can learn more about piloting Office 365 email at *https://support.office.com/ en-nz/article/Pilot-Office-365-with-a-few-email-addresses-on-your-custom-domain-39cee536-6a03-40cf-b9c1-f301bb6001d7.*

Service descriptions

Office 365 is made up of multiple separate services. Service descriptions provide information about what the service does. The service descriptions for these Office 365 services are as follows:

- **Office 365 Platform Service**   The Office 365 platform combines the Microsoft Office suite of desktop applications with cloud-hosted versions of Microsoft communications and collaboration products. You can find the complete service description at *https://technet.microsoft.com/en-us/library/jj819274.aspx*.

- **Exchange Online**   Exchange online provides the capabilities of an on-premises Microsoft Exchange Server deployment, including access to email, calendar, contacts, and tasks, as a cloud-based service. You can find the complete service description at *https://technet.microsoft.com/en-us/library/exchange-online-service-description.aspx*.

- **Exchange Online Archiving**   A cloud-based archiving solution to assist organizations with meeting their archiving, compliance, regulatory, and e-discovery responsibilities. You can find the complete service description at *https://technet.microsoft.com/en-us/library/exchange-online-archiving-service-description.aspx*.

- **Exchange Online Protection**   A cloud-based email-filtering service that protects against spam and malware. This can also be used to enforce data-loss protection policies. You can find the complete service description at *https://technet.microsoft.com/en-us/library/exchange-online-protection-service-description.aspx*.

- **SharePoint Online**   Provides a cloud-hosted SharePoint deployment. You can find the complete service description at *https://technet.microsoft.com/en-us/library/sharepoint-online-service-description.aspx*.

- **OneDrive for Business**   This is an organization-based personal online storage space hosted in the cloud. You can find the complete service description at *https://technet.microsoft.com/en-us/library/onedrive-for-business-service-description.aspx*.

- **Skype for Business**   A hosted communications service that allows instant messaging, file transfer, person-to-person audio/visual communication, and conference hosting. You can find the complete service description at *https://technet.microsoft.com/en-us/library/skype-for-business-online-service-description.aspx*.

- **Office Online**   This allows you to open and edit Word, Excel, PowerPoint, and OneNote documents in a web browser. You can find the complete service description at *https://technet.microsoft.com/en-us/library/office-online-service-description.aspx*.

- **Office Applications**   A subscription service that provides the most recent version of the Office suite of desktop applications. You can find the complete service description at *https://technet.microsoft.com/en-us/library/office-applications-service-description.aspx*.

- **Project Online**   An online solution for project portfolio management. You can find the complete service description at *https://technet.microsoft.com/en-us/library/project-online-service-description.aspx*.

- **Project Pro for Office 365**   Provides an up-to-date version of the Project Professional software to desktop computers. You can find the complete service description at *https://technet.microsoft.com/en-us/library/project-pro-for-office-365-service-description.aspx*.

- **Yammer**   A cloud-hosted enterprise social network. You can find the complete service description at *https://technet.microsoft.com/en-us/library/yammer-service-description.aspx*.

- **Power BI for Office 365**   An online business intelligence service for managing, sharing, and consuming data queries and Excel workbooks that store data models, queries, and reports. You can find the complete service description at *https://technet.microsoft.com/en-us/library/power-bi-for-office-365-service-description.aspx*.

- **Microsoft Dynamics CRM Online**   Provides online customer relationship management (CRM) capabilities. You can find the complete service description at *https://technet.microsoft.com/en-us/library/microsoft-dynamics-crm-online-service-description.aspx*.

> *MORE INFO* **OFFICE 365 SERVICE DESCRIPTIONS**
>
> You can learn more about Office 365 service descriptions at *https://technet.microsoft.com/en-us/library/office-365-service-descriptions.aspx*.

EXAM TIP

Remember which record type needs to be modified to allow some pilot users to have email hosted in Office 365 without configuring a hybrid Exchange deployment.

Thought experiment
Office 365 email pilot at Contoso

In this thought experiment, apply what you've learned about this objective. You can find the answers to these questions in the "Answers" section at the end of the chapter.

You are planning the pilot of Office 365 at Contoso. As part of this pilot, you want the email of five users to be managed through Office 365 rather than your existing on-premises email solution. Currently, the on-premises solution uses the @contoso.com email suffix. The Office 365 tenancy is configured with the name contoso.onmicrosoft.com. With this information in mind, answer the following questions:

1. Which DNS record do you have to update to allow pilot users' email addresses to be hosted in Office 365?

2. What steps do you have to take with the on-premises email so that email sent to pilot users' email addresses ends up in Office 365?

Objective summary

- Pilot users should provide a representative sample of your organization.
- Not all workloads can be or should be migrated to Office 365. Use the pilot phase to determine which workloads you will not migrate.
- The Office 365 on-ramp readiness tool provides advice for migrating to Office 365.
- A test plan or use case is a document that provides information on each phase of the migration process.
- You can configure pilot users with Office 365 mailboxes through the configuration of SPF records, accepted domains, and email forwarding.
- Office 365 service descriptions provide precise information about Office 365 service functionality.

Objective review

Answer the following questions to test your knowledge of the information in this objective. You can find the answers to these questions and explanations of why each answer choice is correct or incorrect in the "Answers" section at the end of the chapter.

1. Your organization has 200 users. What's the minimum number that should be involved in the Office 365 pilot?

   A. 2

   B. 5

   C. 10

   D. 1

2. Which Office 365 service provides spam filtering?

   A. Exchange Online Protection

   B. Exchange Online Archiving

   C. SharePoint Online

   D. OneDrive for Business

3. You are configuring a custom domain as part of an Office 365 pilot. You want to host some, but not all, pilot user email accounts in Office 365. Which setting should you configure for the custom domain?

   A. Authoritative

   B. Internal Relay

   C. External Relay

   D. Remote Domain

4. The current SPF record for your organization's custom DNS zone is configured as "v=spf1 mx include:tailspintoys.com ~all." What should be the value of the SPF record if you want to have some pilot users use Office 365 as the mailbox for email sent to their @tailspintoys.com email address?

   A. "v=spf1 txt include:tailspintoys.com include:spf.protection.outlook.com ~all"

   B. "v=spf1 txt include:tailspintoys.com include:spf.protection.tailspintoys.com ~all"

   C. "v=spf1 mx include:tailspintoys.com include:spf.protection.tailspintoys.com ~all"

   D. "v=spf1 mx include:tailspintoys.com include:spf.protection.outlook.com ~all"

Answers

This section contains the solutions to the thought experiments and answers to the objective review questions in this chapter.

Objective 1.1: Thought experiment

1. The first user account created for a subscription will be assigned global administrator privileges. This will be the user account of the IT staff member who recently left and who set up Office 365.

2. The license conflict can be resolved by either manually removing licenses from the 10 users who have left the organization, or by deleting their user accounts.

Objective 1.1: Review

1. **Correct answers:** A and B

   A. **Correct:** Tenant name cannot be changed after deployment.

   B. **Correct:** Tenant region cannot be changed after deployment.

   C. **Incorrect:** User accounts assigned the global administrator role can be changed after deployment of an Office 365 tenancy.

   D. **Incorrect:** User accounts assigned the billing administrator role can be altered after deployment of an Office 365 tenancy.

2. **Correct answer:** A

   A. **Correct:** Only users assigned the global administrator role are able to reset the passwords of users assigned the global administrator role.

   B. **Incorrect:** Only users assigned the global administrator role are able to reset the passwords of users assigned the global administrator role. Users assigned the password administrator role cannot perform this task

   C. **Incorrect:** Only users assigned the global administrator role are able to reset the passwords of users assigned the global administrator role. Users assigned the user management administrator role cannot perform this task

   D. **Incorrect:** Only users assigned the global administrator role are able to reset the passwords of users assigned the global administrator role. Users assigned the service administrator role cannot perform this task.

3. **Correct answer:** C

   A. **Incorrect:** Assigning the global administrator role would involve assigning unnecessary privileges.

   B. **Incorrect:** Members of the service administrator role are unable to reset passwords.

C. **Correct:** Assigning the password administrator role will ensure that the passwords of non-privileged Office 365 users can be changed without assigning unnecessary privileges.

D. **Incorrect:** Assigning the user management administrator role would involve assigning unnecessary privileges.

4. **Correct answer:** D

A. **Incorrect:** Assigning the global administrator role would involve assigning unnecessary privileges.

B. **Incorrect:** Members of the service administrator role are unable to create user accounts.

C. **Incorrect:** Users assigned the password administrator role are unable to create user accounts.

D. **Correct:** Assigning the user management administrator role would allow users to create non-privileged Office 365 accounts without assigning unnecessary privileges.

Objective 1.2: Thought experiment

1. A TXT record must be added to confirm ownership of the Fabrikam.com DNS zone.

2. The NS records for the zone must be modified to allow Microsoft to host the Fabrikam.com DNS zone.

Objective 1.2: Review

1. **Correct answer:** B

A. **Incorrect:** To move ownership of DNS to Office 365, you need to configure ns1. bdm.microsoftonline.com and ns2.bdm.microsoftonline.com as authoritative nameservers for the zone.

B. **Correct:** To move ownership of DNS to Office 365, you need to configure ns1.bdm. microsoftonline.com and ns2.bdm.microsoftonline.com as authoritative nameservers for the zone.

C. **Incorrect:** To move ownership of DNS to Office 365, you need to configure ns1. bdm.microsoftonline.com and ns2.bdm.microsoftonline.com as authoritative nameservers for the zone rather than MX2.contoso.com.

D. **Incorrect:** To move ownership of DNS to Office 365, you need to configure ns1. bdm.microsoftonline.com and ns2.bdm.microsoftonline.com as authoritative nameservers for the zone rather than MX1.contoso.com

2. **Correct answer:** A

   A. **Correct:** You need to reconfigure MX records to route email from a custom domain to Office 365 once domain ownership has been confirmed.

   B. **Incorrect:** You don't need to reconfigure a TXT record. You need to reconfigure MX records to route email from a custom domain to Office 365 once domain ownership has been confirmed.

   C. **Incorrect:** You don't need to reconfigure a NS record. You need to reconfigure MX records to route email from a custom domain to Office 365 once domain ownership has been confirmed.

   D. **Incorrect:** You don't need to reconfigure a SRV record. You need to reconfigure MX records to route email from a custom domain to Office 365 once domain ownership has been confirmed.

3. **Correct answers:** A and B

   A. **Correct:** You need to configure SRV and CNAME records to use Skype for Business with your confirmed custom DNS zone.

   B. **Correct:** You need to configure SRV and CNAME records to use Skype for Business with your confirmed custom DNS zone.

   C. **Incorrect:** You need to configure SRV and CNAME records, rather than MX records, to use Skype for Business with your confirmed custom DNS zone.

   D. **Incorrect:** You need to configure SRV and CNAME records, rather than TXT records, to use Skype for Business with your confirmed custom DNS zone.

4. **Correct answer:** A

   A. **Correct:** You need to configure a custom TXT record in your custom DNS zone to allow Office 365 to confirm that your organization owns a specific DNS zone.

   B. **Incorrect:** You need to configure a custom TXT record and not an SRV record in your custom DNS zone to allow Office 365 to confirm that your organization owns a specific DNS zone.

   C. **Incorrect:** You need to configure a custom TXT record and not a CNAME record in your custom DNS zone to allow Office 365 to confirm that your organization owns a specific DNS zone.

   D. **Incorrect:** You need to configure a custom TXT record and not an AAAA record in your custom DNS zone to allow Office 365 to confirm that your organization owns a specific DNS zone.

Objective 1.3: Thought experiment

1. You need to update the SPF record to allow pilot users' email addresses to be hosted in Office 365.

2. You need to configure email forwarding to the users' @contoso.onmicrosoft.com accounts.

Objective 1.3: Review

1. **Correct answer:** C

    A. **Incorrect:** A minimum of 5% of users should be involved in the Office 365 pilot. In an organization with 200 users, this is 10 people and not 2.

    B. **Incorrect:** A minimum of 5% of users should be involved in the Office 365 pilot. In an organization with 200 users, this is 10 people and not 5.

    C. **Correct:** A minimum of 5% of users should be involved in the Office 365 pilot. In an organization with 200 users, this is 10 people.

    D. **Incorrect:** A minimum of 5% of users should be involved in the Office 365 pilot. In an organization with 200 users, this is 10 people and not 1.

2. **Correct answer:** A

    A. **Correct:** Exchange Online Protection offers spam filtering and malware protection.

    B. **Incorrect:** Exchange Online Archiving does not provide spam filtering and malware protection.

    C. **Incorrect:** SharePoint Online does not provide spam filtering and malware protection.

    D. **Incorrect:** OneDrive for Business does not provide spam filtering and malware protection.

3. **Correct answer:** B

    A. **Incorrect:** You must configure the domain as an Internal Relay domain when configuring mail flow for pilot mail users rather than as an Authoritative domain.

    B. **Correct:** You must configure the domain as an Internal Relay domain when configuring mail flow for pilot mail users.

    C. **Incorrect:** You must configure the domain as an Internal Relay domain when configuring mail flow for pilot mail users rather than as an External Relay domain.

    D. **Incorrect:** You must configure the domain as an Internal Relay domain when configuring mail flow for pilot mail users rather than as a Remote domain.

4. **Correct answer:** D

   A. **Incorrect:** The SPF record should be set to "v=spf1 mx include:tailspintoys.com include:spf.protection.outlook.com ~all", it should not include a the TXT record type.

   B. **Incorrect:** The SPF record should be set to "v=spf1 mx include:tailspintoys.com include:spf.protection.outlook.com ~all" not include:spf.protection.tailspintoys.com.

   C. **Incorrect:** The SPF record should be set to "v=spf1 mx include:tailspintoys.com include:spf.protection.outlook.com ~all" not include:spf.protection.tailspintoys.com.

   D. **Correct:** The SPF record should be set to "v=spf1 mx include:tailspintoys.com include:spf.protection.outlook.com ~all."

CHAPTER 2

Plan and implement networking and security in Office 365

I f you are using a custom DNS domain with Office 365, you must configure this domain with appropriate DNS records to ensure that your organization's clients are able to find the appropriate Office 365 servers on the Internet. Office 365 requires that clients be able to connect directly to the Office 365 servers on the Internet using a variety of protocols and ports. If the clients cannot make these connections, Office 365 functionality may be limited. As is the case with on-premises Active Directory, Office 365 supports different administrative roles. In large organizations, these roles can be used to allow IT staff, such as those who work on the service desk, to perform support tasks without being granted unnecessary privileges.

Objectives in this chapter:

- Objective 2.1: Configure DNS records for services
- Objective 2.2: Enable client connectivity to Office 365
- Objective 2.3: Administer rights management
- Objective 2.4: Manage administrator roles in Office 365

Objective 2.1: Configure DNS records for services

This objective deals with the configuration of DNS records in custom DNS domains, allowing those domains to be used with Office 365 services. To master this objective, you'll need to understand the types of records that need to be added to a custom DNS domain to support Exchange, Skype for Business, and SharePoint Online.

> **This objective covers the following topics:**
> - Exchange DNS records
> - Skype for Business Online DNS records
> - SharePoint Online DNS records

Exchange DNS records

When you provision Office 365 for your organization, Microsoft takes care of ensuring that the DNS records for your organization's tenant domain, which is the onmicrosoft.com domain, are configured properly so that email addresses that use the tenant domain as an email domain suffix have mail routed properly.

For example, if you provision an Office 365 tenant and the tenant domain is contoso. onmicrosoft.com, then email sent to users at this email domain, such as an email sent to don.funk@contoso.onmicrosoft.com, will arrive at the correct location because Office 365 will provision the appropriate DNS records automatically when the tenancy is provisioned.

When you add a custom domain to Office 365, you need to configure an appropriate set of DNS records to ensure that mail flows properly to Office 365 mailboxes that use the custom domain. For example, if your custom domain is tailspintoys.com, you need to configure DNS so that email will function properly for Office 365 mailboxes that are configured to use the tailspintoys.com email domain. When properly configured, the user associated with the Office 365 mailbox don.funk@tailspintoys.com will receive email sent from other hosts on the Internet.

As you learned in "Chapter 1: Provision Office 365," if your custom DNS zone is hosted by GoDaddy, Office 365 can configure the appropriate DNS records for you automatically. If your custom DNS zone is hosted by another DNS hosting provider, you'll have to configure DNS records manually.

You need to configure the following DNS records:

- Autodiscover CNAME record for Autodiscover service
- MX record for mail routing
- Sender Policy Framework (SPF) record to verify identity of mail server
- TXT record for Exchange federation
- CNAME record for Exchange federation

Autodiscover CNAME record

You need to create a CNAME record that uses the alias Autodiscover to point to the hostname Autodiscover.outlook.com so that Outlook clients have their settings automatically provisioned for Office 365. For example, if the custom domain you assigned to Office 365 was tailspintoys.com, you would need to create the CNAME record Autodiscover.tailspintoys.com and have it point to Autodiscover.outlook.com. Figure 2-1 shows this type of record being created in the DNS console of a DNS server running the Windows Server 2012 R2 operating system.

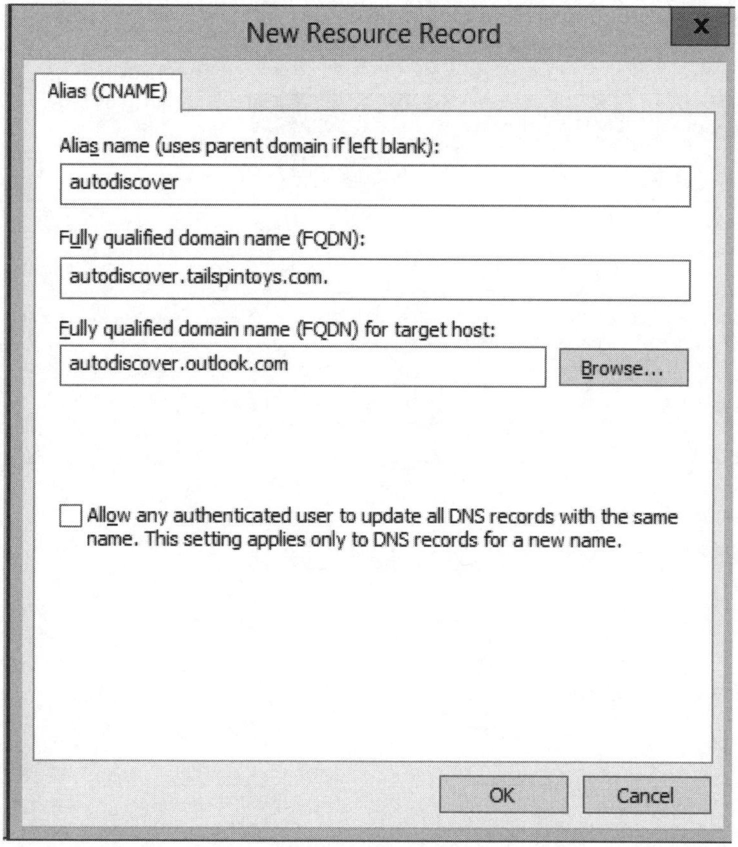

FIGURE 2-1 Autodiscover record

MX record

You need to configure an MX record in your custom domain to point to an Office 365 target mail server. The address of this target mail server will depend on the name of the custom domain and is described in the documentation and in the form <mx token>.mail.protection.outlook.com. You can determine the value for MX token by performing the following steps:

1. In the Office 365 Admin Center, navigate to the Domains node.

2. Select the custom domain, and then click Find and Fix Issues.

3. In the MX records section, select What Do I Fix?

4. Follow the directions provided on the page to determine the MX token value.

To ensure that mail routes properly, you need to configure the MX priority for the record to be a lower value than any other MX records configured for the custom domain. When mail is being routed, a check is performed to determine which MX record has the lowest value for the priority field. For example, an MX record with a priority of 10 will be chosen as a destination for mail routing over an MX record with a priority of 20.

Figure 2-2 shows the MX record for the tailspintoys.com custom domain. The mail server priority is set to 10 and the MX token is tailspintoys-com.

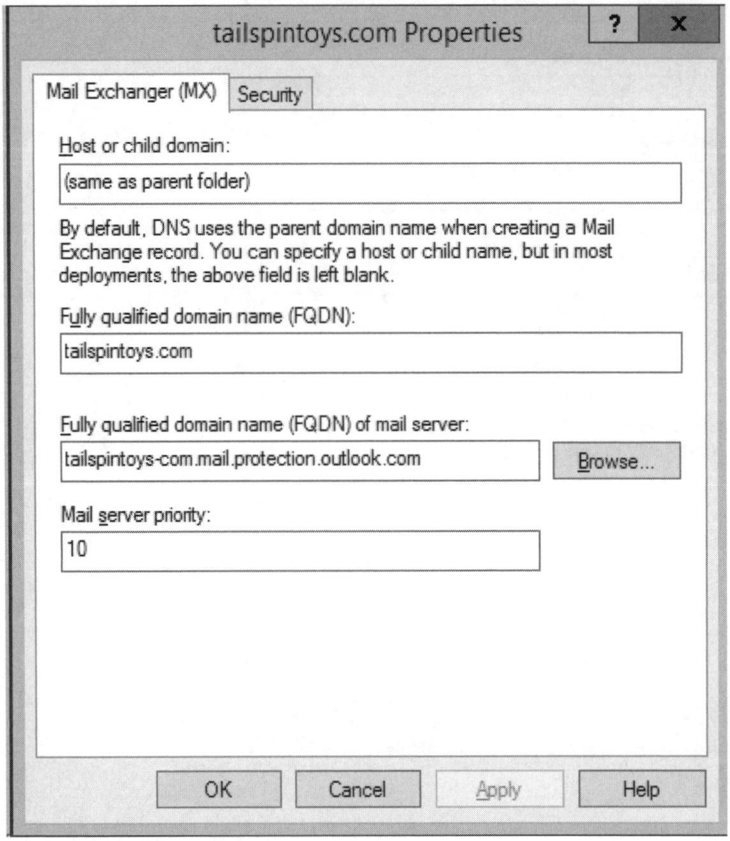

FIGURE 2-2 MX record

SPF record

The Sender Protection Framework (SPF) record is a special TXT record that reduces the possibility of malicious third parties using the custom domain to send spam or malicious email. An SPF record is used to validate which email servers are authorized to send messages on behalf of the custom domain. The SPF record must be a TXT record where the TXT value must include v=spf1 include:spf.protection.outlook.com –all. The record should also be set with a TTL value of 3600. Figure 2-3 shows an SPF record for Office 365 created in the DNS console for Windows Server 2012 R2 where the tailspintoys.com custom domain is being used.

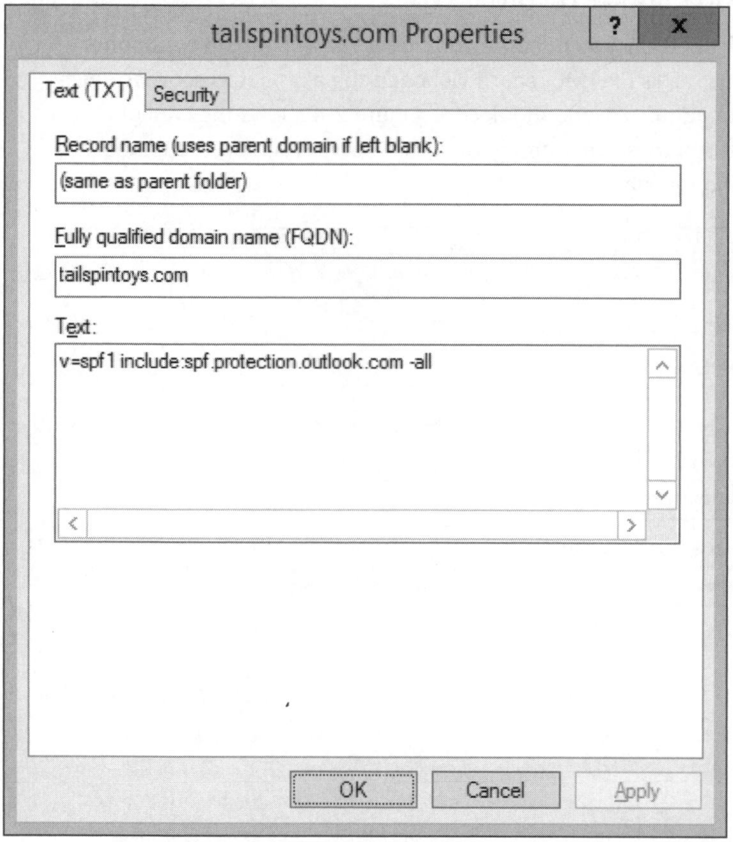

FIGURE 2-3 SPF record

MORE INFO **SPF RECORDS**

You can learn more about DNS records for Exchange in Office 365 at *https://support.office. com/en-in/article/External-Domain-Name-System-records-for-Office-365-c0531a6f-9e25- 4f2d-ad0e-a70bfef09ac0.*

Exchange federation TXT records

If you are configuring federation between an on-premises Exchange deployment and Office 365, you need to create two special TXT records that will include a custom-generated domain-proof hash text.

The first record will include the custom domain name and the hash text, such as tailspintoys. com and Y96nu89138789315669824, respectively. The second record will include the name exchangedelegation with the custom domain name and then the custom generated domain-proof hash text for example, exchangedelegation.tailspintoys.com and Y3259071352452626169.

Exchange federation CNAME record

If you are configuring federation, you need an additional CNAME record to support federation with Office 365. This CNAME record will need the alias autodiscover.service and should also point to autodiscover.outlook.com. Figure 2-4 shows the configuration of this record for the tailspintoys.com domain on a DNS server running the Windows Server 2012 R2 operating system.

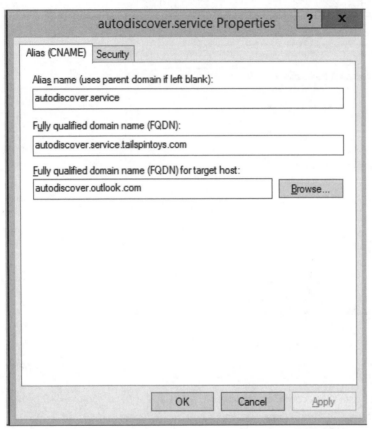

FIGURE 2-4 Autodiscover record

MORE INFO **DNS RECORDS FOR EXCHANGE IN OFFICE 365**

You can learn more about DNS records for Exchange in Office 365 at *https://support.office. com/en-in/article/External-Domain-Name-System-records-for-Office-365-c0531a6f-9e25- 4f2d-ad0e-a70bfef09ac0.*

Skype for Business Online DNS records

Skype for Business requires you to configure two types of DNS records if you have a custom domain. You need to configure two SRV records and two CNAME records to get Skype for Business working properly.

Skype for Business Online SRV records

Skype for Business Online requires two SRV records. The first record is used to coordinate the flow of data between Skype for Business clients. This record should have the following properties:

- Service: _sip
- Protocol: _TCP
- Priority: 100
- Weight: 1
- Port: 443
- Target: sipdir.online.lync.com

An example of this record created in the DNS console on a computer running Windows Server 2012 R2 for the tailspintoys.com custom domain is shown in Figure 2-5.

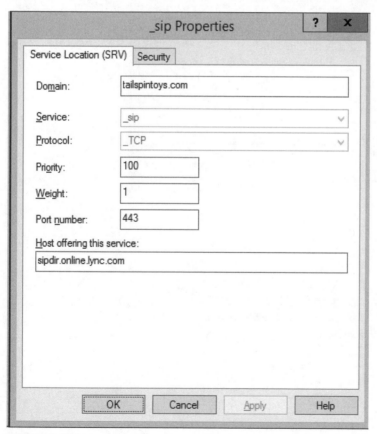

FIGURE 2-5 SRV record

The second record is used by Skype for Business to share instant messaging features with clients other than Lync for Business by allowing SIP federation. This record should have the following properties:

- Service: _sipfederationtls
- Protocol: _TCP
- Priority: 100
- Weight: 1
- Port: 5061
- Target: sipfed.online.lync.com

This record, configured for the tailspintoys.com custom domain, is shown in Figure 2-6.

FIGURE 2-6 SRV record for federation

Skype for Business Online CNAME records

If you want to use Skype for Business with a custom domain, you need to create two separate CNAME records. The first CNAME record uses the alias "sip" and points to sipdir.online.lync.com. This CNAME record allows the client to find the Skype for Business service and assists in the process of signing in. A version of this record, created for the tailspintoys.com custom domain, is shown in Figure 2-7.

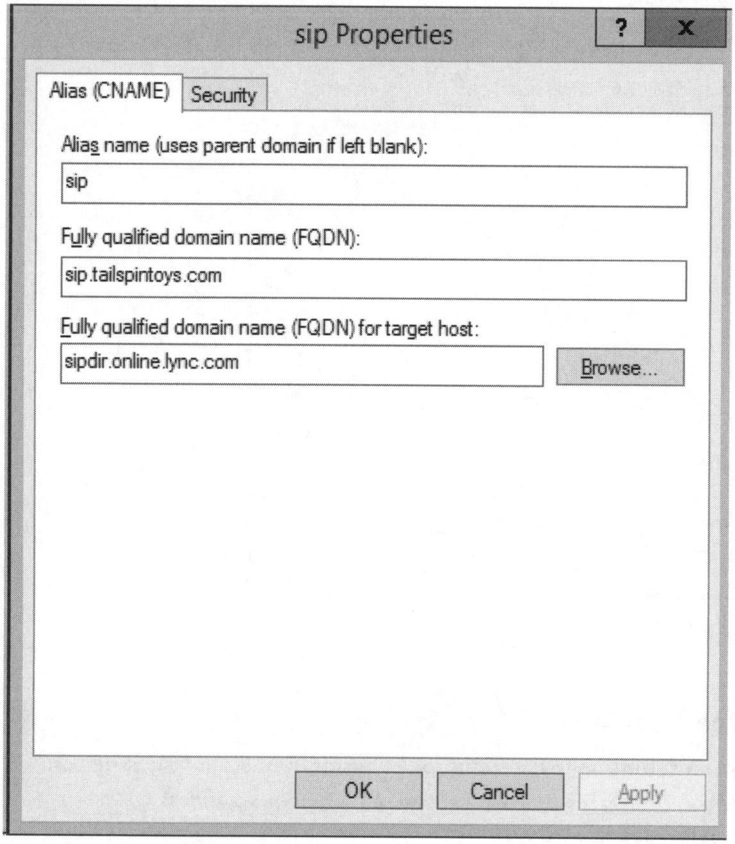

FIGURE 2-7 CNAME record

The second CNAME record assists the Skype for Business mobile device client to find the Skype for Business service and also assists with sign-in. The alias for this record is lyncdiscover and the record target is webdir.online.lync.com. An example of this record for the custom domain tailspintoys.com is shown in Figure 2-8.

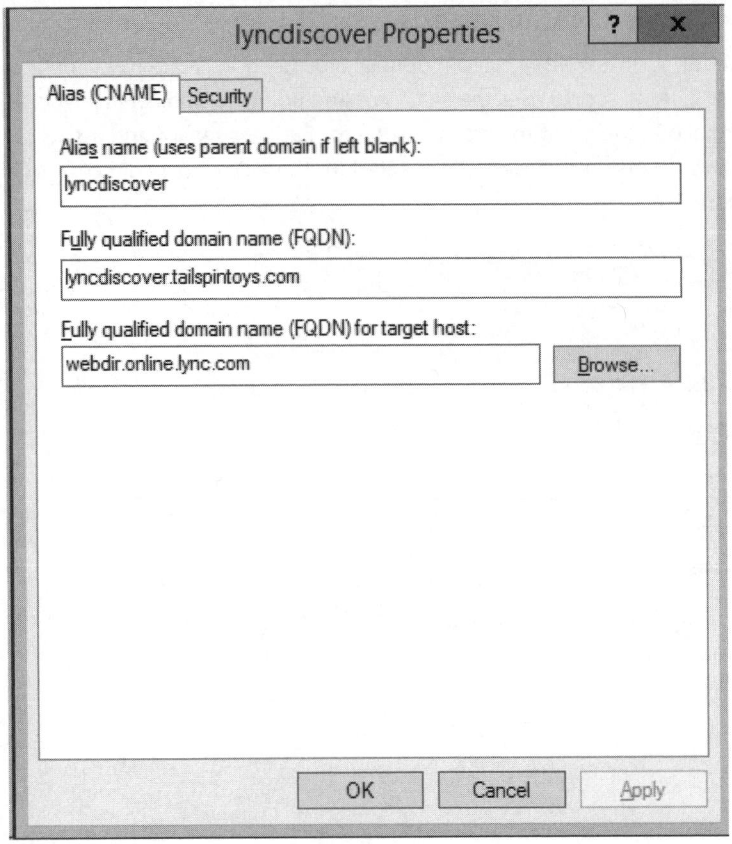

FIGURE 2-8 CNAME for Skype for Business

> *MORE INFO* **SKYPE FOR BUSINESS**
>
> You can learn more about setting up DNS records for Skype for Business at *https://support. office.microsoft.com/en-us/article/Set-up-your-network-for-Skype-for-Business-Online-81fa5e16-418d-4698-a5f0-e666211c5c66.*

SharePoint Online DNS records

You only have to configure a DNS record in a custom domain for SharePoint Online if you are going to allow SharePoint Online to send email to people outside your organization. If you are doing this, you'll need to update the SPF record that you configured for your custom domain to include the text **include:sharepointonline.com**. For example, Figure 2-9 shows the SPF record configured for the tailspintoys.com DNS zone modified to now include the value include:sharepointonline.com.

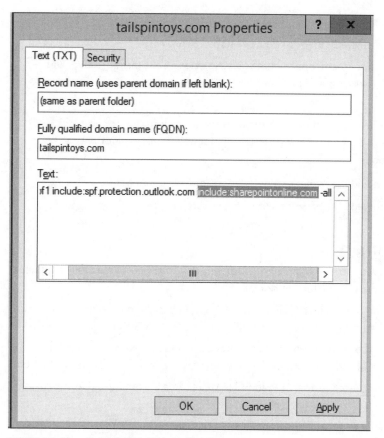

FIGURE 2-9 SharePoint Online SPF modification

MORE INFO **SPF RECORDS FOR SHAREPOINT ONLINE**

You can learn more about configuring SPF records for SharePoint Online at *https:// support.office.com/en-in/article/External-Domain-Name-System-records-for-Office-365-c0531a6f-9e25-4f2d-ad0e-a70bfef09ac0*.

EXAM TIP

Remember which type of DNS record is required for each Office 365 service. Also try to remember the values that should be associated with these records.

> ### *Thought experiment*
> ### Skype for Business SRV records at Tailspin Toys
>
> In this thought experiment, apply what you've learned about this objective. You can find the answers to these questions in the "Answers" section at the end of the chapter.
>
> You are in the process of configuring SRV records in the tailspintoys.com custom domain to support Skype for Business at Tailspin Toys. With this in mind, answer the following questions:
>
> 1. Which port should the _sipfederationtls SRV record be configured to use?
>
> 2. Which port should the _sip SRV record be configured to use?

Objective summary

- If you are using a custom domain with Office 365, you will need to manually configure certain DNS records in the custom domain.

- The configuration of DNS records in custom DNS domains can be configured to occur automatically if an organization has its DNS zones hosted on GoDaddy.

- Exchange DNS records that require configuration include a CNAME record for Autodiscover, an MX record for mail routing, and an SPF record for spam protection.

- Skype for Business requires that SRV and CNAME records be configured in the custom DNS domains.

- If sending email to external users from SharePoint Online, the SPF record will need to be updated with SharePoint specific information.

Objective review

Answer the following questions to test your knowledge of the information in this objective. You can find the answers to these questions and explanations of why each answer choice is correct or incorrect in the "Answers" section at the end of the chapter.

1. The SPF record for a custom DNS domain is currently configured with the value v=spf1 include:spf.protection.outlook.com –all. You want to allow mail to be sent from SharePoint Online. SharePoint will be configured to use the same custom DNS domain as the one that uses the SPF record. Which of the following must be added to the SPF record to accomplish this goal?

   A. Include:office365.com

   B. Include:sharepoint.com

   C. Include:sharepointonline.com

   D. Include:exchange.com

2. What type of record must you configure for the tailspintoys.com custom DNS zone so that email is routed to tailspintoys-com.mail.protection.outlook.com?

   A. SPF record

   B. MX record

   C. CNAME record

   D. SRV record

3. You are configuring CNAME records in your custom domain for Skype for Business Online. Which of the following hosts should the CNAME record for sip point to?

   A. Sipdir.online.outlook.com

   B. Sipdir.online.sharepoint.com

   C. Sipdir.online.exchange.com

   D. Sipdir.online.lync.com

4. You need to create an SPF record for your custom domain. What type of DNS record is an SPF record?

   A. SRV record

   B. TXT record

   C. MX record

   D. CNAME record

Objective 2.2: Enable client connectivity to Office 365

This objective deals with enabling client connectivity to Office 365 servers on the Internet. To master this objective, you'll need to understand how to configure a proxy server to allow anonymous access to Office 365, how to configure outbound firewalls to allow traffic to pass on the appropriate ports, understand which tools to use to calculate Office 365 bandwidth requirements, understand common client Internet connectivity problems, and how to configure previous versions of Office clients to connect to Office 365.

> **This objective covers the following topics:**
> - Proxy server configuration
> - Outbound firewall ports
> - Recommend bandwidth
> - Internet connectivity for clients
> - Deploy desktop setup for previous versions of Office clients

Proxy server configuration

Clients are unable to make connections to Office 365 if their Internet traffic passes through a proxy server that requires authentication. If your organization has a proxy server that requires authentication, you must either choose to disable authentication entirely, or selectively disable authentication for traffic to Office 365-related resources on the Internet.

The number of URLs that you need to configure for exclusion is substantial and a complete list is beyond the scope of this Exam Ref. The URLs and IP address ranges that are associated with Office 365 are always changing and it is possible to subscribe to an RSS feed that will provide notification when URLs and IP addresses change.

> **MORE INFO** **OFFICE 365 URLS AND IP ADDRESSES**
>
> You can learn more about Office 365 URLS and IP addresses at *https://support.office.com/en-us/article/Office-365-URLs-and-IP-address-ranges-8548a211-3fe7-47cb-abb1-355ea5aa88a2.*

Outbound firewall ports

Clients need to be able to make connections to the Office 365 servers on the Internet using certain protocols and ports. If certain ports and protocols are blocked by a perimeter network firewall, clients will be unable to use specific Office 365 services. Table 2-1 lists the protocols and ports that need to be open for clients on an internal network to host on the Internet.

TABLE 2-1: Office 365 Outbound Port requirements

Protocol	Port	Used by
TCP	443	■ Office 365 portal ■ Outlook ■ Outlook Web App ■ SharePoint Online ■ Skype for Business client ■ ADFS Federation ■ ADFS Proxy
TCP	25	Mail routing
TCP	587	SMTP relay
TCP	143/993	IMAP Simple Migration Tool
TCP	80/443	■ Microsoft Azure Active Directory Sync tool ■ Exchange Management Console ■ Exchange Management Shell
TCP	995	POP3 secure
PSOM/TLS	443	Skype for Business Online: Outbound data sharing
STUN/TCP	443	Skype for Business Online: Outbound audio, video, and application sharing sessions

STUN/UDP	3478	Skype for Business Online: Outbound audio and video sessions
TCP	5223	Skype for Business mobile client push notifications
UDP	20000-45000	Skype for Business Online outbound phone
RTC/UDP	50000-59000	Skype for Business Online: Outbound audio and video sessions.

> **MORE INFO** OFFICE 365 PORTS
>
> You can learn more about Office 365 ports at *https://support.office.com/en-in/article/Office-365-URLs-and-IP-address-ranges-8548a211-3fe7-47cb-abb1-355ea5aa88a2.*

Recommend bandwidth

There are many factors that influence the amount of bandwidth that an organization will require to successfully use Office 365. These factors include:

- The specific Office 365 services to which the organization has subscribed.
- The number of clients connecting to Office 365 from a site at any point in time.
- The type of interaction the client is having with Office 365.
- The performance of the Internet browser software on each client computer.
- The capacity of the network connection available to each client computer.
- Your organization's network topology.

Microsoft provides a number of tools that can be used to estimate the bandwidth requirements of an Office 365 deployment. These include:

- **Exchange Client Network Bandwidth Calculator** This tool allows you to estimate the bandwidth required for Outlook, Outlook Web App, and mobile device users.
- **Skype for Business Online Bandwidth Calculator** This tool allows you to estimate the amount of bandwidth you will require based on the number of Skype for Business users and the specific features those users will be leveraging.
- **OneDrive for Business Synchronization calculator** This tool provides network bandwidth estimates based on how users use OneDrive for Business.

> **MORE INFO** BANDWIDTH PLANNING
>
> You can learn more about bandwidth planning for Office 365 at *https://support.office.com/en-us/article/Network-and-migration-planning-for-Office-365-f5ee6c33-bcd7-4b0b-b0f8-dc1d9fb8d132?ui=en-US&rs=en-US&ad=US#estimatebandwidthrequirements.*

Internet connectivity for clients

To use Office 365, clients need to be able to establish unauthenticated connections over port 80 and port 443 to the Office 365 servers on the Internet. On some networks, especially those configured for small businesses, you may run into the following network connectivity problems:

- **Clients configured with APIPA addresses**   If clients are configured with IP addresses in the APIPA range (169.254.0.0 /16), they most likely cannot make a connection to the Internet. They should be configured with IP addresses in the private range with an appropriate default gateway configured to connect either directly or indirectly to the Internet.

- **No default gateway**   Clients need to be configured with a default gateway address of a device that can route traffic to the Internet. The default gateway device doesn't need to be directly connected to the Internet, but it needs to be able to route traffic to a device that eventually does connect to the Internet.

- **Firewall configuration**   Clients require access to the Internet on the ports outlined earlier in the chapter.

- **Proxy server authentication**   Office 365 does not work if an intervening proxy server requires authentication for connections. You'll have to configure an authentication bypass for Office 365 addresses, or disable proxy server authentication.

Deploy desktop setup for previous versions of Office clients

Versions of Office prior to Office 2007, such as Office 2003, needed special configuration to work with Office 365. Office 2003 extended support expired on the same date that Windows XP extended support expired in April 2014. Products that are no longer supported by Microsoft will not appear on Microsoft exams.

Office 2007 is supported with Office 365. For example, Outlook 2007 supports configuration through the Autodiscover protocol, which means that it is possible to configure Outlook 2007 by providing an Office 365 username and password, just as it is possible to configure Outlook 2010 and Outlook 2013 in this manner.

> *MORE INFO* **USING OFFICE 2007 WITH OFFICE 365**
>
> You can learn more about configuring Outlook 2007 for Office 365 at *https://support.office. com/en-us/article/Set-up-email-in-Outlook-2007-1cf5c44a-43c1-4332-bb54-0d7545322cc0.*

EXAM TIP

Remember that clients will be unable to access Office 365 if client traffic passes through a proxy server that requires authentication.

Thought experiment

Office 365 Bandwidth Requirements at Adatum

In this thought experiment, apply what you've learned about this objective. You can find the answers to these questions in the "Answers" section at the end of the chapter.

You are in the process of attempting to ascertain the bandwidth requirements of a potential Office 365 deployment at Adatum. With this information in mind, answer the following questions:

1. Which tool should you use to estimate Skype for Business bandwidth requirements?

2. Which tool should you use to estimate OneDrive for Business bandwidth requirements?

Objective summary

- Office 365 does not work if proxy servers between the client and the Office 365 servers require authentication.

- A variety of outbound firewall ports must be open between the client and the Office 365 servers for all Office 365 functionality to be available.

- Microsoft provides a number of tools that can be used to estimate the client bandwidth requirements.

- Clients must be able to connect to the Internet to use Office 365.

Objective review

Answer the following questions to test your knowledge of the information in this objective. You can find the answers to these questions and explanations of why each answer choice is correct or incorrect in the "Answers" section at the end of the chapter.

1. Which of the following services does not use TCP port 443 between the client computer and the Office 365 servers on the Internet?

   A. Office 365 Portal

   B. SharePoint Online

   C. Outlook Web App

   D. IMAP Simple Migration Tool

2. Which of the following will cause connectivity problems for clients attempting to connect to Office 365 through a proxy server and firewall on the organization's perimeter network? (Choose two.)

   A. Proxy server that requires authentication

   B. Proxy server that does not require authentication

   C. TCP Port 443 open on the external firewall

   D. TCP Port 443 closed on the external firewall

3. Which of the following client IP addresses is likely to require reconfiguration to ensure that connectivity could be established to the Office 365 servers on the Internet?

   A. 10.10.10.10

   B. 169.254.10.10

   C. 192.168.10.10

   D. 172.16.10.10

Objective 2.3: Administer rights management

This objective deals with rights management in Office 365, which allows you to control who is able to access information and the tasks that they can perform with that information. For example, allowing someone to open a document, but not to modify that document or copy the contents of that document. To master this objective, you'll need to understand the basics of rights management, how Microsoft Office integrates with rights management, the roles for Microsoft Azure Active Directory rights management, and how to recover a protected document.

> **This objective covers the following topics:**
> - Activate rights management
> - Office integration with rights management
> - Assign roles for Microsoft Azure Active Directory RM
> - Enable recovery of protected document

Activate Azure Rights Management

Azure Rights Management allows Azure to function as a rights management provider. This provides Office 365 subscribers with the ability to control how documents are consumed and who can access those documents, even if they are inadvertently sent to unauthorized third parties. Azure Rights Management isn't enabled by default on Office 365 subscriptions and does attract additional per user charges once activated.

To activate Azure Rights Management, perform the following steps:

1. Ensure that you are signed in to the Office 365 Admin Center with an account that has global administrator permissions.

2. In the Office 365 Admin Center,, click Rights Management under the Service Settings node as shown in Figure 2-10.

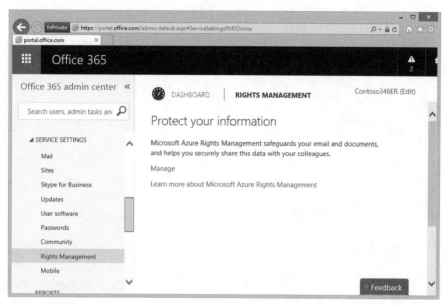

FIGURE 2-10 Rights management

3. On the Protect Your Information page, click Manage.

4. On the Rights Management page, shown in Figure 2-11, click Activate.

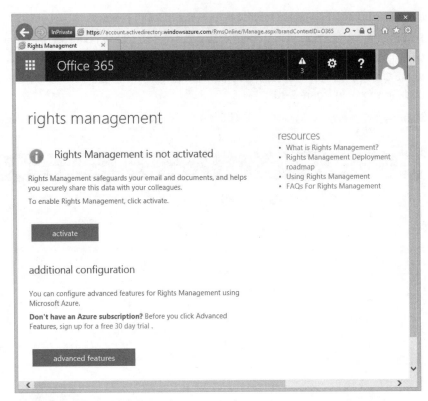

FIGURE 2-11 Active Rights Management

5. On the Do You Want to Activate Rights Management page, shown in Figure 2-12, click Activate.

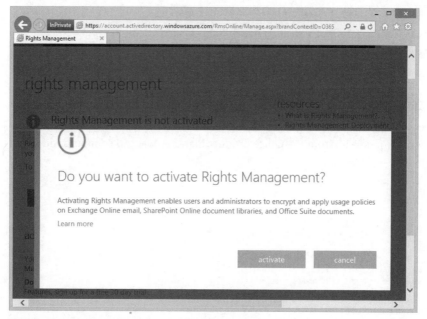

FIGURE 2-12 Do You Want to Activate Rights Management

6. After a few minutes, the message that Rights Management is activated will be displayed, as shown in Figure 2-13.

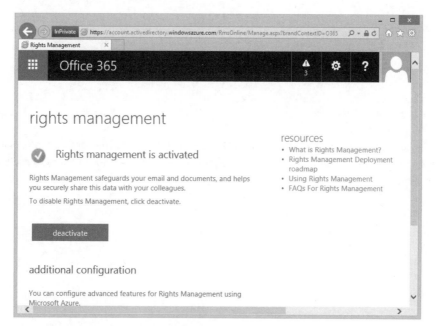

FIGURE 2-13 Rights Management activated

Office integration with Rights Management

It is necessary for users wanting to utilize Rights Management to be signed in to Office 365, as shown in Figure 2-14, from the Office product that they want to configure with Rights Management.

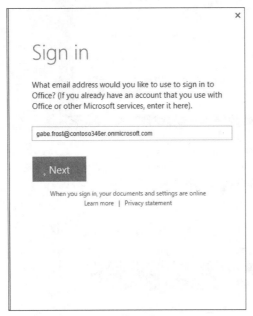

FIGURE 2-14 Sign in to Office 365

A user can verify that they are signed in to Office 365 by checking their account information. Figure 2-15 shows the account information for a user signed in to Word with their Office 365 user account.

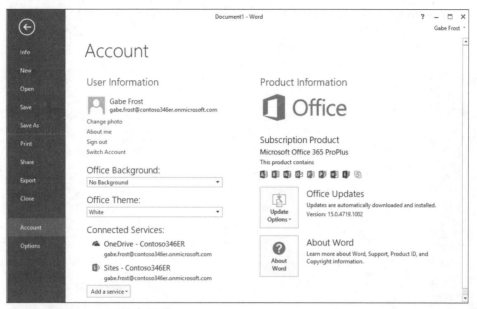

FIGURE 2-15 User account information

Once a user is signed in, they will have access to the Protect Document menu on the Info page of the Stage menu as shown in Figure 2-16.

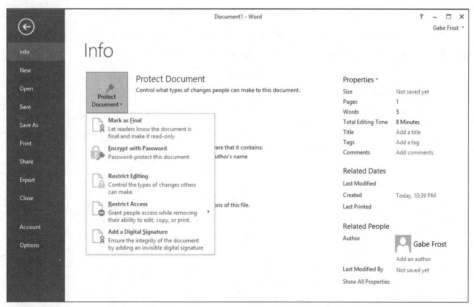

FIGURE 2-16 Protect Document

It may be necessary to connect to the Azure Rights Management servers to get templates. This can be done by clicking Restrict Access and then clicking Connect to Rights Management Servers and Get Templates as shown in Figure 2-17.

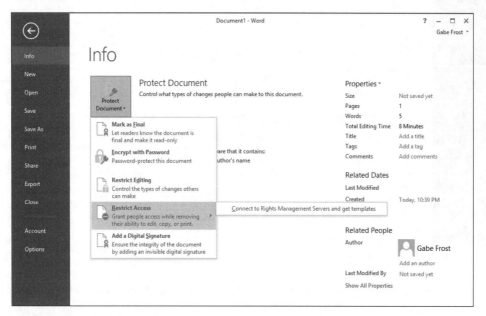

FIGURE 2-17 Restrict Access

Once the templates have been retrieved from the server, these organization-specific templates will be visible in the Restrict Access menu, as shown in Figure 2-18.

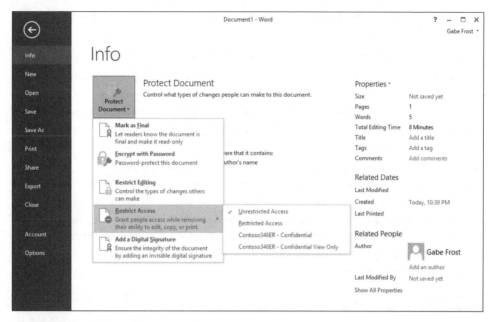

FIGURE 2-18 Available templates

***MORE INFO* CONFIGURE APPLICATIONS FOR AZURE RIGHTS MANAGEMENT**

You can learn more about configuring applications for Azure Rights Management at *https://technet.microsoft.com/en-us/library/jj585031.aspx.*

Assign roles for Microsoft Azure Active Directory RM

Azure Rights Management administrators are able to control the Azure Rights Management service, but are unable to view data protected by the service. You can add a user or group as an Azure Rights Management administrator using the Add-AadrmRoleBasedAdministrator cmdlet.

The Azure Rights Management super user feature allows authorized people and services to view the data that is protected by the Azure Rights Management Service. An Azure Rights Management super user is able to modify the protection applied to a protected document. An Azure Rights Management super user is able to:

- Access documents protected by a user that has left the organization.

- Alter the protection policy applied to existing files.

- Be configured to allow Exchange Server to index mailboxes containing protected content.

- Be configured to allow Data Loss Prevention products and anti-malware products to scan protected documents.
- Perform bulk decryption of files for auditing, legal, or compliance reasons.

The Azure Rights Management super user feature is not enabled by default. It will be enabled automatically when the Rights Management connector is configured for Exchange Server. A user who is configured as an Azure Rights Management administrator can enable the super user role and add users to this role, but cannot by themselves access the protected content unless their account is a member of this role.

You enable the Azure Rights Management super user role using the Enable-AadrmSuperUserFeature cmdlet. You can add user and service accounts to this role using the Add-AadrmSuperUser cmdlet. You can only add individual accounts to the super user role, you can't add security groups to this role. You can disable the super user feature using the Disable-AadrmSuperUserFeature cmdlet. You can view which users have been assigned Azure Rights Management super user privileges using the Get-AadrmSuperUser cmdlet.

> **MORE INFO AZURE ACTIVE DIRECTORY ROLES**
>
> You can learn more about Azure Active Directory Roles at *https://technet.microsoft.com/en-us/library/mt147272.aspx*.

Enable recovery of protected document

A user that has been assigned Azure Rights Management super user role is able to remove protection from a document using the Unprotect-RMSFile cmdlet. A user that has these privileges is able to reapply Rights Management protection using the Protect-RMSFile cmdlet.

EXAM TIP

Remember which cmdlet you use to add users to the Azure Rights Management super user role and which cmdlet enables the role.

Thought experiment

Azure Rights Management at Margie's Travel

In this thought experiment, apply what you've learned about this objective. You can find the answers to these questions in the "Answers" section at the end of the chapter.

You are investigating the features of Azure Rights Management on behalf of Margie's Travel. You want to know about how it might be possible for an authorized person to remove rights management protection from a document. You are also interested in learning about managing the super user functionality. With this information in mind, answer the following questions:

1. Which Windows PowerShell cmdlet removes Azure Rights Management protection?

2. Which Windows PowerShell cmdlet disables the Azure Rights Management super user functionality?

Objective summary

- Azure Rights Management isn't activated by default on Office 365 tenancies and must be enabled in the Office 365 Admin Center.

- Office 365 users must be signed in to Office 365 from Office applications before they are able to access Azure Rights Management functionality.

- Azure Rights Management administrators are able to control the Azure Rights Management Service, but are unable to view data protected by Azure Rights Management.

- Azure Rights Management super users are able to access protected content, as well as modify protection settings applied to documents.

- Azure Rights Management super user functionality must be manually enabled.

- Users who have Azure Rights Management super user permissions can remove protection from a document using the Unprotect-RMSFile Windows PowerShell cmdlet.

Objective review

Answer the following questions to test your knowledge of the information in this objective. You can find the answers to these questions and explanations of why each answer choice is correct or incorrect in the "Answers" section at the end of the chapter.

1. Which Windows PowerShell cmdlet would you use to add an Office 365 user account to the Azure Rights Management administrator role?

   A. Enable-AadrmSuperUserFeature

   B. Add-AadrmSuperUser

   C. Add-AadrmRoleBasedAdministrator

   D. Disable-AadrmSuperUser

2. Which Windows PowerShell cmdlet would you use to enable the Azure Rights Management super user role?

A. Add-AadrmRoleBasedAdministrator

B. Enable-AadrmSuperUserFeature

C. Add-AadrmSuperUser

D. Disable-AadrmSuperUser

3. Which Windows PowerShell cmdlet would you use to add a user account to the Azure Rights Management super user role?

A. Enable-AadrmSuperUserFeature

B. Get-AadrmSuperUser

C. Add-AadrmRoleBasedAdministrator

D. Add-AadrmSuperUser

4. Which Windows PowerShell cmdlet would you use to determine which users have been added to the Azure Rights Management super users role?

A. Add-AadrmSuperUser

B. Disable-AadrmSuperUser

C. Get-AadrmSuperUser

D. Add-AadrmRoleBasedAdministrator

Objective 2.4: Manage administrator roles in Office 365

This objective deals with the different administrator roles that are available in Office 365. In Chapter 1, you learned basic information about some of these roles. To master this objective, you'll need to understand the differences between each of the roles, and understand how you can assign and revoke role membership.

> **This objective covers the following topics:**
> - Global administrator
> - Billing administrator
> - User management administrator
> - Service administrator
> - Password administrator
> - Delegated administrator
> - Manage role membership

Global administrator

As you learned in the previous chapter, global administrators have the most permissions over an Office 365 tenancy. A global administrator has the following permissions:

- View organization and user information
- Manage support tickets
- Reset user passwords
- Perform billing and purchasing operations
- Create and manage user views
- Create, edit, and delete users
- Create, edit, and delete groups
- Manage user licenses
- Manage domains
- Manage organization information
- Delegate administrative roles to others
- User directory synchronization

Users who have the global administrator role in the Office 365 tenancy have the following roles in Exchange Online:

- Exchange Online admin
- Company admin
- SharePoint Online admin
- Skype for Business Online admin

> *MORE INFO* **GLOBAL ADMINISTRATOR ROLE**
>
> You can learn more about the global administrator role at *https://support.office.com/en-us/article/Assigning-admin-roles-eac4d046-1afd-4f1a-85fc-8219c79e1504.*

Billing administrator

Members of the billing administrator role are responsible for making purchases, managing Office 365 subscriptions, managing support tickets, and monitoring the health of Office 365 services. Members of the billing administrator role have the following permissions:

- View organization and user information
- Manage support tickets
- Perform billing and purchasing operations

Members of this role do not have any equivalent roles in Exchange Online, SharePoint Online, or Skype for Business Online.

User management administrator

Members of the user management administrator role are able to reset some user passwords; monitor service health; and manage some user accounts, groups, and service requests. Members of this role have the following permissions:

- View organization and user information
- Manage support tickets
- Reset the passwords of all user accounts except those assigned the global administrator, billing administrator, or service administrator roles
- Create and manage user views
- Can create, edit, and delete users and groups except users who are assigned global administrator privileges
- Can manage user licenses
- Have the Skype for Business Online admin role

Service administrator

Members of the service administrator role are able to manage service requests and monitor the health of services. Before a global administrator can assign the service administrator role to a user, the user must be assigned administrative permissions to one of the Office 365 services, such as SharePoint Online or Exchange Online. Service administrators have the following permissions over the assigned service:

- View organization and user information
- Manage support tickets

Password administrator

Members of the password administrator role are responsible for resetting passwords for non-privileged users and other members of the password administrator role. Members of this role are also able to manage service requests and monitor service health. Members of this role have the following permissions:

- View organization and user information
- Manage support tickets
- Can reset non-privileged user passwords as well as passwords of other password administrators; cannot reset passwords of global administrators, user management administrators, or billing administrators
- Exchange Online Help Desk admin role
- Skype for Business Online admin role

> *MORE INFO* **PASSWORD ADMINISTRATOR**
>
> You can learn more about topic at *https://support.office.com/en-us/article/Assigning-admin-roles-eac4d046-1afd-4f1a-85fc-8219c79e1504.*

Delegated administrator

Delegated administrators are people outside the organization who perform administrative duties within the Office 365 tenancy. Administrators of the tenancy control who has delegated administrator permissions. You can only assign delegated administrator permissions to users who have Office 365 accounts in their own tenancy.

When you configure delegated administration, you can choose one of the following permission levels:

- **Full administration**   When you assign the full administration role to a delegated administrator, that administrator has the same privileges as a member of the global admin role.
- **Limited administration**   When you assign the limited administration role to a delegated administrator, that administrator has the same privileges as a member of the password admin role.

Delegated admins are managed in the Delegated Admins node of the Office 365 Admin Center as shown in Figure 2-19.

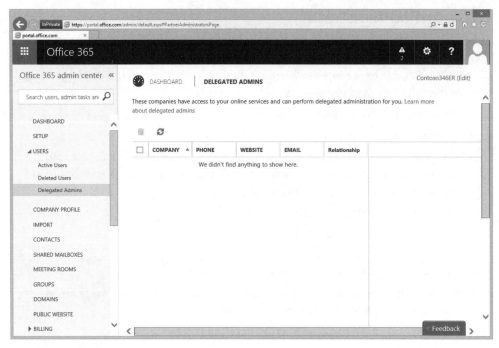

FIGURE 2-19 Delegated Admins

MORE INFO **DELEGATED ADMINISTRATORS**

You can learn more about delegated administrators at *https://support.office.microsoft. com/en-us/article/Partners-Offer-delegated-administration-26530dc0-ebba-415b-86b1- b55bc06b073e.*

Manage role membership

You can assign an administrative role on the Settings page of an Office 365 user's properties, as shown in Figure 2-20. When you assign an administrative role, you specify the role that you want to assign and an alternate email address allows someone assigned the role to perform password recovery. You can only add Office 365 users to a role. You cannot add an Office 365 group to a role.

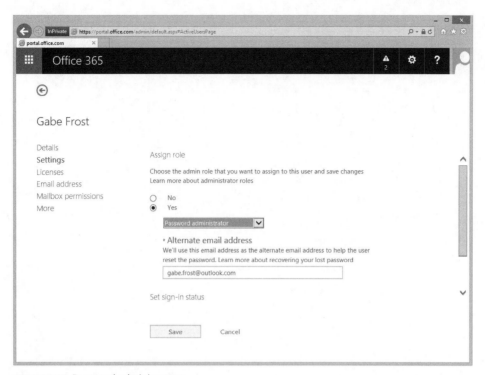

FIGURE 2-20 Password administrator

You can use the Settings page of a user's account to remove an assigned role. To do this, select the role that you want to remove and select the No option and then click Save, as shown in Figure 2-21.

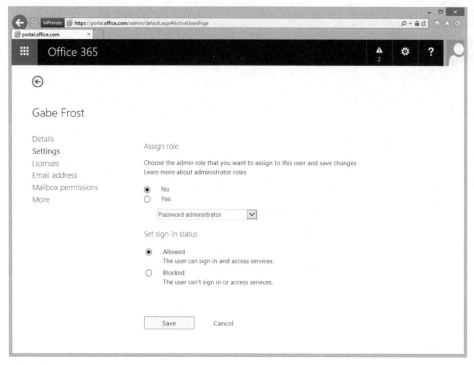

FIGURE 2-21 Remove role

You can view a list of users assigned a particular role by using the Active Users node in the Office 365 Admin Center and selecting the role whose membership you wish to view. Figure 2-22 shows the members of the password admins role.

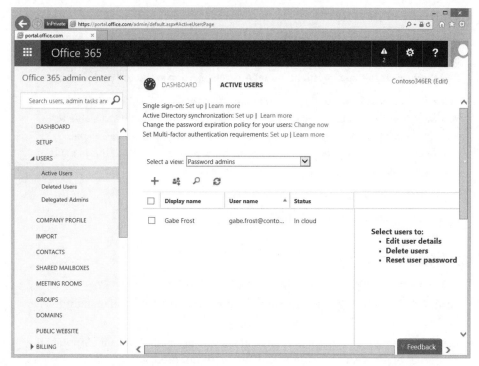

FIGURE 2-22 List of password administrators

You can use the following Windows PowerShell cmdlets to manage Office 365 administrative roles:

- **Add-MsolRoleMember**   Use this cmdlet to add a user to a role.
- **Remove-MsolRoleMember**   Use this cmdlet to remove a user from a role.
- **Get-MsolRole**   Use this cmdlet to retrieve a list of administrative roles.
- **Get-MsolRoleMember**   Use this cmdlet to list the members of a specific administrative role.

MORE INFO **ASSIGNING ADMINISTRATIVE ROLES**

You can learn more about assigning administrative roles at *https://support.office.com/en-us/article/Assigning-admin-roles-eac4d046-1afd-4f1a-85fc-8219c79e1504*.

EXAM TIP

Remember the PowerShell cmdlets that you use to manage administrative role membership.

Thought experiment

Administrative roles at Contoso

In this thought experiment, apply what you've learned about this objective. You can find the answers to these questions in the "Answers" section at the end of the chapter.

You are in the process of configuring administrative role memberships at Contoso. You want to allow Sam to create new Office 365 users, but he shouldn't be able to modify administrative roles. You want Don to be able to pay the Office 365 bills, but he shouldn't be assigned any other unnecessary permissions. With this in mind, answer the following questions.

1. Which role should you add Sam to?

2. Which role should you add Don to?

Objective summary

- Global administrators have full permissions over an Office 365 tenancy.
- Billing administrators can manage subscriptions, support tickets and monitor tenancy health.
- User management administrators can manage user accounts, but cannot modify the properties of users who are members of administrator groups.
- Service administrators are able to manage service requests and can monitor service health for services that they have been granted permission over.
- Password administrators can reset passwords of non-privileged users.
- Delegated administrators are users from other Office 365 tenancies that have been granted administrator access over the tenancy. They can be assigned global administrator or password administrator permissions.
- Administrator roles can be managed through the Office 365 console or by using the Add-MsolRoleMember, Remove-MsolRoleMember, Get-MsolRole, and Get-MsolRoleMember cmdlets.

Objective review

Answer the following questions to test your knowledge of the information in this objective. You can find the answers to these questions and explanations of why each answer choice is correct or incorrect in the "Answers" section at the end of the chapter.

1. Which Windows PowerShell cmdlet would you use to add an Office 365 user to the global administrator role?

   A. Get-MsolRole

   B. Get-MsolRoleMembers

   C. Add-MsolRoleMember

   D. Remove-MsolRoleMember

2. Which Windows PowerShell cmdlet would you use to remove a user from a specific administrative role?

   A. Get-MsolRole

   B. Remove-MsolRoleMember

   C. Add-MsolRoleMember

   D. Get-MsolRoleMembers

3. Which Windows PowerShell cmdlet would you use to view the administrative roles associated with an Office 365 tenancy?

   A. Remove-MsolRoleMember

   B. Add-MsolRoleMember

   C. Get-MsolRoleMembers

   D. Get-MsolRole

4. Which Windows PowerShell cmdlet would you use to determine the membership of a specific Office 365 administrative role?

   A. Get-MsolRole

   B. Get-MsolRoleMembers

   C. Add-MsolRoleMember

   D. Remove-MsolRoleMember

Answers

This section contains the solutions to the thought experiments and answers to the objective review questions in this chapter.

Objective 2.1: Thought experiment

1. The _sipfederationtls SRV record should be configured to use TCP port 5061.
2. The _sip SRV record should be configured to use TCP port 443.

Objective 2.1: Review

1. **Correct answer:** C

   A. **Incorrect:** The record must have the text include:sharepointonline.com added, not office365.com.

   B. **Incorrect:** The record must have the text include:sharepointonline.com added, not sharepoint.com.

   C. **Correct:** The record must have the text include:sharepointonline.com added.

   D. **Incorrect:** The record must have the text include:sharepointonline.com added, not exchange.com.

2. **Correct answer:** B

   A. **Incorrect:** SPF records are not used to route email. MX records are used to route email.

   B. **Correct:** MX records are used to route email.

   C. **Incorrect:** CNAME records are not used to route email. MX records are used to route email.

   D. **Incorrect:** SRV records are not used to route email. MX records are used to route email.

3. **Correct answer:** D

   A. **Incorrect:** The alias should not point at sipdir.online.exchange.com. The sip alias in the custom domain should point at sipdir.online.lync.com.

   B. **Incorrect:** The alias should not point at sipdir.online.sharepoint.com. The sip alias in the custom domain should point at sipdir.online.lync.com.

   C. **Incorrect:** The alias should not point at sipdir.online.exchange.com. The sip alias in the custom domain should point at sipdir.online.lync.com.

   D. **Correct:** The sip alias in the custom domain should point at sipdir.online.lync.com.

4. **Correct answer:** B

   A. Incorrect: An SPF record is a TXT record, not a SRV record.

   B. Correct: An SPF record is a TXT record.

   C. Incorrect: An SPF record is a TXT record, not a MX record.

   D. Incorrect: An SPF record is a TXT record, not a CNAME record.

Objective 2.2: Thought experiment

1. You should use the Skype for Business bandwidth calculator to estimate Skype for Business bandwidth requirements.

2. You should use the OneDrive for Business Synchronization calculator to estimate OneDrive for Business bandwidth requirements.

Objective 2.2: Review

1. **Correct answer:** D

   A. Incorrect: The Office 365 Portal uses TCP port 443.

   B. Incorrect: SharePoint Online uses TCP port 443.

   C. Incorrect: Outlook Web App uses TCP port 443.

   D. Correct: The IMAP Simple Migration Tool uses TCP ports 143 and 993.

2. **Correct answers:** A and D

   A. Correct: The proxy server should be configured not to require authentication as proxy servers that require authentication will cause problems when placed between clients and the Office 365 servers on the Internet.

   B. Incorrect: The proxy server should be configured not to require authentication as proxy servers that require authentication will cause problems when placed between clients and the Office 365 servers on the Internet.

   C. Incorrect: TCP Port 443 must be open on the external firewall.

   D. Correct: TCP Port 443 must be open on the external firewall.

3. **Correct answer:** B

   A. Incorrect: The IP address 10.10.10.10 is in the private IP address range used by many organizations on their internal networks.

   B. Correct: The IP address 169.254.10.10 is in the APIPA address range. This address range is automatically assigned when clients are not configured with an IP address and usually indicates that Internet connectivity will be unable to be established.

   C. Incorrect: The IP address 192.168.10.10 is in the private IP address range used by many organizations on their internal networks.

   D. Incorrect: The IP address 172.16.10.10 is in the private IP address range used by many organizations on their internal networks.

Objective 2.3: Thought experiment

1. The Unprotect-RMSFile cmdlet will remove Azure Rights Management protection from a file.

2. The Disable-AadrmSuperUserFeature cmdlet will disable the Azure Rights Management super user functionality.

Objective 2.3: Review

1. **Correct answer:** C

   A. **Incorrect:** You enable the Azure Rights Management super user role using the Enable-AadrmSuperUserFeature cmdlet.

   B. **Incorrect:** You can add user and service accounts to this role using the Add-AadrmSuperUser cmdlet.

   C. **Correct:** You can add a user or group as an Azure Rights Management administrator using the Add-AadrmRoleBasedAdministrator cmdlet. Azure Rights Management administrators are able to control the Azure Rights Management service, but are unable to view data protected by the service.

   D. **Incorrect:** You can disable the super user feature using the Disable-AadrmSuperUserFeature cmdlet.

2. **Correct answer:** B

   A. **Incorrect:** You can add a user or group as an Azure Rights Management administrator using the Add-AadrmRoleBasedAdministrator cmdlet. Azure Rights Management Administrators are able to control the Azure Rights Management service, but are unable to view data protected by the service.

   B. **Correct:** You enable the Azure Rights Management super user role using the Enable-AadrmSuperUserFeature cmdlet.

   C. **Incorrect:** You can add user and service accounts to this role using the Add-AadrmSuperUser cmdlet.

   D. **Incorrect:** You can disable the super user feature using the Disable-AadrmSuperUserFeature cmdlet.

3. **Correct answer:** D

   A. **Incorrect:** You enable the Azure Rights Management super user role using the Enable-AadrmSuperUserFeature cmdlet.

   B. **Incorrect:** You can view which users have been assigned Azure Rights Management super user privileges using the Get-AadrmSuperUser cmdlet.

   C. **Incorrect:** You can add a user or group as an Azure Rights Management administrator using the Add-AadrmRoleBasedAdministrator cmdlet. Azure Rights Management administrators are able to control the Azure Rights Management service, but are unable to view data protected by the service.

   D. **Correct:** You can add user and service accounts to this role using the Add-AadrmSuperUser cmdlet.

4. **Correct answer:** C

   A. **Incorrect:** You can add user and service accounts to this role using the Add-AadrmSuperUser cmdlet.

   B. **Incorrect:** You can disable the super user feature using the Disable-AadrmSuperUserFeature cmdlet.

   C. **Correct:** You can view which users have been assigned Azure Rights Management super user privileges using the Get-AadrmSuperUser cmdlet.

   D. **Incorrect:** You can add a user or group as an Azure Rights Management administrator using the Add-AadrmRoleBasedAdministrator cmdlet. Azure Rights Management administrators are able to control the Azure Rights Management service, but are unable to view data protected by the service.

Objective 2.4: Thought experiment

1. You should add Sam to the user management administrator role.

2. You should add Don to the billing administrator role.

Objective 2.4: Review

1. **Correct answer:** C

   A. **Incorrect:** The Get-MsolRole cmdlet allows you to view the available administrative roles.

   B. **Incorrect:** The Get-MsolRoleMembers cmdlet allows you to view the members of a specific role.

   C. **Correct:** The Add-MsolRoleMember cmdlet is used to add users to a role.

   D. **Incorrect:** The Remove-MsolRoleMember cmdlet allows you to remove a user from a specific administrative role.

2. **Correct answer:** B

   A. **Incorrect:** The Get-MsolRole cmdlet allows you to view the available administrative roles.

   B. **Correct:** The Remove-MsolRoleMember cmdlet allows you to remove a user from a specific administrative role.

   C. **Incorrect:** The Add-MsolRoleMember cmdlet is used to add users to a role.

   D. **Incorrect:** The Get-MsolRoleMembers cmdlet allows you to view the members of a specific role.

3. **Correct answer:** D

   A. **Incorrect:** The Remove-MsolRoleMember cmdlet allows you to remove a user from a specific administrative role.

   B. **Incorrect:** The Add-MsolRoleMember cmdlet is used to add users to a role.

   C. **Incorrect:** The Get-MsolRoleMembers cmdlet allows you to view the members of a specific role.

   D. **Correct:** The Get-MsolRole cmdlet allows you to view the available administrative roles.

4. **Correct answer:** B

   A. **Incorrect:** The Get-MsolRole cmdlet allows you to view the available administrative roles.

   B. **Correct:** The Get-MsolRoleMembers cmdlet allows you to view the members of a specific role.

   C. **Incorrect:** The Add-MsolRoleMember cmdlet is used to add users to a role.

   D. **Incorrect:** The Remove-MsolRoleMember cmdlet allows you to remove a user from a specific administrative role.

CHAPTER 3

Manage cloud identities

Cloud identities is the term used to refer to Office 365 user accounts. These accounts are stored within Azure Active Directory. Users authenticate against Azure Active Directory when signing in to the Office 365 portal or when required to authenticate to use other Office 365 resources. Just as you need to manage user accounts, password policies, and security groups when managing an on-premises environment where users authenticate against Active Directory domain controllers, the 70-346 exam requires you to know how to manage Office 365 user accounts, password policies, and security groups using both the Office 365 Admin Center as well as Windows PowerShell.

Objectives in this chapter:

- Objective 3.1: Configure password management
- Objective 3.2: Manage user and security groups
- Objective 3.3: Manage cloud identities with Windows PowerShell

Objective 3.1: Configure password management

This objective deals with configuring the properties of passwords for users of Office 365. Password policies allow you to set rules about how complex a password must be, configure the number of days that need to elapse before a user's password expires, and set the number of days prior to expiry before a warning is sent. This objective also deals with resetting both user account and administrator passwords.

> **This objective covers the following topics:**
> - Expiry policy
> - Password complexity
> - Password resets

Working with cloud identities

Cloud identities, including Office 365 user accounts and security groups, are stored within Azure Active Directory rather than in a separate Office 365 specific account database. This means that user identities are subject to Azure Active Directory policies, such as the Azure Active Directory password and account lockout policies. A big adjustment for administrators of traditional on-premises environments is that many settings, such as how complex a password must be, or how many incorrect passwords must be entered before a lockout is triggered, and what the duration of the account lockout will be, are configured by Microsoft and cannot be configured by administrators of Office 365 through the Office 365 Admin Center. When studying for the 70-346 exam, candidates need to be familiar with the settings that they are able to configure as well as the settings that are non-configurable and are applied by Microsoft.

Configuring password policies

Password policies determine how often an Office 365 user must change their password. The default Office 365 settings require a user to change their password every 90 days, with a warning issued 14 days prior to password expiration.

You configure Office 365 password policies using the Office 365 Admin Center. To perform this action, navigate to the Passwords section under the SERVICE SETTINGS and specify the following options as shown in Figure 3-1:

- **Passwords Never Expire** Enabling this setting means that the password does not expire.
- **Days Before Passwords Expire** The maximum number of days that a password remains valid. You can set this to values between a minimum of 14 and a maximum of 730 days.
- **Days Before a User is Notified That Their Password Will Expire** This setting determines the number of days prior to password expiration that the user will receive notification. The value can be set to between 1 and 30 days.

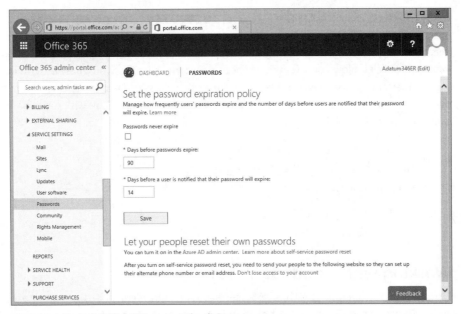

FIGURE 3-1 Default Office 365 password policies

Password expiration duration and password expiration notification settings can be configured using the Set-MsolPasswordPolicy Windows PowerShell cmdlet, which is included in the Azure Active Directory module for Windows PowerShell. Password expiration can be set with the Set-MsolUser cmdlet. Use a value of FALSE to ensure that the password will expire and a value of TRUE to configure the account so that the password will not expire. Using Windows PowerShell to manage cloud identities is covered in more detail later in this chapter.

Following password complexity policies

Password complexity policies in Office 365 are not able to be configured by administrators and are instead set by Microsoft. The password complexity policies specified by Microsoft require passwords to have the following properties:

- 8 character minimum
- 16 character maximum
- Can include the following characters: A–Z, a–z, 0–9, @ # $ % ^ & * - _ + = [ ] { } | \ : ' , . ? / ` ~ " ( ) ;
- Cannot include Unicode characters
- Cannot include spaces
- Cannot contain a dot character (.) immediately preceding an at sign (@)

Although you cannot disable Office 365 password complexity requirements using Office 365 Admin Center, you can disable complex password requirements on a per-user basis using Windows PowerShell.

Office 365 requires that the last password used cannot be used again. This differs from Active Directory, where a configurable number of recent passwords cannot be reused. This means that a user can rotate their password between a small number of passwords. The lack of a lengthier password history is a good reason to enable multi-factor authentication on Office 365 user accounts. Multi-factor authentication is covered in more detail later in this chapter.

Office 365 account lockout policies are also managed by Microsoft. If 10 sequential unsuccessful login attempts are made, a user will need to respond to a CAPTCHA dialog box. A CAPTCHA is a test used to protect Office 365 user accounts from automated password attacks.

After an additional 10 sequential unsuccessful login attempts, the user will be locked out for a time period starting at 90 seconds and increasing with each subsequent incorrect login attempt. At no point will the account be locked out in such a way that it can only be unlocked by an Office 365 administrator.

> **MORE INFO** **PASSWORD POLICIES**
>
> You can learn more about Office 365 password policies at the following address: *https://technet.microsoft.com/library/jj943764.aspx*.

Resetting passwords

Helping users who forget their passwords is a fundamental element of the practice of systems administration. Though Microsoft is hinting at moving away from password-based authentication with Windows 10, services such as Office 365 and Azure Active Directory still use passwords as the primary method of authentication.

The drawback of using passwords is that the more secure you make them, the less likely users are to remember them. While a password policy that requires users to change their passwords every 21 days does marginally increase security, it will also increase the number of calls to the service desk as more users require administrators to reset their forgotten passwords. Office 365 provides two basic methods of dealing with forgotten passwords: the first is to have an administrator perform a manual password reset; the second is to allow the user to reset their own password using the self-service password reset mechanism.

Administrator reset

Office 365 administrators can reset user passwords using the Office 365 Admin Center or by using the Set-MsolUserPassword cmdlet, which is part of the Azure Active Directory module for Windows PowerShell. You'll learn more about performing operations using this module later in the chapter.

When you reset a user password using Office 365 Admin Center, Office 365 assigns a new temporary password. This means that the administrator does not choose the temporary password to be assigned. As a way of remembering this temporary password, Office 365 provides you with the option of emailing the password to one or more email addresses.

Once the password is reset, the reset user password will be displayed on the screen as shown in Figure 3-2. Because the password is displayed on the screen, an administrator can perform a reset and use another method to communicate the reset password to the user. For example, you could choose to send an SMS to the user or provide the password verbally by telephone call. Using an alternative method to communicate the password to the user is more secure than sending the password in clear text using email.

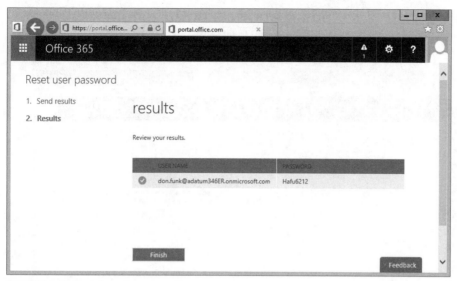

FIGURE 3-2 Password reset

To reset a user password, perform the following steps:

1. In the Office 365 Admin Center, select the Active Users area, which is located under the USERS section.

2. In the Active Users area, select the user account for which you need to reset the password. Figure 3-3 shows the Don Funk user account selected.

FIGURE 3-3 Select the user in the Active Users area

3. Under the user's name, click Reset Password.

4. On the Send Results In Email page, configure the email address to which the new password will be sent. Note that if you choose to email the password, that information will be sent in clear text and will not be protected by encryption. The default option,

shown in Figure 3-4, is that the user will be required to reset their password the next time they sign in. Passwords transmitted in clear text over email should always be reset as expeditiously as possible.

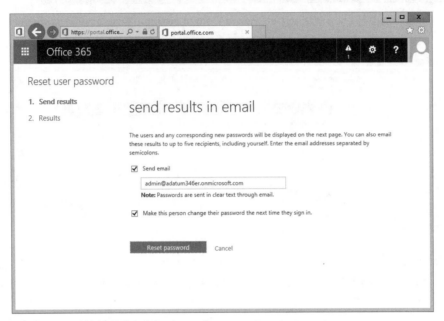

FIGURE 3-4 Send reset information in email

5. When you click Reset Password, the temporary password is displayed on the screen. If you haven't chosen to email the password, you should make a note of it and then forward it to the recipient using another method.

6. Click Finish to complete the password reset operation.

Self-service password reset

Self-service password reset allows users to reset a forgotten password rather than having to contact an administrator to reset the password.

Self-service password reset has the following prerequisites:

- You must use an Azure Active Directory tenant. Office 365 functions as an Azure Active Directory tenant, so if you have Office 365, you have met this prerequisite. This Azure Active Directory tenant must be associated with an Azure subscription.

- You must use Azure Active Directory Premium or Basic. Azure Active Directory comes in Free, Basic, and Premium editions.

- There must be at least one administrator account and one user account in the Azure Active Directory instance.

- The Azure Active Directory Premium or Basic license must be assigned to the administrator and user account.

To configure self-service password reset, perform the following steps:

1. Open the Azure Management Portal and select the Active Directory section in the navigation pane.

2. Select the Active Directory instance for which you want to configure the user password reset policy. Figure 3-5 shows the Adatum346ER directory selected.

FIGURE 3-5 Azure Active Directory instance

3. On the Configure tab, select Yes next to Users Enabled For Password Reset as shown in Figure 3-6.

FIGURE 3-6 Enable password reset

4. You can choose to allow all standard users to reset passwords, or restrict the reset to a specific group of users. Administrative users don't use the same password mechanism as standard users. The administrative user password reset policy is controlled by Microsoft and is not configurable by an Office 365 or Azure Active Directory administrator.

Figure 3-7 shows the user password reset policy configured so that only members of the SSPRSecurityGroupUsers group are able to perform self-service password reset.

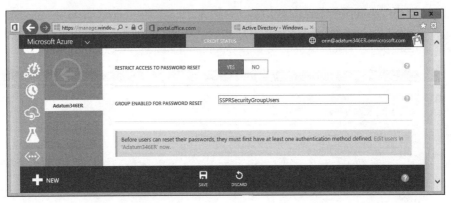

FIGURE 3-7 Limit password reset

5. You can opt to enable one or more of the following authentication methods, as shown in Figure 3-8. You can also require that more than one authentication method be used to perform a password reset, such as answering a security question and providing a code that is sent via SMS message. The contact settings will be taken from the settings stored with the user's Office 365/Azure Active Directory user account. You can also provide users with a link to the following webpage, *http://aka.ms/ssprsetup*, which allows authenticated users to alter their authentication information.

- **Office Phone** The user's office phone number. This option supports the phone call method of verification.

- **Mobile Phone** The user's mobile phone number. This option supports the phone call and SMS method of verification.

- **Alternate Email Address** Verification information is sent to a previously specified email address.

- **Security Questions** Question and answer pairs are selected by the user at the Authentication Information Registration page. You can configure which questions are asked through the Azure Management console.

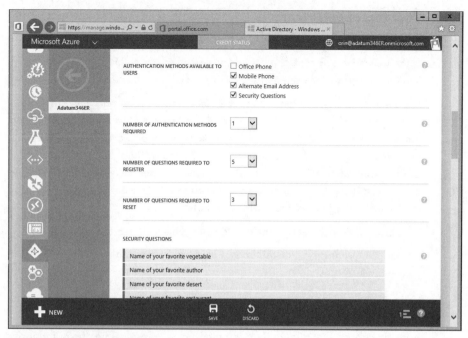

FIGURE 3-8 Limit password reset

Once you have enabled the self-service password reset policy, users will be able to perform self-service password resets by clicking the Can't Access Your Account? link on the Office 365 sign-in portal, *portal.microsoftonline.com*.

> **MORE INFO** **AZURE ACTIVE DIRECTORY SELF-SERVICE PASSWORD RESET**
>
> You can learn more about enabling self-service password reset at *https://msdn.microsoft. com/en-us/library/azure/dn683881.aspx*.

EXAM TIP

Remember the password complexity requirements and limitations.

Thought experiment

Password reset at Adatum

In this thought experiment, apply what you've learned about this objective. You can find the answers to these questions in the "Answers" section at the end of this chapter.

You are in the process of configuring the user password reset policy for Office 365 users at Adatum. All users at Adatum have been issued mobile phones, and they do not have traditional landlines. Each user at Adatum has only a single email account. Company policy requires that email accounts hosted by third-party providers not be used for Adatum-related business or activities. Within these constraints, you want to configure the strongest user password reset policy possible. With this information in mind, answer the following questions:

1. Which password reset options should you enable for Adatum?

2. How many authentication methods should be required in the user password reset policy?

Objective summary

- Administrators can configure how complex a password must be, the number of days that need to elapse before a user's password expires, and set the number of days prior to expiry before a warning is sent.

- Office 365 password complexity policies are not configurable by tenant administrators.

- Passwords must be between 8 and 16 characters, must have a mix of three uppercase, lowercase, numbers and symbols, and cannot include a dot character (.) preceding an at sign (@).

- Administrators can reset passwords or configure self-service password reset.

- Self-service password reset options include office phone, mobile phone, alternate email address, and security questions.

Objective review

Answer the following questions to test your knowledge of the information in this objective. You can find the answers to these questions and explanations of each answer choice in the "Answers" section at the end of this chapter.

1. Which of the following authentication methods can you enable in a user password reset policy? (Choose all that apply.)

    A. Office phone

    B. Mobile phone

    C. Multi-factor authentication

    D. Security questions

2. Which of the following passwords conform with the Office 365 password policy?

   A. Sydney123

   B. AbC.@2345

   C. 5432@.AbC

   D. 31337

3. Which of the following settings can Office 365 administrators configure?

   A. Maximum password length

   B. Minimum password length

   C. Minimum password age

   D. Maximum password age

4. Which of the following characters cannot be included in an Office 365 user password?

   A. " " (space)

   B. @

   C. %

   D. ^

Objective 3.2: Manage user and security groups

This objective deals with how you can manage Office 365 user and security groups. You'll also learn how to bulk import users into Office 365, configure multi-factor authentication, perform a soft delete of a user account, and leverage the Azure Active Directory Graph API for user and group management.

> **This objective covers the following topics:**
> - Bulk import
> - Soft delete
> - Multi-factor authentication
> - Azure Active Directory Graph API

Using the bulk import process

The bulk import process allows you to import a list of users from a specially formatted CSV file into Office 365. This CSV file must have the following fields in the first row:

- User name
- First name
- Last name

- Display name
- Job title
- Department
- Office number
- Office phone
- Mobile phone
- Fax
- Address
- City
- State or province
- ZIP or postal code
- Country or region

Each of these fields must be on the first line and each must be separated by a comma (','). Both a sample and a blank CSV file can be downloaded from the Bulk Add Users page.

Once you have populated the CSV file with the account information you want to import, you can complete this operation by performing the following steps:

1. In the Office 365 Admin Center, click the Active Users node under the USERS node.

2. Click the Bulk Add icon next to the Add icon.

3. On the Select a CSV File page, shown in Figure 3-9, select the specially formatted file that has the user account information and click Next.

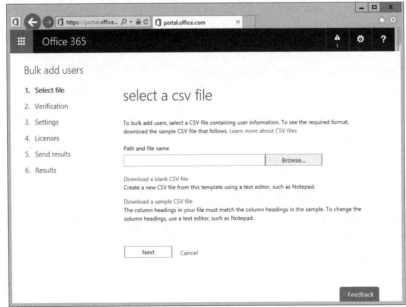

FIGURE 3-9 Select a CSV file

4. On the Verification Results page, shown in Figure 3-10, ensure that all users have passed verification. If some users have not passed verification, you can view the import log file. Click Next to continue.

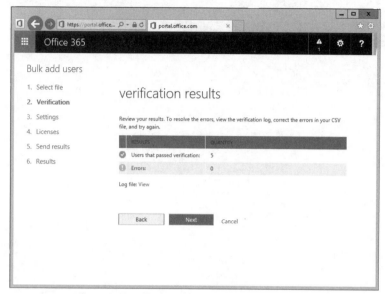

FIGURE 3-10 Verification results

5. On the Settings page, you will specify whether users are allowed to sign in and access services. You will also need to specify the user location on this page. Figure 3-11 shows that users are allowed to sign in and their user location is set to United States. Click Next.

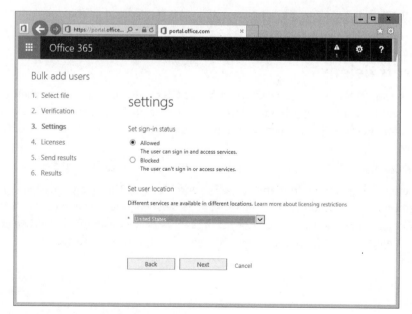

FIGURE 3-11 Set sign-in status

6. On the Assign Licenses page, shown in Figure 3-12, you will specify which services the imported users are licensed for and click Next.

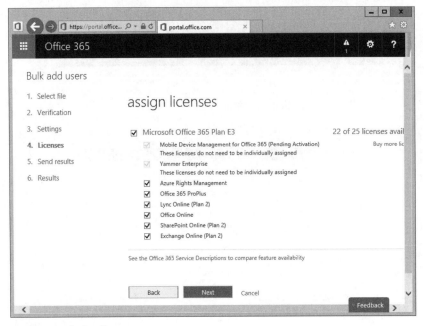

FIGURE 3-12 Assign licenses

7. On the Send Results page, you can send the results to an email address if you choose. Click Create to make the new Office 365 user accounts.

8. On the Results page, you will see a list of the users created and a list of the temporary passwords assigned.

Using soft delete

There are several methods that you can use to delete Office 365 user accounts. Whether the user account is permanently deleted, termed a "hard delete," or is moved to the Azure Active Directory Recycle Bin, termed a "soft delete," depends on the method used to delete the account.

You can use the following methods to delete an Office 365 user account:

- Delete the user account from the Office 365 admin portal. This involves navigating to the Users node, selecting the Active Users node, selecting the user that you want to delete, and selecting Delete from the list of tasks associated with the user. When you click Delete, you will be prompted with the warning shown in Figure 3-13.

Warning

Are you sure that you want to delete the selected users?

Yes   No

FIGURE 3-13 Delete a user account warning box

- Delete using the Remove-MsolUser cmdlet located in the Azure Active Directory module for Windows PowerShell. More detail on this cmdlet, including how to use it to perform a hard user deletion rather than just a soft deletion, is provided later in this chapter.

- User accounts can be deleted through the Exchange Admin Center in Exchange Online.

- If directory synchronization is configured, users can be deleted when removed from the on-premises Active Directory Services instance.

You can view a list of soft deleted users in the Deleted Users section, under the USERS area of the Office 365 Admin Center.

Figure 3-14 shows the deleted Office 365 user account of Gabe Frost. Soft-deleted users remain visible for 30 days and can be recovered during this period. After this period expires, the user account is deleted and is unrecoverable.

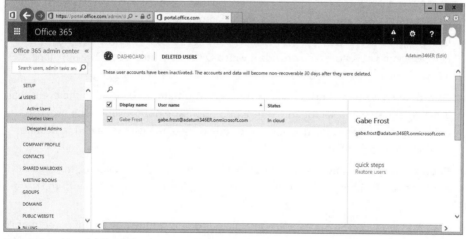

FIGURE 3-14 List of deleted users

You can restore a user that is in the Azure Active Directory Recycle Bin by selecting the user in the list of deleted users and then clicking Restore Users. When you take this action, you will be presented with a message indicating that the user has been successfully restored, as shown in Figure 3-15.

FIGURE 3-15 Restoring a user

> **MORE INFO** **DELETING USER ACCOUNTS IN OFFICE 365**
>
> You can learn more about deleting Office 365 user accounts at *http://support.microsoft.com/en-us/kb/2619308*.

Enabling multi-factor authentication

When you enable multi-factor authentication for Office 365 users, a user must utilize two or more forms of authentication before being able to sign in. For example, when signing in, a user may have to provide a username and password combination as well as a code generated by an application.

A username and password remains the primary method of authenticating to Office 365. Office 365 supports the following secondary multi-factor authentication options:

- **Use of a Mobile Device App** This is an app that can be downloaded from each mobile device vendor's app store. You provide it with a QR or numerical code. The app generates a new number every 30 seconds. The user enters this code when signing in.

- **One-time Password** This is a single-use password that can be used in the event that other secondary multi-factor authentication options are not available. The user can enter this code when signing in. Once the code is used, the user will need to acquire a new one-time password.

- **Phone Call** This involves a phone call to a pre-configured phone number. The user must answer the phone call by entering a code displayed on the screen into the handset.

- **SMS Message** An SMS message containing a code is sent to a pre-configured mobile phone number. The user enters this code when signing in to Office 365.

Enable multi-factor authentication

To enable multi-factor authentication in Office 365, perform the following steps:

1. In the Office 365 Admin Center, navigate to the Users section and click the Active Users section, as shown in Figure 3-16.

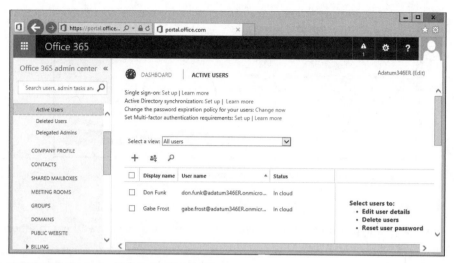

FIGURE 3-16 Set up multi-factor authentication

2. Next to Set Multi-Factor Authentication Requirements, click Set Up.
3. On the Multi-Factor Authentication page, shown in Figure 3-17, select the user for which you want to enable multi-factor authentication and then click Enable.

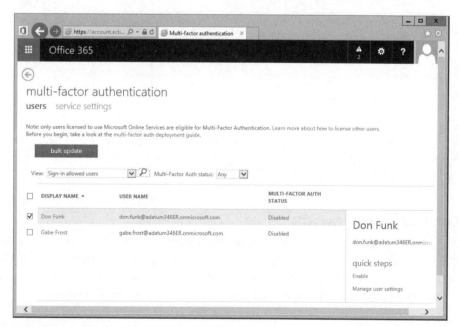

FIGURE 3-17 Enable multi-factor authentication

4. Review the About Enabling Multi-Factor Auth dialog box shown in Figure 3-18 and then click Enable Multi-Factor Auth.

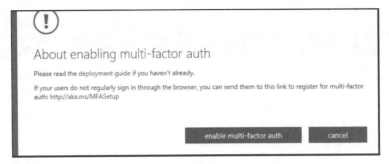

FIGURE 3-18 Enable multi-factor authentication dialog box

5. Click Close when notified that multi-factor auth has been enabled.

At their next sign in, users will be redirected to a webpage that allows them to set up multi-factor authentication.

You can choose between enabling multi-factor authentication, which gives the user the option of using multi-factor authentication, or enforcing multi-factor authentication, which requires the user to use multi-factor authentication. When you enforce multi-factor authentication for a user, you are presented with the warning dialog box shown in Figure 3-19. This warning informs you that the user will need to create app passwords.

FIGURE 3-19 Enforce multi-factor auth warning dialog box

Configure app passwords

App passwords allow you to configure application-specific passwords for non-browser clients that might not support multi-factor authentication. App-specific passwords are enabled by default when you enable multi-factor authentication. App passwords are separate from user passwords and remain valid even when a user changes their user account password.

You can enable or disable application passwords by performing these steps.

1. In the Office 365 Admin Center, select the Active Users node under the Users node and then click Set Up next to Set Multi-Factor Authentication Requirements.

2. On the Multi-Factor Authentication page, click Service Settings.

3. On the Service Settings page, choose to allow or disallow app passwords. You can also use this page, shown in Figure 3-20, to allow users to suspend multi-factor authentication on a per-device basis by allowing Office 365 to remember the device. You can configure how long the device will be remembered before requiring reauthentication. The default value is 14 days.

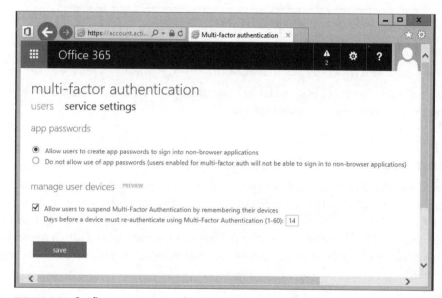

FIGURE 3-20 Configure app password settings

Although administrators cannot view or change app passwords, they can force users to recreate app passwords by deleting all existing app passwords. To perform this task, complete the following steps:

1. In the Office 365 Admin Center, select the Active Users node under the Users node and then click Set Up next to Set Multi-Factor Authentication Requirements.

2. On the Multi-Factor Authentication page, select the check box next to the user for which you want to delete all existing app passwords and then click Manage User Settings.

3. On the Manage User Settings dialog box, shown in Figure 3-21, select Delete All Existing App Passwords Generated by the Selected Users and click Save.

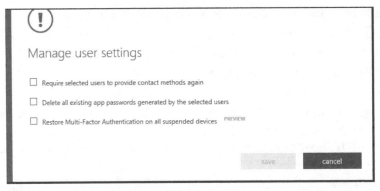

FIGURE 3-21 Manage user settings dialog box

MORE INFO **MULTI-FACTOR AUTHENTICATION**

You can learn more about multi-factor authentication for Office 365 at *https://msdn.micro-soft.com/en-us/library/azure/dn383636.aspx*.

Using Azure Active Directory Graph API

The Azure Active Directory Graph API (Application Programming Interface) provides organizations with REST API endpoints through which they can programmatically access Azure Active Directory. Azure Active Directory Graph API allows applications to perform create, read, update, and delete operations on objects and data stored within Azure Active Directory. Azure Active Directory Graph API can be leveraged to perform the following operations:

- Create, disable, or delete a user account.
- Retrieve user properties, such as group membership and licensing status.
- Modify user properties, including changing a user's password.

Before it can perform actions, an application must be both registered with and configured with access to the Azure Active Directory. To register an application, perform the following steps:

1. Sign in to the Azure Management portal.
2. In the Azure Management portal, click on the Active Directory item and then ensure that the appropriate directory is selected. Figure 3-22 shows the Adatum346ER directory selected.

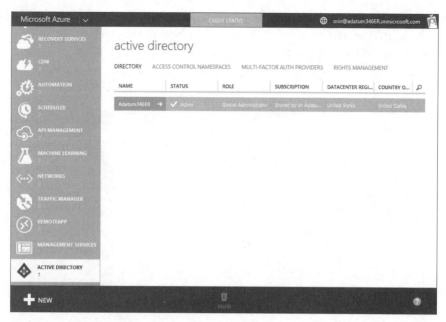

FIGURE 3-22 Select appropriate Azure Active Directory

3. Click the directory. On the top menu, click Applications. Figure 3-23 shows what is displayed when Applications is selected.

FIGURE 3-23 Azure Active Directory applications

4. Click the Add button on the command bar.

5. On the What Do You Want To Do? page, click Add an Application My Organization Is Developing.

6. On the Tell Us About Your Application page, shown in Figure 3-24, specify an application name and select whether the application is a web application and/or web API or a native client application. Click on the arrow to move to the next page.

FIGURE 3-24 Add an application

7. On the App Properties page, shown in Figure 3-25, enter the sign-in URL and the App ID URI. Click the Check button to finish adding the app.

FIGURE 3-25 Application properties

8. Once the application has been added, the application's Quick Start page will open. This will allow you to add additional capabilities to the application, such as allowing user sign-in and access to web APIs in other applications.

EXAM TIP

Remember the different multi-factor authentication options that are available for Office 365 user accounts.

Thought experiment
Multi-factor authentication at Contoso

In this thought experiment, apply what you've learned about this objective. You can find the answers to these questions in the "Answers" section at the end of this chapter.

You are configuring the Office 365 deployment at Contoso. As a security measure, you intend to require multi-factor authentication for all users who are authenticating to the organization's Office 365 deployment. You have the following objectives:

- You want to ensure that users always use multi-factor authentication when connecting to Office 365.

- You only want to allow applications that support multi-factor authentication to be able to connect to your organization's Office 365 deployment. Users should not be able to configure a special password for each app.

With this information in mind, answer the following questions:

1. How should you configure multi-factor authentication?

2. How should you configure app passwords?

Objective summary

- You can use the Office 365 Admin Center to bulk import users from a specially formatted CSV file.

- When you delete a user from Office 365, their account remains in the Azure Active Directory Recycle Bin for 30 days. The account can be recovered during this period.

- Multi-factor authentication can be configured to allow or require users to use a second form of authentication, including an office phone, a mobile phone, an alternate email address, or by answering a set of security questions.

- Azure Active Directory Graph API provides programmatic access to Azure Active Directory.

Objective review

Answer the following questions to test your knowledge of the information in this objective. You can find the answers to these questions and explanations of each answer choice in the "Answers" section at the end of this chapter.

1. You delete a user using the Office 365 Admin Center. How many days does a user's account remain in the Azure Active Directory Recycle Bin before it is permanently deleted?

   A. 120 days

   B. 90 days

   C. 60 days

   D. 30 days

2. Which of the following multi-factor authentication methods are supported for Office 365? (Choose all that apply.)

   A. Mobile app

   B. Telephone call

   C. Skype for Business

   D. Skype

3. Which of the following must you supply when registering a web app application or web API with Azure Active Directory? (Choose all that apply.)

   A. Sign-in URL

   B. IP address

   C. App ID URI

   D. SSL certificate

4. Sam, one of the users of your organization's Office 365 deployment, has multi-factor authentication enforced on his account. Sam uses an app password with a custom email application on his mobile device, which doesn't support multi-factor authentication. Sam believes that he may have left his mobile device on public transportation and has asked you to block the email application from accessing his mailbox. Which of the following steps could you take to accomplish this goal?

   A. Disable multi-factor authentication on Sam's account.

   B. Configure Sam's account so that his device will be remembered for 14 days.

   C. Change Sam's user account password.

   D. Delete all of Sam's app passwords.

5. If you want to bulk import a user's details file into Office 365, which file format must you use to perform this operation using the Office 365 Admin Center?

   A. TXT

   B. DOC

   C. XLS

   D. CSV

Objective 3.3: Manage cloud identities with Windows PowerShell

This objective deals with how you can manage Office 365 user identities using Windows PowerShell. Although the web-based Office 365 Admin Center enables you to quickly perform Office 365 user management tasks on individual users, this method is not suited to performing management tasks across a large number of user accounts.

The advantage of using Windows PowerShell is that you can use it to perform user management tasks across some or all of the user accounts stored in Office 365 with one or two lines of code as opposed to manually performing the same set of actions on each user account when using the Office 365 Admin Center.

This objective covers the following topics:

- Configure passwords to never expire
- Hard delete users
- Bulk user creation
- Bulk user license management
- Bulk update of user properties
- Additional Azure Active Directory cmdlets

Managing user passwords with Windows PowerShell

If you have the Azure Active Directory Module for Windows PowerShell installed and properly configured, you can use the cmdlets that it contains to manage Office 365 cloud identities. As new features are introduced to Office 365, they often become configurable through Windows PowerShell before the Office 365 Admin Center is updated to allow configuration of new features.

You can perform the following Office 365 user administration tasks using Windows PowerShell:

- Modify a user's password
- Configure the password policy for the Office 365 tenant (number of days to expire and notification settings)
- Configure whether a user's password will expire
- Remove password complexity requirements
- You can also use Windows PowerShell to generate lists of users based on their password-setting properties, such as a list of users who have accounts with passwords configured not to expire or a list of users who have accounts that are configured not to require strong passwords.

Changing users' passwords

You can change a user's password using the Set-MsolUserPassword Windows PowerShell cmdlet. You can also use this cmdlet to force a password change the next time a user signs in. If a user is unable to perform a self-service password reset due to a forgotten password, you can use the Set-MsolUserPassword Windows PowerShell cmdlet to assign a new, temporary password to access the service. A password change will be required the next time the user signs into adhere to the Office 365 password policies.

For example, to change the password of Don Funk to Pa$$w0rd and require him to change it the next time he signs in, issue the following command:

```
Set-MsolUserPassword -UserPrincipalName don.funk@adatum365er.onmicrosoft.com
-NewPassword Pa$$w0rd -ForceChangePassword $true
```

> **MORE INFO** SET-MSOLUSERPASSWORD
>
> You can learn more about the Set-MsolUserPassword Windows PowerShell cmdlet at the following address: *https://technet.microsoft.com/en-us/library/dn194140.aspx*.

Configure password expiration

You can use the Set-MsolUser cmdlet from the Azure Active Directory module for Windows PowerShell to configure whether an Office 365 user's password will expire. This is not recommended from a security perspective because a password that is not changed is more likely to be compromised. If you do choose or are required to configure an Office 365 user's password to not expire, consider implementing multi-factor authentication as a way of increasing the user's account authentication requirements.

To configure the password of the user Don Funk to never expire, use the command:

```
Set-MsolUser -UserPrincipalName don.funk@adatum365er.onmicrosoft.com
-PasswordNeverExpires $true
```

You can configure the Office 365 tenancy so that passwords don't expire for any users' accounts by using the Set-MsolUser cmdlet in conjunction with the Get-MsolUser cmdlet. For example, to configure all users' accounts so that passwords do not expire, use the following command:

```
Get-MsolUser | Set-MsolUser -PasswordNeverExpires $true
```

You can change this back so that the password does expire by setting the PasswordNeverExpires parameter to $false. For example, to configure Don Funk's user account so that the password follows the existing password policy, use the following command:

```
Set-MsolUser -UserPrincipalName don.funk@adatum365er.onmicrosoft.com
-PasswordNeverExpires $false
```

You can configure the Office 365 tenancy so that all passwords expire according to the tenancy password policy by issuing the following command:

Get-MsolUser | Set-MsolUser –PasswordNeverExpires $false

MORE INFO **SET-MSOLUSER**

You can learn more about the Set-MsolUser Windows PowerShell cmdlet at the following address: *https://technet.microsoft.com/en-us/library/dn194136.aspx.*

Password complexity

Office 365 user accounts stored in Azure Active Directory are subject to the Azure Active Directory password policy. As you learned earlier in this chapter, this means that all user account passwords need to be between 8 and 16 characters long and need to contain three of the following four characteristics: uppercase letters, lowercase letters, numbers, and symbols. You cannot change the Azure Active Directory password policy because this is set by Microsoft. You cannot use the Office 365 Admin Center to exempt a user account from the Azure Active Directory password policy. You can, however, use a PowerShell command to exempt a user account from the requirement of having a strong password. You can do this with the Set-MsolUser cmdlet and the StrongPasswordRequired parameter. For example, to configure Don Funk's Office 365 user account so that it does not have to conform to the Azure Active Directory password complexity policy, issue the following command:

```
Set-MsolUser –UserPrincipalName don.funk@adatum365er.onmicrosoft.com
–StrongPasswordRequired $false
```

To switch an account back, pass $true to the parameter instead of $false. For example, to configure Don Funk's Office 365 user account so that it must conform to the Azure Active Directory password complexity policy, issue the following command:

```
Set-MsolUser –UserPrincipalName don.funk@adatum365er.onmicrosoft.com
–StrongPasswordRequired $true
```

Even though you can exempt a user from the Azure Active Directory password policy using Windows PowerShell and not the Office 365 Admin Center, from a security perspective it would be difficult to find an adequate justification for doing so.

Hard deleting users

As mentioned earlier in this chapter, most user deletion operations move user accounts into the Azure Active Directory Recycle Bin rather than deleting those accounts entirely. Only after a user's account has been stored in the recycle bin for a period of 30 days will it be completely deleted. Once a user has been removed from the Azure Active Directory Recycle Bin, all licenses assigned to that user are reclaimed. Deleting a user's account so it ends up in the Recycle Bin is sometimes referred to as "soft deleting."

You can view users that have been soft deleted using the following Windows PowerShell command:

```
Get-MsolUser -ReturnDeletedUsers
```

If you want to empty all users from the Azure Active Directory Recycle Bin, you can use the following command:

```
Get-MsolUser -ReturnDeletedUsers | Remove-MsolUser -RemoveFromRecycleBin -Force
```

In some cases, you may want to delete a user's account entirely, bypassing the Azure Active Directory Recycle Bin. This is called a "hard delete." You can hard delete a specific user as long as you know their UPN. For example, to hard delete the user with the UPN don.funk@adatum346ER.onmicrosoft.com, you would issue the following command:

```
Remove-MsolUser -UserPrincipalName don.funk@adatum346ER.onmicrosoft.com -Force
```

> **MORE INFO REMOVE-MSOLUSER**
>
> You can learn more about using Remove-MsolUser at *https://technet.microsoft.com/en-us/library/dn194132.aspx.*

Performing bulk account operations

Earlier in the chapter, you learned how to import users stored in a CSV file into Office 365 using the Office 365 Admin Center. You can also perform bulk operations, such as a bulk user import or a bulk change of user properties, using the Azure Active Directory module for Windows PowerShell.

Importing users

You can perform a bulk import of users from a specially formatted CSV file. The CSV file used for bulk import operations requires the fields to be formatted in the following manner.

```
UserPrincipalName,DisplayName,FirstName,LastName,Password,Department,UsageLocation
```

Once you have the CSV file that needs to be imported into Office 365, you can use the following command to place the contents of the file NewUsers.csv into the variable $NewUsers:

```
$NewUsers = Import-Csv -path .\NewUsers.csv
```

If you want to license the users during the import process, the next thing you'll need to have is the SKU ID information. You can store this information in a variable and use with the bulk import command. You can place the SKU ID information into a variable by issuing the following command:

```
$Sku = Get-MsolAccountSku
```

Once you have the $Sku variable configured, you can enact the following command to import this account information into Office 365:

```
ForEach($NewUser in $NewUsers){New-MsolUser -UserPrincipalName $NewUser.
UserPrincipalName -DisplayName $NewUser.DisplayName -FirstName $NewUser.Firstname
-LastName $NewUser.LastName -Password $NewUser.Password -Department $NewUser.Department
-UsageLocation $NewUser.UsageLocation -LicenseAssignment $Sku.AccountSkuId}
```

You can also choose to not include password information. If you do that, Office 365 will assign a random password to each user. The drawback of this is that you will need to make a note of each password, whereas by including it in the CVS file, you can assign a standard first password to all users and then use a second command to require a password change upon their next sign in.

Bulk licensing users

In the previous example, you learned how to bulk import users and assign licenses at the same time. You can also choose not to license users at the time of import and instead perform a bulk license operation. If you are going to use this method, you must ensure that the Usage Location property of the user's account is already set. You cannot perform this operation if this property has not been configured.

You can bulk license users by generating a CSV file that has a single header titled UPN and contains a list of users by UPN, one UPN per line.

To import this list into a variable, use the Import-Csv cmdlet in the following manner:

```
$LicenseUsers = Import-Csv =Path .\LicenseUsers.csv
```

The next step is to get the appropriate SKU and place it into a second Windows PowerShell variable. You can do this by issuing the following command:

```
$Sku=Get-MsolAccountSku
```

Once this is done, you can apply the license information by issuing the following command:

```
ForEach($LicenseUser in $LicenseUsers){Set-MsolUserLicense -UserPrincipalName
$LicenseUser.UPN -AddLicenses $Sku.AccountSkuId}
```

Bulk update user properties

You can perform a bulk update of users' properties using a combination of the Get-MsolUser and the Set-MsolUser cmdlets. Depending on how you want to update the properties, you can pipe the results of the Get-MsolUser cmdlet straight into the Set-MsolUser cmdlet. As an alternative, you can also read the output of the Get-MsolUser cmdlet into a variable and then use a foreach loop to update the users' properties using the Set-MsolUser cmdlet.

For example, to update the city property of each user in the HR department to Melbourne, issue the command:

```
Get-MsolUser -Department "HR" | Set-MsolUser -City "Melbourne"
```

Using Azure Active Directory cmdlets

When loaded, the Azure Active Directory module for Windows PowerShell allows you to manage an Office 365 tenancy as well as the Azure Active Directory instance that supports that tenancy. For organizations that have just implemented a simple Office 365 deployment, only some of these cmdlets will be relevant. For organizations that want to take greater advantage of the integration between Office 365 and Azure Active Directory, understanding of which cmdlets are available and what they can accomplish is important.

The Azure Active Directory cmdlets can be separated into the following categories:

- User management
- Group and role management
- Service principal management
- Domain management
- Single sign-on management
- Subscription and license management
- Company information and service management
- Administrative unit management

User management cmdlets

There are nine cmdlets in the Azure Active Directory module for Windows PowerShell, which can be used to manage Office 365 and Azure Active Directory user accounts. Several of these cmdlets were covered earlier in this chapter but are included here to assist with exam revision.

- **Convert-MsolFederatedUser** This cmdlet allows you to update a user in a domain that originally used single sign-on/identity federation authentication, but which has been converted to standard authentication. When using this cmdlet, it is necessary to provide a new password for the user.
- **Get-MsolUser** This cmdlet allows you to retrieve information for one or a number of users
- **New-MsolUser** This cmdlet allows you to create a new Office 365 or Azure Active Directory user. To grant a user access to Office 365 services, the user must be assigned a license.
- **Remove-MsolUser** You can use this cmdlet to remove an Office 365 or Azure Active Directory user. This cmdlet allows you to remove the user, associated licenses, and data.

- **Restore-MsolUser**   You can use this cmdlet to restore a user who is in the Azure Active Directory Recycle Bin. Deleted user accounts are only stored in the Azure Active Directory Recycle Bin for 30 days.

- **Set-MsolUser**   You can use this cmdlet to modify the properties of an existing Office 365 or Azure Active Directory user. You would not use this cmdlet to set licenses, passwords, or users' principal names. Separate cmdlets exist for these tasks.

- **Set-MsolUserPassword**   You can use this cmdlet to change a user's password. You can only use this cmdlet for Office 365 and Azure Active Directory users with standard identities. You cannot use this cmdlet to change the password of users from domains that use single sign-on or identity federation.

- **Set-MsolUserPrincipalName**   You can use this cmdlet to alter the user principal name of a user. You can also use this cmdlet to move a user between a domain that uses standard identities and a domain that uses single sign-on/identity federation.

- **Redo-MsolProvisionUser**   You can use this cmdlet to reattempt provisioning of an Office 365 or Azure Active Directory user in the event that a prior attempt to create the user object generated a validation error.

> ***MORE INFO*** **USER MANAGEMENT CMDLETS**
>
> You can learn more about using PowerShell to manage Office 365 and Azure Active Directory users at *https://technet.microsoft.com/en-us/library/b7727a57-b002-4d84-a20c-3192b1d6b1b4#BKMK_ManageUsers.*

Group and role management cmdlets

The Azure Active Directory module for Windows PowerShell includes a number of cmdlets that you can use to manage roles and groups. These include the following:

- **Add-MsolGroupMember**   You can use this cmdlet to add members to an Office 365 or Azure Active Directory security group. You can add user accounts to security groups or have one security group as a member of another security group.

- **Add-MsolRoleMember**   You can use this cmdlet to add users to an Office 365 or Azure Active Directory role.

- **Get-MsolGroup**   You can use this cmdlet to get group information from Office 365 or Azure Active Directory.

- **Get-MsolGroupMember**   You can use this cmdlet to get membership information for an Office 365 or Azure Active Directory group.

- **Get-MsolRole**   You can use this cmdlet to get a list of administrator roles for Office 365 or Azure Active Directory.

- **Get-MsolRoleMember**   You can use this cmdlet to determine membership information for a specific role.

- **Get-MsolUserRole** You can use this cmdlet to determine to which administrator roles a specific Office 365 or Azure Active Directory user belongs.

- **New-MsolGroup** You can use this cmdlet to add a new security group to Office 365 or Azure Active Directory.

- **Redo-MsolProvisionGroup** You can use this cmdlet to reattempt the provisioning of a group if you previously received a validation error when attempting this task.

- **Remove-MsolGroup** You can use this cmdlet to delete a security group from Office 365 or Azure Active Directory.

- **Remove-MsolGroupMember** You can use this cmdlet when you want to remove a user or security group account from an existing Office 365 or Azure Active Directory security group.

- **Remove-MsolRoleMember** You can use this cmdlet to remove a user account from an existing administrator role.

- **Set-MsolGroup** You can use this cmdlet to modify the properties of an existing security group.

> **MORE INFO** **GROUP AND ROLE MEMBERSHIP**
>
> You can learn more about using PowerShell to manage Office 365 and Azure Active Directory users at *https://technet.microsoft.com/en-us/library/321d532e-407d-4e29-a00a-8afbe23008dd#BKMK_ManageGroups*.

Service principal management cmdlets

The Azure Active Directory module for Windows PowerShell includes a number of cmdlets that you can use to manage the configuration of service principals in Azure Active Directory. These cmdlets include:

- **Set-MsolServicePrincipal** You can use this cmdlet to update an Azure Active Directory service principal. For example, you can use it to update the display name, configure the service principal name, and enable or disable the service principal.

- **New-MsolServicePrincipal** You can use this cmdlet to create a new service principal. You would do this when you need a representation of "service principal" objects in Azure Active Directory of a Line Of Business (LOB) Application or an on-premises server like Exchange, SharePoint, or Skype for Business.

- **Get-MsolServicePrincipal** You can use this cmdlet to retrieve a list of service principals stored in Azure Active Directory or obtain information about a specific service principal.

- **New-MsolServicePrincipalAddress** You can use this cmdlet to create a new service principal address object. You can then use this new object when updating the address of a service principal.

- **Get-MsolServicePrincipalCredential** You use this cmdlet to view a list of credentials that are tied to a specific service principal.

- **New-MsolServicePrincipalCredential**   You can use this cmdlet to add new credentials to a service principal. You can also use this cmdlet to add credential keys for an application.
- **Remove-MsolServicePrincipalCredential**   You can use this cmdlet to remove a credential key from a specific service principal.

> **MORE INFO** **SERVICE PRINCIPAL MANAGEMENT**
>
> You can learn more about service principal management cmdlets at *https://technet.micro-soft.com/en-us/library/81cc7f03-75d3-4343-aec4-57116017683a#BKMK_ManageService.*

Domain management cmdlets

The Azure Active Directory module for Windows PowerShell includes a number of cmdlets that you can use to manage domains stored within Azure Active Directory. These cmdlets include the following:

- **Confirm-MsolDomain**   You can use this cmdlet to confirm that you own a specific domain. You can do this by adding a special TXT DNS record to the domain. You can use this cmdlet after first adding the domain to Azure Active Directory with the New-MsolDomain cmdlet.
- **Get-MsolDomain**   You can use this cmdlet to retrieve company domains.
- **Get-MsolDomainVerificationDns**   You can use this cmdlet to determine which DNS records you need to configure to confirm a domain.
- **New-MsolDomain**   You can use this cmdlet to create a new domain that uses managed identities. Although you can use this cmdlet to create a domain that uses federated identities, Microsoft recommends using the New-MsolFederatedDomain cmdlet for this task.
- **Remove-MsolDomain**   You can use this cmdlet to remove a domain from Azure Active Directory. You can only remove a domain if it has no users or groups with email addresses stored.
- **Set-MsolDomain**   You can use this cmdlet to update settings for a domain.
- **Set-MsolDomainAuthentication**   You can use this cmdlet to alter the authentication model for the Azure Active Directory domain between single sign-on/federated and standard identities. This cmdlet updates Azure Active Directory settings. Microsoft recommends using the Convert-MsolDomainToStandard or Convert-MsolDomainToFederated cmdlets when performing a domain conversion operation.
- **Get-MsolPasswordPolicy**   You can use this cmdlet to view the current password policy.
- **Set-MsolPasswordPolicy**   You can use this cmdlet to change the current password policy.

Single sign-on management cmdlets

The Azure Active Directory module for Windows PowerShell includes a number of cmdlets
related to managing federated, also known as single sign-on, domains.

- **New-MsolFederatedDomain**   You can use this cmdlet to add a new identity
  federated/single sign-on domain and to configure the relying party trust settings
  between Azure Active Directory and the on-premises Active Directory Federation
  Services 2.0 server.

- **Convert-MsolDomainToStandard**   You can use this cmdlet to convert an Azure
  Active Directory domain between identity federation/single sign-on to standard
  authentication. This will remove relying party trust settings between the on-premises
  Active Directory Federation Services 2.0 server and Azure Active Directory. Once the
  conversion is complete, all existing users will have their authentication switched from
  single sign-on to standard authentication. When this process occurs, each converted
  user will be assigned a temporary password. These passwords are stored in a file that
  is accessible by the administrator and can be forwarded to users who need to sign in
  to Office 365.

- **Convert-MsolDomainToFederated**   You can use this cmdlet to convert an Azure
  Active Directory domain from standard authentication to identity federation/single
  sign-on. Performing this action will also configure the relying party trust settings
  between Azure Active Directory and the on-premises Active Directory Federation
  Services 2.0 server.

- **Get-MsolFederationProperty**   You can use this cmdlet to get key settings from
  Azure Active Directory and the on-premises Active Directory Federation Services 2.0
  server.

- **Get-MsolDomainFederationSettings**   You can use this cmdlet to get key settings
  from Azure Active Directory.

- **Remove-MsolFederatedDomain**   You can use this cmdlet to remove a specific
  identity federated/single sign-on domain from Azure Active Directory. Executing
  this cmdlet also removes relying party trust settings from the on-premises Active
  Directory Federation Services 2.0 server.

- **Set-MsolDomainFederationSettings**   You can use this cmdlet to update the settings
  of an identity federated/single sign-on domain.

- **Set-MsolADFSContext**   You can use this cmdlet to configure the credentials that
  connect the on-premises Active Directory Federation Services 2.0 server and Azure
  Active Directory.

- **Update-MsolFederatedDomain** You can use this cmdlet to alter settings in both Azure Active Directory and Active Directory Federation Services. For example, you would use this cmdlet to update the URLs or certificate information when you need to renew certificates.

> **MORE INFO** **SINGLE SIGN-ON MANAGEMENT**
>
> You can learn more about single sign-on management cmdlets at *https://technet.microsoft.com/en-us/library/5d903388-0355-447a-8be8-8598e0435bdf#BKMK_sso*.

Subscription and license management cmdlets

The Azure Active Directory module for Windows PowerShell includes a number of cmdlets related to subscription and license management. These cmdlets allow you to view and manage organizational subscription information, and also allow you to manage the licenses assigned to Office 365 users. Cmdlets in this category include the following:

- **Get-MsolSubscription** You can use this cmdlet to view all of the subscriptions that your organization has purchased.
- **Get-MsolAccountSku** You can use this cmdlet to generate a list of all of the SKUs that your organization owns.
- **New-MsolLicenseOptions** You can use this cmdlet to allow you to create a new License Options object.
- **Set-MsolUserLicense** You can use this cmdlet to adjust the licenses assigned to a user, including assigning a new license and removing or updating a license.

> **MORE INFO** **SUBSCRIPTION AND LICENSE MANAGEMENT CMDLETS**
>
> You can learn more about subscription and license management cmdlets at *https://technet.microsoft.com/en-us/library/3c205980-2610-4a89-b204-1994cdf7d10f#BKMK_subs*.

Company information and service management cmdlets

The Azure Active Directory module for Windows PowerShell includes a number of cmdlets you can use to manage company and service information. You can use the following cmdlets for this task:

- **Add-MsolForeignGroupToRole** You can use this cmdlet when you want to add a partner tenant security group to an Office 365 or Azure Active Directory role.
- **Connect-MsolService** You can use this cmdlet to initiate a connection to Azure Active Directory. You use this cmdlet in a command at the start of each Windows PowerShell session when you want to manage Office 365 or Azure Active Directory.
- **Get-MsolCompanyInformation** You can use this cmdlet to retrieve company-level information from Azure Active Directory.

- **Get-MsolContact**   You can use this cmdlet to get information about a specific contact object, or to generate a list of contacts.

- **Get-MsolPartnerContract**   This cmdlet is used by partner organizations to generate a list of partner-specific contracts.

- **Get-MsolPartnerInformation**   This cmdlet is used by partner organizations to generate partner-specific information.

- **Redo-MsolProvisionContact**   You can use this cmdlet if you receive a validation error when attempting to provision a contact object.

- **Remove-MsolContact**   You can use this cmdlet when you want to delete an object from Azure Active Directory.

- **Set-MsolCompanyContactInformation**   You can use this cmdlet when you want to configure company-level contact preferences, such as email addresses for billing, marketing, and technical notifications.

- **Set-MsolCompanySecurityComplianceContactInformation**   You can use this cmdlet when you want to configure company-level contact preferences for security and compliance correspondence.

- **Set-MsolCompanySettings**   You can use this cmdlet to modify company-level configuration settings.

- **Set-MsolDirSyncEnabled**   You can use this cmdlet to enable or disable directory synchronization.

- **Set-MsolPartnerInformation**   This cmdlet is used by partners to configure partner-specific settings. These settings are visible by all tenants to which the partner has access.

> *MORE INFO* **COMPANY INFORMATION AND SERVICE MANAGEMENT CMDLETS**
>
> You can learn more about company information and service management cmdlets at *https://technet.microsoft.com/en-us/library/0fe48277-4713-4c05-8f39-efc534814eea#BKMK_ManageContacts.*

Administrative unit management cmdlets

The Azure Active Directory module for Windows PowerShell includes a number of cmdlets that you can use to manage administrative units. These include the following cmdlets:

- **Add-MsolAdministrativeUnitMember**   You can use this cmdlet to add an account to an administrative unit.

- **Add-MsolScopedRoleMember**   You can use this cmdlet to add an account to a specific role that is scoped to a specific administrative unit.

- **Get-MsolAdministrativeUnit**   You can use this cmdlet to generate a list of administrative units stored in Azure Active Directory.

- **Get-MsolAdministrativeUnitMember**   You can use this cmdlet to get a list of all of the members of a specific administrative unit.

- **Get-MsolScopedRoleMember** You can use this cmdlet to get a membership list of a specific role that is scoped to a specific administrative unit.

- **New-MsolAdministrativeUnit** You can use this cmdlet to add a new administrative unit to Azure Active Directory.

- **Remove-MsolAdministrativeUnit** You can use this cmdlet to remove an administrative unit from Azure Active Directory.

- **Remove-MsolAdministrativeUnitMember** You can use this cmdlet to remove a user account from a specific administrative unit.

- **Remove-MsolScopedRoleMember** You can use this cmdlet to remove a user account from a specific role that is scoped to a specific administrative unit.

- **Set-MsolAdministrativeUnit** You can use this cmdlet to modify the properties of an administrative unit stored in Azure Active Directory.

> **MORE INFO** **MANAGING ADMINISTRATIVE UNITS**
>
> You can learn more about managing Azure Active Directory administrative units at the following address: *https://technet.microsoft.com/en-us/library/421056d5-0d4a-4278-9c8c-4c656b9de9e2#BKMK_adminunits*.

EXAM TIP

Remember each of the different PowerShell cmdlets and how you can use them to manage different aspects of Office 365 tenant users and groups.

Thought experiment
Managing cloud identities from Windows PowerShell at Adatum

In this thought experiment, apply what you've learned about this objective. You can find the answers to these questions in the "Answers" section at the end of this chapter.

You are responsible for managing Adatum's Office 365 deployment. You need to add 1,000 new user accounts to Office 365. These user accounts are stored in an appropriately formatted CSV file. Additionally, all users who are in the Sydney office are being moved to the Melbourne office. As there are 500 users, you would rather use Windows PowerShell to perform a bulk user account property update. With this information in mind, answer the following questions:

1. Which cmdlets would you use to bulk import user accounts from the CSV file using Windows PowerShell?

2. Which cmdlets would you use to bulk update the properties of existing Office 365 user accounts?

Objective summary

- Use the Set-MsolUser cmdlet with the –PasswordNeverExpires parameter to configure users' passwords that will never expire.

- Use the Remove-MsolUser cmdlet with the –Force parameter to hard delete users.

- Use the Import-CSV cmdlet to import users in a properly formatted spreadsheet into a variable, and then use a foreach command with the New-MsolUser cmdlet to import these users into Office 365/Azure Active Directory.

- Use the Set-MsolUser cmdlet with the –AddLicenses parameter to perform bulk licensing operations.

- Use the Get-MsolUser cmdlet with the Set-MsolUser cmdlet to bulk update user properties.

Objective review

Answer the following questions to test your knowledge of the information in this objective. You can find the answers to these questions and explanations of each answer choice in the "Answers" section at the end of this chapter.

1. You want to configure Don Funk's Office 365 user account so that his password does not expire. The password expiration settings of other accounts in the Office 365 tenancy should not change. With the Azure Active Directory module for Windows PowerShell loaded, which of the following Windows PowerShell commands would you use to accomplish this goal?

   A. Set-MsolUser –UserPrincipalName don.funk@adatum365er.onmicrosoft.com –PasswordNeverExpires $true

   B. Get-MsolUser | Set-MsolUser –PasswordNeverExpires $true

   C. Set-MsolUser –UserPrincipalName don.funk@adatum365er.onmicrosoft.com – PasswordNeverExpires $false

   D. Get-MsolUser | Set-MsolUser –PasswordNeverExpires $false

2. Several user accounts in your organization's Office 365 tenancy have been configured so that the passwords do not expire. You want to reconfigure all accounts so that the passwords expire in alignment with the password policy configured for the Office 365 tenancy. With the Azure Active Directory module for Windows PowerShell installed, which of the following commands would you use to accomplish this goal?

   A. Set-MsolUser –UserPrincipalName don.funk@adatum365er.onmicrosoft.com –PasswordNeverExpires $false

   B. Set-MsolUser –UserPrincipalName don.funk@adatum365er.onmicrosoft.com –PasswordNeverExpires $true

   C. Get-MsolUser | Set-MsolUser –PasswordNeverExpires $false

   D. Get-MsolUser | Set-MsolUser –PasswordNeverExpires $true

3. Don Funk has called the service desk. He has forgotten his password and needs someone in the IT department to reset it for him. You decide to reset the password to the temporary password "Pa$$w0rd," but also want to require Don to change his password the next time he signs in. When the Azure Active Directory module for Windows PowerShell module is loaded, which of the following cmdlets could you use to accomplish this goal?

   A. Set-MsolUser –UserPrincipalName don.funk@adatum365er.onmicrosoft.com –NewPassword Pa$$w0rd –ForceChangePassword $true

   B. Set-MsolUserPassword –UserPrincipalName don.funk@adatum365er.onmicrosoft.com –NewPassword Pa$$w0rd –ForceChangePassword $false

   C. Set-MsolUserPassword –UserPrincipalName don.funk@adatum365er.onmicrosoft.com –NewPassword Pa$$w0rd –ForceChangePassword $true

   D. Set-MsolUser –UserPrincipalName don.funk@adatum365er.onmicrosoft.com –NewPassword Pa$$w0rd –ForceChangePassword $false

4. You need to allow Don Funk to use a 7-character password. The Azure Active Directory password policy does not allow 7-character passwords. Which of the following Windows PowerShell commands would you use to exempt Don Funk's Office 365 user account from the Azure Active Directory password policy?

   A. Set-MsolUser –UserPrincipalName don.funk@adatum365er.onmicrosoft.com –StrongPasswordRequired $true

   B. Set-MsolUser –UserPrincipalName don.funk@adatum365er.onmicrosoft.com –StrongPasswordRequired $false

   C. Set-MsolUser –UserPrincipalName don.funk@adatum365er.onmicrosoft.com –PasswordNeverExpires $false

   D. Set-MsolUser –UserPrincipalName don.funk@adatum365er.onmicrosoft.com –PasswordNeverExpires $true

5. Which cmdlet must you use each time you use a Windows PowerShell session to manage an Office 365 tenancy?

   A. Connect-MsolService

   B. Get-MsolContact

   C. Get-MsolUser

   D. Get-MsolGroup

Answers

This section contains the solutions to the thought experiments and answers to the lesson review questions in this chapter.

Objective 3.1: Thought experiment

1. Because users do not have traditional landlines and Adatum-related business should not be sent to external email accounts, the remaining password reset options are Mobile Phone and Security Question.

2. Because you want to configure the strongest user password reset policy and you only have two available methods, requiring both the Mobile Phone and the Security Question provides you with the strongest possible option.

Objective 3.1: Review

1. **Correct answers:** A, B, and D

   A. **Correct:** You can use Office Phone as an authentication method in a user password reset policy.

   B. **Correct:** You can use Mobile Phone as an authentication method in a user password reset policy.

   C. **Incorrect:** You wouldn't use multi-factor authentication for password reset, however, you can use it as an additional authentication method when signing in.

   D. **Correct:** You can use Security Questions as an authentication method in a user password reset policy.

2. **Correct answers:** A and C

   A. **Correct:** This password has an uppercase letter, a lowercase letter, numerals, and is between 8 and 16 characters in length.

   B. **Incorrect:** Office 365 does not support passwords where the period character (.) immediately precedes the at character (@).

   C. **Correct:** This password has a mix of numerals, symbols, uppercase letters, and lowercase letters. It is 9 characters in length and the period character (.) does not precede the at character (@).

   D. **Incorrect:** This password is only 5 characters in length.

3. **Correct answer:** D

   A. **Incorrect:** Office 365 administrators cannot configure the maximum password length for Office 365 users in their tenancy. This value is set by Microsoft at 16 characters.

   B. **Incorrect:** Office 365 administrators cannot configure the minimum password length for Office 365 users in their tenancy. This value is set by Microsoft at 8 characters.

   C. **Incorrect:** Office 365 administrators cannot configure the minimum password age for Office 365 users in their tenancy.

   D. **Correct:** Office 365 administrators can configure the maximum password age for Office 365 users in their tenancy.

4. **Correct answer:** A

   A. **Correct:** You cannot use a space in an Office 365 user password.

   B. **Incorrect:** You can use the at sign (@) in an Office 365 user password.

   C. **Incorrect:** You can use the percent character (%) in an Office 365 user password.

   D. **Incorrect:** You can use the caret character (^) in an Office 365 user password.

Objective 3.2: Thought experiment

1. You should enforce multi-factor authentication for all Office 365 users. This means that they must use multi-factor authentication; it is not optional.

2. You should disable app passwords so that they cannot be used.

Objective 3.2: Review

1. **Correct answer:** D

   A. **Incorrect:** User accounts remain in the Azure Active Directory Recycle Bin for 30 days before they are permanently deleted.

   B. **Incorrect:** User accounts remain in the Azure Active Directory Recycle Bin for 30 days before they are permanently deleted.

   C. **Incorrect:** User accounts remain in the Azure Active Directory Recycle Bin for 30 days before they are permanently deleted.

   D. **Correct:** User accounts remain in the Azure Active Directory Recycle Bin for 30 days before they are permanently deleted.

2. **Correct answers:** A and B

   A. **Correct:** A Mobile App is a supported multi-factor authentication method for Office 365.

   B. **Correct:** A Telephone Call is a supported multi-factor authentication method for Office 365.

   C. **Incorrect:** Skype for Business is not a supported multi-factor authentication method for Office 365.

   D. **Incorrect:** Skype is not a supported multi-factor authentication method for Office 365.

3. **Correct answers:** A and C

   A. **Correct:** You must provide a sign-in URL and App ID URI when registering a web application or web API with Azure Active Directory.

   B. **Incorrect:** You do not need to provide an IP address when registering a web application or web API with Azure Active Directory.

   C. **Correct:** You must provide a sign-in URL and App ID URI when registering a web application or web API with Azure Active Directory.

   D. **Incorrect:** You do not need to provide an IP address when registering a web application or web API with Azure Active Directory.

4. **Correct answer:** D

   A. **Incorrect:** Disabling multi-factor authentication on Sam's account will not remove his app password.

   B. **Incorrect:** Configuring Sam's account so that his device can be remembered for 14 days will not remove his app password. Also, this setting is not configured on a per-user basis.

   C. **Incorrect:** Changing a user's password does not mean that existing app passwords become invalid. You can only make an app password invalid by deleting it.

   D. **Correct:** Deleting all of Sam's existing app passwords means that all of Sam's current app passwords will become invalid.

5. **Correct answer:** D

   A. **Incorrect:** To import user accounts into Office 365 using the Office 365 Admin Center, the file containing user account information must be in CSV format.

   B. **Incorrect:** To import user accounts into Office 365 using the Office 365 Admin Center, the file containing user account information must be in CSV format.

   C. **Incorrect:** To import user accounts into Office 365 using the Office 365 Admin Center, the file containing user account information must be in CSV format.

   D. **Correct:** To import user accounts into Office 365 using the Office 365 Admin Center, the file containing user account information must be in CSV format.

Objective 3.3: Thought experiment

1. You can use the Import-CSV cmdlet, foreach, and the New-MsolUser cmdlets to bulk import user accounts from a specially formatted CSV file.

2. You can use the Get-MsolUser cmdlet to retrieve a list of all users in the Sydney office and the Set-MsolUser cmdlet to update their office information so that it is set to the Melbourne office.

Objective 3.3: Review

1. **Correct answer:** A

   A. **Correct:** This command will configure Don Funk's account so that the password does expire.

   B. **Incorrect:** This command will configure all user accounts in the Office 365 tenancy so that they do not expire.

   C. **Incorrect:** This command will configure Don Funk's account so that the password will expire according to the Office 365 tenancy password policy.

   D. **Incorrect:** This command will configure all accounts in the Office 365 tenancy so that passwords will expire according to the tenancy password policy.

2. **Correct answer:** C

   A. **Incorrect:** This command will configure Don Funk's account so that the password will expire according to the Office 365 tenancy password policy.

   B. **Incorrect:** This command will configure Don Funk's account so that the password does expire.

   C. **Correct:** This command will configure all accounts in the Office 365 tenancy so that passwords will expire according to the tenancy password policy.

   D. **Incorrect:** This command will configure all user accounts in the Office 365 tenancy so that they do not expire.

3. **Correct answer:** C

   A. **Incorrect:** You cannot use the Set-MsolUser cmdlet to change an Office 365 user's password.

   B. **Incorrect:** Although using this command will change Don Funk's password to Pa$$w0rd, it will not force him to change his password the next time he signs in.

   C. **Correct:** Using this command will change Don Funk's password to Pa$$w0rd and force him to change it the next time he signs in.

   D. **Incorrect:** You cannot use the Set-MsolUser cmdlet to change an Office 365 user's password.

4. **Correct answer:** B

    A. **Incorrect:** Using this command ensures that the Azure Active Directory password policy is applied to Don Funk's Office 365 user account.

    B. **Correct:** Using this command ensures that the Azure Active Directory password policy is not applied to Don Funk's Office 365 user account.

    C. **Incorrect:** Using this command configures Don Funk's account so that the password will expire according to the Office 365 tenancy password policy.

    D. **Incorrect:** Using this command configures Don Funk's account so that the password will not expire.

5. **Correct answer:** A

    A. **Correct:** You can use this cmdlet to establish a connection between a local Windows PowerShell session and Office 365/Azure Active Directory.

    B. **Incorrect:** You can use this cmdlet to get information about an Office 365 or Azure Active Directory contact.

    C. **Incorrect:** You can use this cmdlet to get information about an Office 365 or Azure Active Directory user.

    D. **Incorrect:** You can use this cmdlet to get information about an Office 365 or Azure Active Directory group.

CHAPTER 4

Implement and manage identities by using DirSync

A substantial number of organizations integrate their on-premises Active Directory Domain Services deployment with the Azure Active Directory instance that supports their Office 365 tenancy. Unlike a cloud-only deployment where all of the user, group, and contact accounts are stored and managed in Azure Active Directory, integration allows users, groups, and contacts created on-premises to synchronize up to Office 365. Integration can occur through synchronization, which is the subject of this chapter, or through federation, the subject of Chapter 5, "Implement and manage federated identities."

Objectives in this chapter:

- Objective 4.1: Prepare on-premises Active Directory for DirSync
- Objective 4.2: Set up DirSync
- Objective 4.3: Manage Active Directory users and groups with DirSync in place

Objective 4.1: Prepare on-premises Active Directory for DirSync

This objective deals with preparing your on-premises Active Directory environment for synchronization of user accounts, group accounts, and mail-enabled contacts to the Azure Active Directory instance that supports the Office 365 tenancy. To master this objective, you'll need to understand the different Active Directory synchronization tools, the steps needed to prepare an on-premises Active Directory instance for DirSync, what to do if your on-premises Active Directory uses a non-routable domain name, what to think about when it comes to planning filtering of user account objects for synchronization, and what to do if you have a multiple-forest environment.

Using Active Directory synchronization tools

One of the challenges of studying for an Office 365 or Microsoft Azure exam is that the technology is always changing and the resources you use to study for the exam could be outdated. Your study material might lack reference to newer tools that have superseded the tools listed on the exam objectives at the time of authoring. For example, the published 70-346 exam objectives do not refer to Azure Active Directory Connect, the successor to DirSync and Azure Active Directory Sync.

DirSync

DirSync, also known as Azure Active Directory Synchronization Tool, is the tool used for on-premises Azure Active Directory account and group synchronization listed in the 70-346 exam objectives. This chapter's primary coverage is around how to deploy and manage this tool.

DirSync allows replication of Active Directory user, group, and contact objects to Azure Active Directory. Any new user, group, or contact object added to the on-premises Active Directory database is also added to Azure Active Directory. Similarly, any object that is deleted from an on-premises Active Directory instance is simultaneously deleted from Office 365. DirSync uses a process known as email-address matching to determine whether a new user object needs to be created in the Azure Active Directory instance. If a user account is present in the on-premises Active Directory instance and no user account object exists in the Azure Active Directory instance used by Office 365, DirSync creates a user account in the Office 365 Azure Active Directory instance that has the same email address as the on-premises user account.

When DirSync performs initial synchronization, a check is performed to determine if any existing user objects within the Office 365 Azure Active Directory instance have the same email address as user objects within the on-premises Active Directory instance. If such a pairing is found, these objects become linked.

It's important to understand that when you use DirSync with an Office 365 deployment, new users, groups, and contacts are added to the Azure Active Directory instance that supports Office 365, but they are not automatically assigned Office 365 licenses. It's also important to note that if you disable a user account in the on-premises Active Directory Domain Services instance that has been assigned an Office 365 license, the license will not be released. You'll have to manually remove the license from the disabled user.

DirSync replicates most, but not all, Active Directory attributes of a user, group, or contact object from the on-premises Active Directory database to the Azure Active Directory instance that supports Office 365.

A key concept in synchronization of Active Directory objects between an on-premises deployment of Active Directory and Azure Active Directory is source of authority. When you use DirSync, the source of authority is the on-premises Active Directory instance. With the exception of Office 365 license management, this means that modifications to those objects can only be performed using on-premises tools such as Windows PowerShell, Active Directory Users And Computers, or Active Directory Administrative Center. Users with Office 365 administrative privileges are unable to modify objects stored within the Azure Active Directory used by Office 365 if the source of authority is an on-premises Active Directory instance.

DirSync can be used in a variety of scenarios including:

- Where Office 365 is used as a replacement for an on-premises Exchange deployment.
- Where Exchange and Office 365 are in a hybrid deployment. In this scenario, DirSync enables mail routing for the shared namespace.

> **MORE INFO DIRSYNC AND OFFICE 365**
>
> You can learn more about DirSync and Office 365 at *https://technet.microsoft.com/en-us/library/dn635310.aspx.*

Azure Active Directory Sync

Azure Active Directory Sync is the Microsoft follow-up tool to DirSync, though DirSync continues to be supported and may still be suited for specific scenarios. A comparison of tools is provided later in this chapter.

Azure Active Directory Sync includes the following functionality:

- Support for replication of multi-forest Active Directory and Exchange deployments
- Control over attribute synchronization on a per-cloud service basis
- Selective replication of accounts on the basis of OU and domain
- Reduced privilege requirements when configuring replication
- Synchronization rules that allow attribute mapping and flow

However, as is the case with tools related to Office 365 and Microsoft Azure, product-release cycles move quickly and the successor to Azure Active Directory Sync is available and is known as Azure Active Directory Connect. Azure Active Directory Connect is not referenced by the published 70-346 objectives.

> **MORE INFO AZURE ACTIVE DIRECTORY SYNC**
>
> You can learn more about Azure Active Directory Sync at *http://blogs.technet.com/b/ad/archive/2014/09/16/azure-active-directory-sync-is-now-ga.aspx.*

Azure Active Directory Connect

Azure Active Directory Connect (AAD Connect) is the Microsoft replacement for DirSync and Azure Active Directory Sync. Azure Active Directory Connect is designed to streamline the process of configuring connections between an on-premises deployment and Azure Active Directory. Rather than perform some of the complex tasks outlined in this chapter and the next, the Azure Active Directory Connect tool is designed to make the process of configuring synchronization between an on-premises Active Directory deployment and Azure Active Directory as frictionless as possible.

Azure Active Directory Connect can automatically configure and install simple password synchronization or Federation/Single Sign-on, depending on your organizational needs, as shown in Figure 4-1. When you choose the Federation With AD FS option, Active Directory Federation Services is installed and configured as a Web Application Proxy server to facilitate communication between the on-premises AD FS deployment and Microsoft Azure Active Directory.

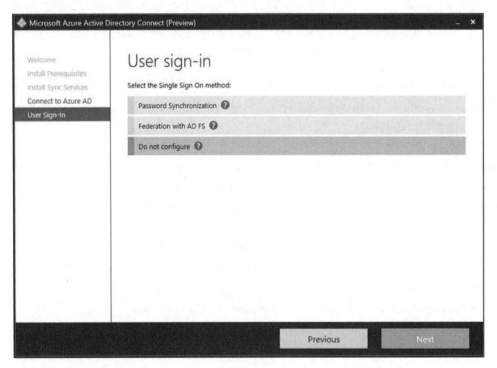

FIGURE 4-1 Azure Active Directory Connect

The Azure Active Directory Connect tool supports the following optional features as shown in Figure 4-2:

- Exchange hybrid deployment
- Azure AD app and attribute filtering
- Password writeback

- User writeback
- Group writeback
- Device writeback
- Device sync
- Directory extension attribute sync

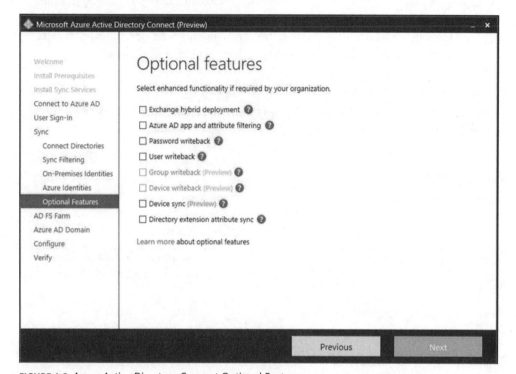

FIGURE 4-2 Azure Active Directory Connect Optional Features

MORE INFO **AZURE ACTIVE DIRECTORY CONNECT**

You can learn more about Azure Active Directory Connect at *http://blogs.technet.com/b/ad/ archive/2014/08/04/connecting-ad-and-azure-ad-only-4-clicks-with-azure-ad-connect.aspx.*

EXAM TIP

Although Azure Active Directory Connect is not currently mentioned on the 70-346 exam objectives, it is not unreasonable to assume that any revision to those objectives at some point will involve a change in focus from using DirSync to using Azure Active Directory Connect. Before taking any exam related to Office 365 and Microsoft Azure, candidates should check to see if changes have been made to address changes in technology that may have occurred.

Forefront Identity Manager 2010 R2

Unlike the other tools listed, Forefront Identity Manager 2010 R2 is a separate product that is purchasable from Microsoft. Forefront Identity Manager enables you to perform identity management tasks beyond that which is possible with the built-in roles and features available to support an on-premises Active Directory instance. With Forefront Identity Manager, you can deploy on-premises self-service password reset, configure a user-provisioning workflow, and provide a centralized interface for certificate management tasks. The next version of Forefront Identity Manager will be known as Microsoft Identity Manager. The 70-346 objectives do not refer to Forefront Identity Manager or Microsoft Identity Manager.

> **MORE INFO FOREFRONT IDENTITY MANAGER 2010 R2**
>
> You can learn more about Forefront Identity Manager 2010 R2 at *https://technet.microsoft.com/en-us/library/jj133852(v=ws.10).aspx.*

Comparison

Table 4-1 provides a comparison between DirSync and the Azure Active Directory Connect tool.

TABLE 4-1   DirSync and Azure Active Directory Connect feature comparison

Feature	DirSync	Azure Active Directory Connect
Support for single on-premises AD DS forest	Yes	Yes
Support for multiple on-premises AD DS forests	No	Yes
Connect to single on-premises LDAP directory	No	Yes
Connect to multiple on-premises LDAP directories	No	Yes
Connect to on-premises AD DS and on-premises LDAP directories	No	Yes
Synchronize directory extensions/customer defined attributes	No	Yes
Writeback of devices	Yes	Yes
Attribute writeback (used with Exchange hybrid deployments)	Yes	Yes
Writeback of users and groups	No	Yes
Writeback of passwords (from self-service password reset and password change in Azure Active Directory)	No	Yes
Writeback of directory extensions/customer defined attributes	No	Yes
Password sync for single on-premises AD DS forest	Yes	Yes
Password sync for multiple on-premises AD DS forests	No	Yes

Single Sign-on/Federation	Yes	Yes
Filtering on Domains and Organizational Units	Yes	Yes
Filtering on object attribute values	Yes	Yes
Allow minimal set of attributes to be synchronized (MinSync)	No	Yes
Allow different service templates to be applied for attribute flows	No	Yes
Allow removing attributes from flowing from AD DS to Azure AD	No	Yes
Allow advanced customization for attribute flows	No	Yes

> **MORE INFO** **DIRECTORY INTEGRATION TOOLS COMPARISON**
>
> You can learn more about directory integration tools at *https://msdn.microsoft.com/library/azure/dn757582.aspx*.

Cleaning up existing Active Directory objects

Before you deploy DirSync, it is prudent to ensure that your on-premises Active Directory environment is healthy. You should also have an excellent understanding of the current state of the Active Directory environment. This should include performing an audit to determine the following:

- Do any Active Directory objects use invalid characters?
- Do any Active Directory objects have incorrect Universal Principal Names (UPNs)?
- What are the current domain and forest functional levels?
- Are any schema extensions or custom attributes in use?

Prior to deploying DirSync, you should ensure that you have performed the following tasks:

- Remove any duplicate proxy-Addresses attributes.
- Remove any duplicate user-Principal-Name attributes.
- Ensure that blank or invalid user-Principal-Name attribute settings have been altered so that the setting contains only a valid UPN.
- Ensure that for user accounts the cn and sAMAccountName attributes have been assigned values.
- Ensure that for group accounts, the member, alias, and display name (for groups with a valid mail or proxy-Addresses attribute) are populated.
- Ensure that the following attributes do not contain invalid characters:
  - givenName
  - sn
  - sAMAccountName
  - givenName

- displayName

- mail

- proxyAddresses

- mailNickName

UPNs that are used with Office 365 can only contain the following characters:

- Letters

- Numbers

- Periods

- Dashes

- Underscores

Rather than having to perform this operation manually, Microsoft provides some tools that allow you to automatically remediate problems that might exist with attributes prior to deploying DirSync.

> **MORE INFO** **LIST OF ATTRIBUTES SYNCED BY DIRSYNC**
>
> You can learn more about the list of attributes synced by DirSync at *http://social.technet. microsoft.com/wiki/contents/articles/19901.dirsync-list-of-attributes-that-are-synced-by-the-azure-active-directory-sync-tool.aspx.*

IdFix

The IdFix tool, which you can download from the Microsoft website, allows you to scan an Active Directory instance to determine if any user accounts, group accounts, or contacts have problems that will cause them not to synchronize between the on-premises instance of Active Directory and the Office 365 instance of Azure Active Directory. IdFix can also perform repairs on objects that would otherwise be unable to sync. IdFix runs with the security context of the currently signed-in user. This means that if you want to use IdFix to repair objects in the forest that have problems, the security account you use to run IdFix must have permissions to modify those objects. The IdFix tool is shown in Figure 4-3 displaying an account detected with an incorrectly configured userPrincipalName.

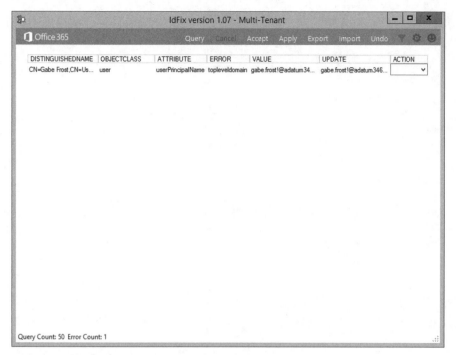

FIGURE 4-3 IdFix finds user with a problematic UPN

> **MORE INFO IDFIX**
>
> You can download IdFix at *http://www.microsoft.com/en-us/download/details.aspx?id=36832*.

ADModify.NET

ADModify.NET is a tool that enables you to make changes to specific attributes for multiple objects simultaneously. If you are using ADSIEdit or the Advanced mode of the Active Directory Users And Computers console, you are only able to modify the attribute of one object at a time. For example, Figure 4-4 shows ADModify.NET being used to modify the format of the userPrincipalName attribute for a number of user accounts such that it conforms to a specific format.

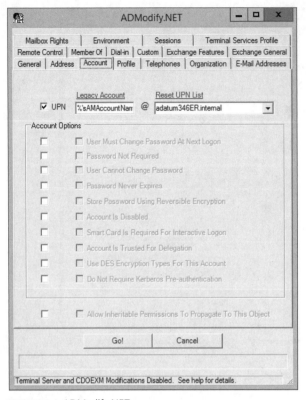

FIGURE 4-4 ADModify.NET

You can also use ADModify.NET to perform other system administration tasks such as disabling multiple accounts or configuring a large number of accounts such that users are required to change their password at next logon.

> **MORE INFO ADMODIFY.NET**
>
> You can learn more about ADModify.NET at *https://technet.microsoft.com/en-us/library/aa996216(v=EXCHG.65).aspx.*

Using UPN suffixes and non-routable domains

Prior to performing synchronization between an on-premises Active Directory environment and an Azure Active Directory instance used to support an Office 365 tenancy, you must ensure that all user account objects in the on-premises Active Directory environment are configured with a value for the UPN suffix that is able to function for both the on-premises environment as well as Office 365.

This is not a problem when the internal Active Directory domain suffix of an organization is a publicly routable domain. For example, a domain name such as contoso.com or adatum.com is resolvable by public DNS servers. Things become more complicated when the internal Active Directory domain suffix is not publicly routable. For example, Figure 4-5 shows the adatum346ER.internal non-routable domain.

FIGURE 4-5 Non-routable domain

If a domain is non-routable, the default routing domain—for example, adatum346ER.onmicrosoft.com—should be used for the Office 365 UPN suffix. This requires modifying the UPN suffix of accounts stored in the on-premises Active Directory instance. Modification of UPN after initial synchronization has occurred is not supported. This means that you need to ensure that on-premises Active Directory UPNs are properly configured prior to performing initial synchronization using DirSync.

To add a UPN suffix to the on-premises Active Directory in the event that the Active Directory domain uses a non-routable namespace, perform the following steps:

1. Open the Active Directory Domains And Trusts console and select Active Directory Domains And Trusts.

2. On the Action menu, click Properties.

3. On the UPN Suffixes tab, enter the UPN suffix to be used with Office 365. Figure 4-6 shows the UPN suffix of adatum346ER.onmicrosoft.com.

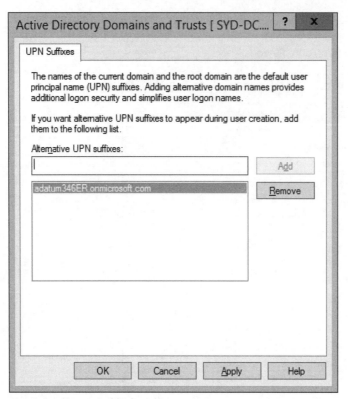

FIGURE 4-6 Non-routable domain

4. Once the UPN suffix has been added in Active Directory Domains And Trusts, you can assign the UPN suffix to user accounts. You can do this manually as shown in Figure 4-7 by using the Account tab of the user's Properties dialog box in Active Directory Users And Computers.

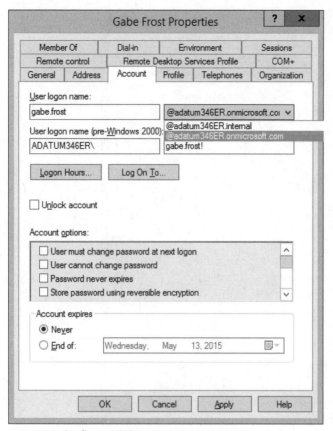

FIGURE 4-7 Configure UPN

5. You can use the ADModify.NET tool to reset the UPNs of multiple accounts as shown in Figure 4-8.

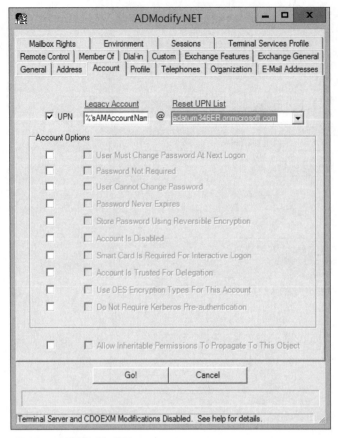

FIGURE 4-8 ADModify.NET

6. You can also use Windows PowerShell scripts to reset the UPNs of multiple user accounts. For example, the following script resets UPN suffixes of all user accounts in the adatum346ER.internal domain to adatum346ER.onmicrosoft.com.

```
Get-ADUser -Filter {UserPrincipalName -like "*@adatum346ER.internal"} -SearchBase
"DC=adatum346ER,DC=internal" |
ForEach-Object {
$UPN =
$_.UserPrincipalName.Replace("adatum346.internal","adatum346ER.onmicrosoft.com")
Set-ADUser $_ -UserPrincipalName $UPN
}
```

Planning for filtering Active Directory

When you use DirSync to synchronize on-premises Active Directory to an Azure Active Directory instance, the default setting is to have all user accounts, group accounts, and mail-enabled contact objects synchronized up to the cloud. For some organizations, synchronizing everything is exactly what they want. Other organizations want to be more selective about which objects are synchronized from the on-premises Active Directory environment to the Azure Active Directory instance that supports the Office 365 tenancy.

With DirSync, you can choose to filter based on the following options:

- **Domain-based**   In a forest with multiple domains, you can configure filtering so that only objects from some domains, and not others, are filtered.
- **Organizational-unit (OU)-based**   With this filtering type, you choose which objects are filtered, based on their location within specific organizational units.
- **User-attribute-based**   You can also create filters based on the attributes of user objects. You can create filters based on any Active Directory user-object attribute.

You can combine filters such that it is possible to use a combination of domain, OU, and attribute-based filtering to limit which user account objects are synchronized from on-premises Active Directory to the Azure Active Directory instance that supports the Office 365 tenancy. Later in the chapter, you'll learn about the specifics of how to implement Active Directory filtering using DirSync.

> **MORE INFO FILTERING**
>
> You can learn more about DirSync filtering at *https://msdn.microsoft.com/en-us/library/azure/jj710171.aspx*.

Supporting multiple forests

By itself, DirSync doesn't support synchronization from two or more Active Directory forests to a single Azure Active Directory instance that supports an Office 365 tenancy. To accomplish this task, you can use the Azure Active Directory Connector for Forefront Identity Manager 2010. When using the Azure Active Directory Connector for Forefront Identity Manager, you need to deploy the Forefront Identity Manager product in its entirety. DirSync includes a stripped-down and optimized version of Forefront Identity Manager, but this only enables a single on-premises forest connection.

Also worth noting is that the Azure Active Directory Connect tool supports synchronization from multiple on-premises Active Directory forests to a single Azure Active Directory instance. This tool debuted after the 70-346 exam objectives were published.

EXAM TIP

Remember that DirSync does not support synchronization from multiple separate Active Directory forests to Azure Active Directory. Use either Forefront Identity Manager with the Azure Active Directory Connector or, if the objectives have been updated by the time you read this, Azure Active Directory Connect.

Thought experiment
Consulting at Adatum

In this thought experiment, apply what you learned about this objective. You can find answers to these questions in the "Answers" section at the end of this chapter.

You are in the process of consulting at Adatum about their planned synchronization solution, which will allow them to replicate user account, group account, and mail-enabled contacts from their on-premises Active Directory environment to an Azure Active Directory instance that supports an Office 365 tenancy. The Adatum environment consists of three forests with 21 separate domains. A preliminary assessment using the IdFix tool has found that it is necessary to make bulk changes to certain attributes used with user accounts before synchronization between the on-premises environment and Azure Active Directory can commence. With this in mind, answer the following questions:

1. Why is DirSync not a suitable solution for Adatum?

2. What tool, besides Windows PowerShell, could be used to bulk modify the attributes of selected user accounts at Adatum?

Objective summary

- DirSync is a tool that allows the replication of user accounts, groups, and mail-enabled contacts from an on-premises Active Directory instance to an Azure Active Directory instance that supports the Office 365 tenancy.

- Prior to deploying DirSync, you should run a tool named IdFix to locate objects in the on-premises Active Directory that have attribute configurations that are incompatible with DirSync.

- If your organization has a non-routable domain, you'll need to update the UPN suffixes used by the accounts that you want to synchronize to Azure Active Directory such that they use routable domain records.

- DirSync does not support synchronization of multiple Active Directory forests to an Azure Active Directory instance that supports the Office 365 tenancy. You can use the Azure Active Directory Connector for Forefront Identity Manager to perform this task.

Objective review

Answer the following questions to test your knowledge of the information in this objective. You can find the answers to these questions and explanations of each answer choice in the "Answers" section at the end of the chapter.

1. You want to add adatum.com as a UPN suffix to the adatum.internal domain in preparation for the deployment of DirSync. Which of the following tools can you use to accomplish this goal?

   A. Active Directory Sites And Services

   B. Active Directory Domains And Trusts

   C. Active Directory Users And Computers

   D. Office 365 Admin Center

2. Which of the following are non-routable domain names?

   A. Adatum.info

   B. Adatum.internal

   C. Adatum.net

   D. Adatum.com

3. Which of the following Active Directory synchronization tools support synchronizing user objects from multiple forests to a single Azure Active Directory instance that supports the Office 365 tenancy? (Choose all that apply.)

   A. DirSync

   B. Azure Active Directory Connect

   C. Active Directory Domains And Trusts

   D. Azure Active Directory Connector For Forefront Identity Manager

4. Which of the following tools can you use to scan Active Directory to locate attributes associated with user objects that will cause problems when you attempt to use DirSync to synchronize those objects with an Azure Active Directory instance that supports an Office 365 tenancy?

   A. Synchronization Service Manager

   B. IdFix

   C. ADModify.NET

   D. ADSI Edit

Objective 4.2: Set up DirSync

This objective deals with the process of deploying DirSync as well as configuring initial DirSync options. To master this objective, you'll need to understand how the on-premises Active Directory environment needs to be configured to support DirSync, the hardware and software specifications of the computer that hosts DirSync, and the privileges required by the account that is used to configure DirSync. You'll also need to understand soft-match filtering, be able to identify synchronized attributes, and be able to configure password synchronization.

> **This objective covers the following topics:**
> - DirSync installation requirements
> - Installing DirSync
> - Filtering
> - Identify synchronized attributes
> - Password sync

Meeting the DirSync installation requirements

Prior to installing DirSync, you should ensure that your environment, DirSync computer, and account used to configure DirSync meet relevant software, hardware, and privilege requirements. This means that you need to ensure that your Active Directory environment is configured at the appropriate level, that the computer on which you will run DirSync has the appropriate software and hardware configuration, and that the account that you use to install DirSync has been added to the appropriate security groups.

Software environment requirements

DirSync requires that the on-premises Active Directory environment be configured at the Windows Server 2003 forest functional level or higher. Forest functional level is dependent on the minimum domain functional level of any domain in a forest. For example, if you have five domains in a forest, with four of them running at the Windows Server 2012 R2 domain functional level and one of them running at the Windows Server 2003 domain functional level, then Windows Server 2003 will be the maximum forest functional level.

You can check the forest functional level using the Active Directory Domains And Trusts console. To do this, perform the following steps:

1. Open the Active Directory Domains And Trusts console.
2. Select the Active Directory Domains And Trusts node.
3. On the Actions menu, click Raise Forest Functional Level.
4. The dialog box displays the current functional level and, if possible, provides you with the option of upgrading the forest functional level. Figure 4-9 shows the forest

functional level configured at Windows Server 2012 R2, which is the highest possible forest functional level for an organization where all domain controllers are running the Windows Server 2012 R2 operating system.

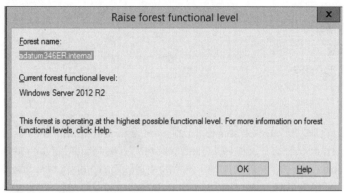

FIGURE 4-9 Forest functional level

You can also check the forest functional level by using the following Windows PowerShell command:

```
(Get-ADForest).ForestMode
```

DirSync is software that you install on a computer for the purpose of managing the process of synchronizing objects between the on-premises Active Directory and the Azure Active Directory instance that supports the Office 365 tenancy. You can install DirSync on computers running the following operating systems:

- Windows Server 2003 with Service Pack 1 (x86 and x64)
- Windows Server 2003 R2 (x86 and x64)
- Windows Server 2008 (x86 and x64)
- Windows Server 2008 R2 (x64)
- Windows Server 2012 (x64)
- Windows Server 2012 R2 (x64)

Prior to attempting to install DirSync, you must ensure that you have installed the following software prerequisites:

- Microsoft .NET Framework 3.5 SP1
- Microsoft .NET Framework 4.0
- Azure Active Directory module for Windows PowerShell

If you are having trouble installing Microsoft .NET Framework 3.5 SP1 on computers running the Windows Server 2012 and Windows Server 2012 R2 operating systems, remember that the installation files for that feature are located in the X:\sources\sxs\ folder (where X is the location of the Windows Server 2012 and Windows Server 2012 R2 installation media).

The computer that hosts DirSync must be a member of a domain in the forest that you want to synchronize and must have connectivity to a writable domain controller in each domain of the forest you want to synchronize on the following ports:

- DNS: TCP/UDP Port 53
- Kerberos: TCP/UDP Port 88
- RPC: TCP Port 135
- LDAP: TCP/UDP Port 389
- SSL: TCP Port 443
- SMB: TCP 445

The computer running DirSync must be able to establish communication with the Microsoft Azure servers on the Internet over TCP port 443. The computer can be located on an internal network as long as it can initiate communication on TCP port 443. The computer hosting DirSync does not need a publicly routable IP address. The computer running DirSync always initiates synchronization communication to Microsoft Azure. Microsoft Azure Active Directory does not initiate synchronization communication to the computer hosting DirSync on the on-premises network.

While you can install DirSync on a domain controller, Microsoft recommends that you deploy DirSync on a computer that does not host the domain controller role. If you are going to be replicating more than 50,000 objects, Microsoft recommends that you deploy SQL Server on a computer that is separate from the computer that will host DirSync. If you plan to host the SQL Server instance on a separate computer, ensure that communication is possible between the computer hosting DirSync and the computer hosting the SQL Instance on TCP port 1433.

If you are going to use a separate SQL Server instance, you must perform installation of DirSync using the command line. A GUI install of DirSync always deploys an instance of SQL Server Express. If you are using a full SQL Server instance, ensure that the account used to install and configure DirSync has "systems administrator" rights on the SQL instance and that the service account used for DirSync has "public" permissions on the DirSync database.

Hardware requirements

The hardware requirements of the computer that hosts DirSync depend on the number of objects in the Active Directory environment that you need to sync. The greater the number of objects that you need to sync, the steeper the hardware requirements. Table 4-2 provides a guide to the requirements, with all configurations requiring at least a 1.6 GHz processor.

TABLE 4-2 DirSync computer hardware requirements

Number of objects in Active Directory	Memory	Storage
Fewer than 10,000	4 GB	70 GB
10,000–50,000	4 GB	70 GB
50,000–100,000	16 GB	100 GB

100,000–300,000	32 GB	300 GB
300,000–600,000	32 GB	450 GB
More than 600,000	32 GB	500 GB

Important to note during the planning phase is that a new Office 365 tenancy has a limit of 50,000 objects. However, once the first domain is verified, this limit is increased to 300,000 objects. Organizations that need to store more than 300,000 objects in an Azure Active Directory instance that supports an Office 365 tenancy should contact Microsoft Support.

Installation account requirements

The accounts that you use to install and configure DirSync have the following requirements:

- The account used to configure Office 365 must have Administrator permissions in the Office 365 tenant. If you create a service account in Office 365 to use in place of the account with Tenant Administrator permissions, ensure that you configure the account with a password that does not expire.

- The account used to install and configure DirSync must have Enterprise Administrator permissions within the on-premises Active Directory forest. This account is only required during installation and configuration. Once DirSync is installed and configured, this account no longer needs Enterprise Administrator permissions. Best practice is to create a separate account for DirSync installation and configuration and to temporarily add this account to the Enterprise Admins group during the installation and configuration process. Once DirSync is installed and configured, this account can be removed from the Enterprise Admins group. You should not attempt to change the account used after DirSync is set up and configured, as DirSync always attempts to run using the original account.

- The account used to install and configure DirSync must be a member of the local Administrators group on the computer on which DirSync is installed.

- Once DirSync is installed, the account used to run the Configuration Wizard must be a member of the FIMSyncAdmins group. The account used to install DirSync is automatically added to this group during the installation process. However, to have these permissions applied, the user account that installs DirSync should sign in and then sign in again so that the new group membership configuration takes effect.

MORE INFO **DEPLOYING DIRSYNC**

You can learn more about deploying DirSync at *https://technet.microsoft.com/en-us/library/dn635310%28v=office.15%29.aspx.*

Office 365 requirements

Before you can install and configure DirSync, you also need to ensure that you have configured an additional domain for Office 365 and enabled Active Directory Synchronization from within the Office 365 Admin console. You can only enable Active Directory Synchronization once an additional domain has been configured. You learned about configuring additional domains in Chapter 1, "Provision Office 365." Figure 4-10 shows the Do You Want To Activate Active Directory Synchronization dialog box.

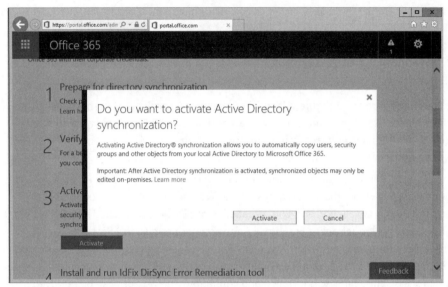

FIGURE 4-10 Activate Active Directory Synchronization

Installing DirSync

To install DirSync, perform the following steps:

1. Sign in to the Office 365 Admin Center with an account that has Administrator privileges.

2. In the Active Users node, under Active Users as shown in Figure 4-11, click Set Up next to Active Directory Synchronization.

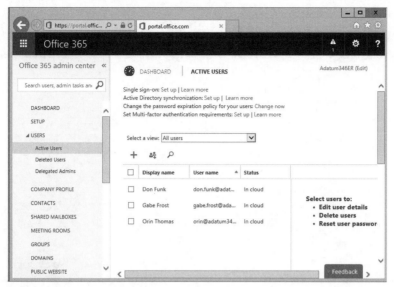

FIGURE 4-11 Active Users node

3. You'll need to have set up a domain already. You learned about setting up domains in Chapter 1. Figure 4-12 shows the adatum346er.com domain configured.

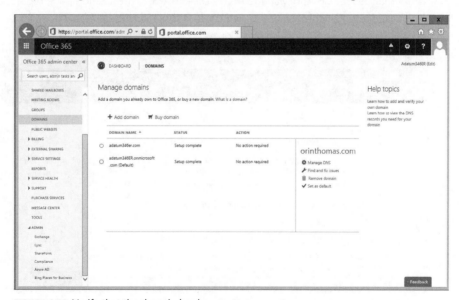

FIGURE 4-12 Verify that the domain has been set up

4. In the Office 365 Admin Center, click back to Active Users under USERS and then click Set Up next to Active Directory Synchronization.

5. On the Set Up And Manage Active Directory Synchronization page, click Activate under Activate Active Directory Synchronization as shown in Figure 4-13.

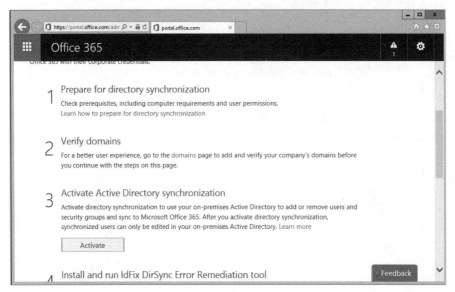

FIGURE 4-13 Activate Active Directory Synchronization

6. On the Do You Want To Activate Active Directory Synchronization page, click Activate.

7. Verify that the Set Up And Manage Active Directory Synchronization page reports that Active Directory Synchronization is Activated as shown in Figure 4-14.

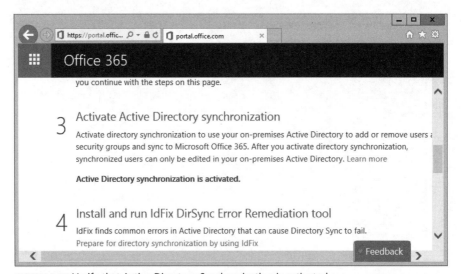

FIGURE 4-14 Verify that Active Directory Synchronization is activated

8. On the Set Up And Manage Active Directory Synchronization page, click Download in the Install And Configure The Directory Sync Tool as shown in Figure 4-15.

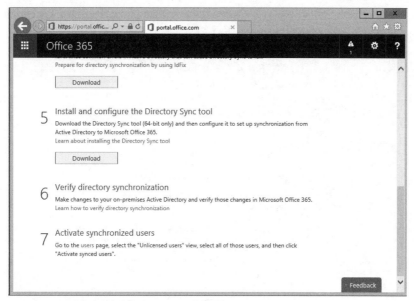

FIGURE 4-15 Download the Directory Sync Tool

9. Save the DirSync.exe executable file to a location on the computer that will host DirSync.

10. When DirSync.exe has downloaded, double-click the file to start installation.

11. On the Welcome page, shown in Figure 4-16, click Next.

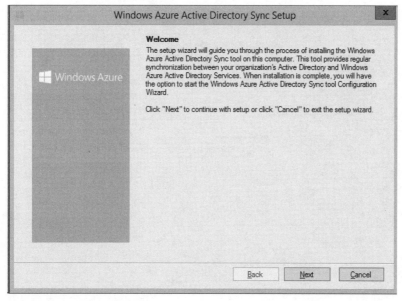

FIGURE 4-16 The Welcome page

12. On the Microsoft Software License Terms page, review the license, click I Accept as shown in Figure 4-17, and then click Next.

FIGURE 4-17 Review license terms

13. On the Select Installation Folder page, either accept the default, as shown in Figure 4-18, or select a different installation folder.

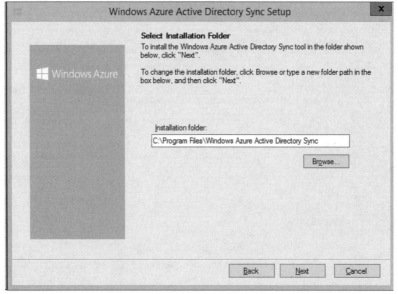

FIGURE 4-18 Installation folder

14. Installation takes between 5 and 15 minutes.

15. Once installation has completed, click Next. Because you log off from the computer on which you have installed DirSync and then log in again to perform configuration, you should clear the Start Configuration Wizard Now check box as shown in Figure 4-19 and click Finished.

FIGURE 4-19 The Finished page

After installation has completed, examine the local groups on the computer on which DirSync has been installed and verify that the following groups are present as shown in Figure 4-20:

- FIMSyncAdmins
- FIMSyncBrowse
- FIMSyncJoiners
- FIMSyncOperators
- FIMSyncPasswordSet

FIGURE 4-20 FIM groups

These groups are used with the stripped-down Forefront Identity Manager (FIM) component used in DirSync. The account used to configure DirSync needs to be a member of the FIMSyncAdmins group as shown in Figure 4-21. If the installation process has completed without error, this occurs automatically.

FIGURE 4-21 Non-routable domain

Initial DirSync configuration

To configure DirSync, perform the following steps:

1. Open Directory Sync Configuration from the icon that is present on the desktop after DirSync is installed.

2. On the Welcome page of the Windows Azure Active Directory Sync Tool Configuration Wizard, click Next.

3. On the Windows Azure Active Directory Credentials page of the Windows Azure Active Directory Sync Tool Configuration Wizard, enter the credentials of the Office 365 Tenant Administrator account. Figure 4-22 shows the credentials for the adatum346ER. onmicrosoft.com tenancy. Click Next.

FIGURE 4-22 Office 365 Administrator Credentials

4. On the Active Directory Credentials page, shown in Figure 4-23, provide the credentials of a user account with Enterprise Administrator credentials. Click Next.

FIGURE 4-23 On-premises Administrator Credentials

5. On the Hybrid Deployment page, shown in Figure 4-24, select Enable Hybrid Deployment if you want to configure a deployment where you want to have Azure Active Directory write data back to your on-premises Active Directory instance.

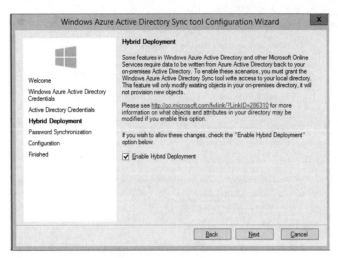

FIGURE 4-24 Enable Hybrid Deployment

6. On the Password Synchronization page, shown in Figure 4-25, select whether or not you want to allow DirSync to synchronize passwords from the on-premises Active Directory to the Azure Active Directory instance that supports the Office 365 tenancy and then click Next.

FIGURE 4-25 Password synchronization

7. The DirSync tool performs configuration. When configuration is complete, click Next.

8. On the Finished page, select Synchronize Your Directories Now and then click Finish.

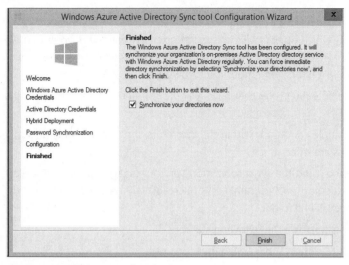

FIGURE 4-26 Directory synchronization

An instance of DirSync can only be used to populate a single cloud tenant. If you wish to populate a second Office 365 tenancy, you'll need to deploy an additional instance of DirSync.

> **MORE INFO INSTALLING DIRSYNC**
>
> You can learn more about installing DirSync at *https://technet.microsoft.com/en-us/library/jj151800.aspx*.

Deploying DirSync in Microsoft Azure

Rather than deploying the computer running DirSync in your on-premises environment, you can deploy the computer hosting DirSync on a virtual machine running Microsoft Azure. To implement this configuration, you need to perform the following general steps:

1. Create an Azure virtual network.
2. Configure a site-to-site VPN connection from the on-premises network to the Azure virtual network.
3. Deploy a virtual machine on the virtual network in Microsoft Azure.
4. Join this Azure virtual machine to the on-premises domain.
5. Install DirSync using the method detailed earlier in this chapter.

> **MORE INFO DEPLOYING DIRSYNC IN MICROSOFT AZURE**
>
> You can learn more about deploying DirSync in Azure at *https://technet.microsoft.com/en-us/library/dn635310%28v=office.15%29.aspx*.

Filtering

You use filters to specify which objects will not synchronize between the on-premises Active Directory and the Azure Active Directory instance that supports the Office 365 tenancy. When creating rules with multiple filters, remember the following:

- If you create multiple filter rules that have a single condition, the filter applies if any rules match.
- If you create multiple conditions within the same rule, the filter will only be applied if all the conditions are true.

You configure filtering using the Synchronization Service Manager, sometimes called Identity Manager, located in the %ProgramFiles%\Microsoft Online Directory Sync\SYNCBUS\ Synchronization Service\UIShell folder.

To configure filtering, perform the following steps:

1. Open the Synchronization Service Manager console.
2. On the Management Agents tab, shown in Figure 4-27, double-click Active Directory Connector.

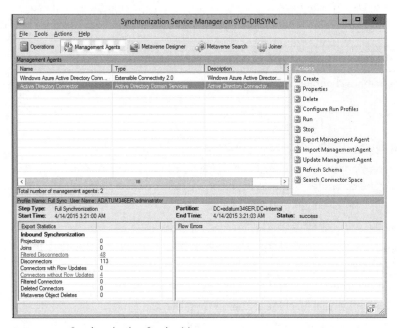

FIGURE 4-27 Synchronization Service Manager

3. In the Actions pane, click Properties.
4. If you want to remove specific organizational units from replication, click Configure Directory Partitions.
5. On the Configure Directory Partitions page, shown in Figure 4-28, click Containers.

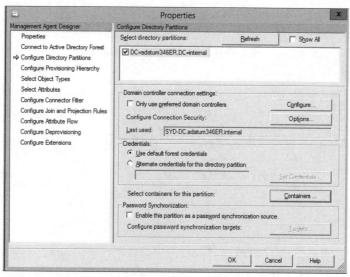

FIGURE 4-28 Configure Directory Partitions

6. On the Select Containers page, shown in Figure 4-29, select the organizational units that you want to allow to replicate during synchronization.

FIGURE 4-29 Select Containers

7. To filter on the basis of attributes, click Configure Connector Filter. Figure 4-30 shows this page selected.

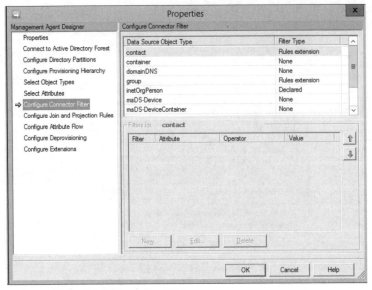

FIGURE 4-30 Configure Connector Filter

8. You can select a User Data Source Object and then configure a filter based on the attribute that you want to configure. You can also click New and create your own filter based on the available data source attributes. Figure 4-31 shows a filter for users who have the Department attribute equal to Research.

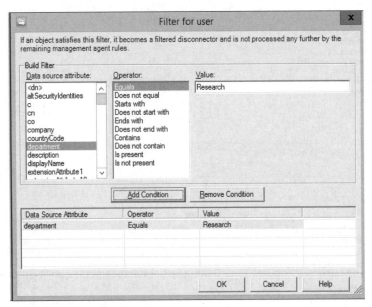

FIGURE 4-31 Create filter

Identifying synchronized attributes

DirSync synchronizes some, but not all, attributes from the on-premises Active Directory instance to Azure Active Directory instance that supports an Office 365 tenancy. One-hundred forty-three separate attributes synchronize, depending on whether the object is a user account, a group account, or a mail-enabled contact object. These attributes are as listed in Table 4-3.

TABLE 4-3 List of attributes synchronized by DirSync

assistant	msExchArchiveStatus	msExchTeamMailboxSharePointUrl
authOrig	msExchAssistantName	msExchUCVoiceMailSettings
C	msExchAuditAdmin	msExchUsageLocation
Cn	msExchAuditDelegate	msExchUserHoldPolicies
Co	msExchAuditDelegateAdmin	msOrg-IsOrganizational
company	msExchAuditOwner	msRTCSIP-ApplicationOptions
countryCode	MsExchBlockedSendersHash	msRTCSIP-DeploymentLocator
department	msExchBypassAudit	msRTCSIP-Line
description	MsExchBypassModerationFromDLMembersLink	msRTCSIP-OwnerUrn
displayName	MsExchBypassModerationLink	msRTCSIP-PrimaryUserAddress
dLMemRejectPerms	msExchCoManagedByLink	msRTCSIP-UserEnabled
dLMemSubmitPerms	msExchDelegateListLink	msRTCSIP-OptionFlags
ExtensionAttribute1	msExchELCExpirySuspensionEnd	objectGUID
ExtensionAttribute10	msExchELCExpirySuspensionStart	oOFReplyToOriginator
ExtensionAttribute11	msExchELCMailboxFlags	otherFacsimileTelephone
ExtensionAttribute12	MsExchEnableModeration	otherHomePhone
ExtensionAttribute13	msExchExtensionCustomAttribute1	otherIpPhone
ExtensionAttribute14	msExchExtensionCustomAttribute2	otherMobile
ExtensionAttribute15	msExchExtensionCustomAttribute3	otherPager
ExtensionAttribute2	msExchExtensionCustomAttribute4	otherTelephone
ExtensionAttribute3	msExchExtensionCustomAttribute5	pager

ExtensionAttribute4	MsExchGroupDepartRestriction	photo
ExtensionAttribute5	MsExchGroupJoinRestriction	physicalDeliveryOfficeName
ExtensionAttribute6	msExchHideFromAddressLists	postalCode
ExtensionAttribute7	MsExchImmutableID	postOfficeBox
ExtensionAttribute8	msExchLitigationHoldDate	PreferredLanguage
ExtensionAttribute9	msExchLitigationHoldOwner	proxyAddresses
Facsimiletelephonenumber	MsExchMailboxGuid	PublicDelegates
givenName	msExchMailboxAuditEnable	pwdLastSet
GroupType	msExchMailboxAuditLogAgeLimit	reportToOriginator
hideDLMembership	MsExchModeratedByLink	ReportToOwner
homephone	MsExchModerationFlags	samAccountName
Info	MsExchRecipientDisplayType	sn
Initials	msExchRecipientTypeDetails	st
ipPhone	MsExchRemoteRecipientType	streetAddress
L	msExchRequireAuthToSendTo	targetAddress
legacyExchangeDN	MsExchResourceCapacity	TelephoneAssistant
Mail	MsExchResourceDisplay	telephoneNumber
mailnickname	MsExchResourceMetaData	thumbnailphoto
managedBy	MsExchResourceSearchProperties	title
manager	msExchRetentionComment	unauthOrig
member	msExchRetentionURL	url
middleName	MsExchSafeRecipientsHash	userAccountControl
Mobile	MsExchSafeSendersHash	userCertificate
msDS-HABSeniorityIndex	MsExchSenderHintTranslations	UserPrincipalName
msDS-PhoneticDisplay-Name	msExchTeamMailboxExpiration	userSMIMECertificate
MsExchArchiveGUID	msExchTeamMailboxOwners	wWWHomePage
MsExchArchiveName	msExchTeamMailboxSharePoint-LinkedBy	

MORE INFO ATTRIBUTES SYNCHRONIZED BY DIRSYNC

You can learn more about which attributes are synchronized by DirSync at *http://social. technet.microsoft.com/wiki/contents/articles/19901.dirsync-list-of-attributes-that-are- synced-by-the-azure-active-directory-sync-tool.aspx.*

Syncing passwords

Password Sync allows the synchronization of user account passwords from on-premises Active Directory to the Azure Active Directory instance that supports the Office 365 tenancy. The advantage of this is that users can sign in to Office 365 using the same password that they use to sign in to computers on the on-premises environment. Password Sync does not provide single sign-on or federation. This topic is covered in more detail in Chapter 5.

When you enable Password Sync, the on-premises password complexity policies override password complexity policies configured for the Azure Active Directory instance that supports the Office 365 tenancy. This means that any password that is valid for an on-premises user will be valid within Office 365 even if it would otherwise be invalid.

Password expiration works in the following way: the password of the account of the cloud user object is set to never expire. Each time the user account password is changed in the on-premises Active Directory instance, that change replicates to the Azure Active Directory instance that supports the Office 365 tenancy. This means that it is possible for a user account password to expire on the on-premises Active Directory instance, but that user can still use the same password to sign in to Office 365. The next time they sign in to the on-premises environment, they are required to change their password and that change replicates to the Azure Active Directory instance that supports the Office 365 tenancy.

When Password Sync is enabled and you disable a user's account in the on-premises Active Directory instance, the user's account in the Azure Active Directory instance that supports the Office 365 tenancy is disabled within a few minutes. If Password Sync is not enabled and you disable a particular user account in the on-premises Active Directory instance, then the same user account in the Azure Active Directory instance that supports the Office 365 tenancy is not disabled until the next full synchronization.

MORE INFO PASSWORD SYNCHRONIZATION

You can learn more about password synchronization at *https://msdn.microsoft.com/en-us/ library/azure/dn246918.aspx.*

EXAM TIP

Remember the DirSync prerequisites.

Thought experiment

DirSync at Tailspin Toys

In this thought experiment, apply what you learned about this objective. You can find answers to these questions in the "Answers" section at the end of this chapter.

You are in the process of planning the deployment of DirSync at Tailspin Toys. All accounts at Tailspin Toys are in geography-based OUs. Attributes, such as the Department attribute, denote the departments with which the users are associated. With this information in mind, answer the following questions:

1. How can you ensure that members of the Research department don't have their accounts synchronized to the Azure Active Directory instance that supports the Office 365 tenancy?

2. You have installed the Azure Active Directory module for Windows PowerShell and enabled the .NET Framework 4.0 on the computer running Windows Server 2012 R2 that will host DirSync. What other software must be installed before you can install DirSync?

Objective summary

- You can only install DirSync on joined computers in a forest that is at the Windows Server 2003 forest functional level or higher.

- DirSync requires .NET Framework 3.5 SP1 and .NET Framework 4.0.

- Two accounts are required to install and configure DirSync. The first account must be a member of the Enterprise Administrators group of the local Active Directory forest. The second account must have administrator privileges to the Office 365 tenancy.

- Filtering allows you to control which user account, group account, and mail-enabled contact objects are replicated to the Azure Active Directory instance that supports the Office 365 tenancy.

- Password Sync allows users to use the password they use with their on-premises Active Directory user account to sign in to Office 365.

Objective review

Answer the following questions to test your knowledge of the information in this objective. You can find the answers to these questions and explanations of why each answer choice in the "Answers" section at the end of the chapter.

1. What's the minimum forest functional level required to deploy DirSync?

   A. Windows Server 2003

   B. Windows Server 2008

   C. Windows Server 2008 R2

   D. Windows Server 2012 R2

2. Which of the following groups must be a member of an account to run DirSync configuration?

   A. Schema Admins

   B. Enterprise Admins

   C. Domain Admins

   D. Account Operators

3. Which tool do you use to configure DirSync filtering?

   A. Active Directory Administrative Center

   B. Active Directory Domains And Trusts

   C. Synchronization Service Manager

   D. ADModify.NET

4. You are planning the deployment of DirSync at your organization. At what number of objects replicating from the on-premises Active Directory instance to Azure Active Directory instance that supports the Office 365 tenancy does Microsoft recommend using a SQL Server instance deployed on a separate computer to support DirSync rather than using SQL Server Express?

   A. 10,000

   B. 20,000

   C. 25,000

   D. 50,000

Objective 4.3: Manage Active Directory users and groups with DirSync in place

This objective deals with managing Active Directory users and groups once you have configured DirSync. To master this objective you'll need to understand the concept of source of authority and that, in most cases, you'll need to continue to manage users and groups using your on-premises Active Directory tools and either wait for or force synchronization for those changes to become apparent within Office 365.

> **This objective covers the following topics:**
> - Create users and groups
> - Modify users and groups
> - Delete users and groups
> - Schedule synchronization
> - Force synchronization

Creating users and groups

Source of authority is a very important concept when it comes to creating users and groups in an environment where DirSync is configured to synchronize an on-premises Active Directory instance with the Azure Active Directory instance that supports the Office 365 tenancy. When you create a user or group in the on-premises Active Directory instance, the on-premises Active Directory instance retains authority over that object. Objects created within the on-premises Active Directory instance that are within the filtering scope of objects synchronized via DirSync will replicate to the Azure Active Directory instance that supports the Office 365 tenancy.

Newly created on-premises user and group objects will only be present within the Azure Active Directory instance that supports the Office 365 tenancy after synchronization has occurred. By default, synchronization occurs every three hours. You can force synchronization to occur using the Synchronization Service Manager tool, sometimes called Identity Manager, or by using Windows PowerShell.

It is important to remember that to remember is that user accounts created in Office 365 by the synchronization process will not automatically be assigned Office 365 licenses. This means that when you are creating new user accounts in the on-premises environment after you've initially configured DirSync, you'll also need to use either Office 365 Admin Center or Windows PowerShell to provision those accounts with Office 365 licenses.

One of the simplest methods to assign licenses to a large number of accounts is by using Windows PowerShell. To accomplish this task using Windows PowerShell, you need to first ensure that a usage location is set for each unlicensed user, and then to assign a license using the proper SKU identifier.

To determine which Office 365 users have not been properly configured with a license, enact the following Windows PowerShell command:

```
Get-MsolUser -UnlicensedUsersOnly
```

To assign all unlicensed users to a specific location use the following command where <location> is the location to which you want to assign the unlicensed users:

```
Get-MsolUser -UnlicensedUsersOnly | Set-MsolUser -UsageLocation <location>
```

You'll need to apply the account SKU ID to each account. The way to do this is by first assigning SKU information to a variable with the following command:

```
$Sku=Get-MsolAccountSku
```

Once you have this information, you can use the following command to apply the appropriate account SKU ID to correctly license each account:

```
Get-MsolUser -UnlicensedUsersOnly | Set-MsolUser -AddLicenses $Sku.AccountSkuID
```

Modifying users and groups

Source of authority is again important when it comes to making modifications to users and groups. Remember that modifications that occur in the on-premises Active Directory instance overwrite the current state of the objects within the Azure Active Directory instance that supports the Office 365 tenancy. The only exception to this rule is with the assignment of licenses, which only occurs using the Office 365 Admin Center tool or Windows PowerShell.

Modifications made to on-premises user and group objects will only be present within the Azure Active Directory instance that supports the Office 365 tenancy after synchronization has occurred. By default, synchronization occurs every three hours. You can force synchronization to occur using the Synchronization Service Manager tool or by using Windows PowerShell.

Deleting users and groups

With deletion, the concept of source of authority is again very important. When you want to delete a user or group account that was created in the on-premises Active Directory instance, you should use tools such as Active Directory Users And Computers or Active Directory Administrative Center to remove that user. When you use this method to delete the user or group, the user will be deleted from the on-premises Active Directory instance and then, when synchronization occurs, will be deleted from the Azure Active Directory instance that supports the Office 365 tenancy. As discussed earlier, synchronization occurs by default every three hours, but you can force a synchronization, which you'll learn how to do later in this chapter, to make the deletion occur more quickly.

When you delete a user from Office 365, their account remains in the Azure Active Directory Recycle Bin for 30 days. This means that you can recover the account online should it be necessary to do so. If you delete a user from your on-premises Active Directory environment, but have enabled the on-premises Active Directory Recycle Bin, recovering the user from the on-premises Active Directory Recycle Bin will automatically recover the user account in Office 365. If you don't have Active Directory Recycle Bin enabled, you'll need to create another account with a new GUID.

In some cases, synchronization doesn't work properly and objects that are deleted from the on-premises Active Directory instance don't automatically get deleted from the Azure Active Directory instance that supports the Office 365 tenancy. In this circumstance, you can use the Remove-MsolUser, Remove-MsolGroup, or Remove-MsolContact Windows PowerShell cmdlets to manually remove the orphaned object.

> **MORE INFO** **REMOVING OBJECTS THAT WON'T DELETE**
>
> You can learn more about removing objects created through synchronization that won't delete from Office 365 at *https://support.microsoft.com/en-us/kb/2619062*.

Scheduling synchronization

Scheduled synchronization occurs every three hours. You can change the synchronization frequency by modifying the Microsoft.Online.DirSync.Scheduler.exe.Config configuration file, which is located in the %programfiles%\Windows Azure Active Directory Sync folder. Once you have modified this file, shown in Figure 4-32, you need to restart the synchronization service on the computer that hosts DirSync.

```
<?xml version="1.0" encoding="utf-8"?>
<configuration>
  <appSettings>
    <!--the interval in hours-->
    <!--refer for valid values:http://msdn2.microsoft.com/en-us/library/system.timespan.parse.aspx-->
    <add key="SyncTimeInterval" value="3:0:0" />
  </appSettings>
  <startup>
    <supportedRuntime version="v4.0" />
  </startup>
</configuration>
```

FIGURE 4-32 Change synchronization schedule

Forcing synchronization

In some cases, such as when you make a change to a user account or create a collection of user accounts and want to get those changes or new accounts up into the Azure Active Directory instance that supports the Office 365 tenancy as fast as possible, rather than waiting the default three hours, you need to force a synchronization. You can force a synchronization using the Synchronization Service Manager tool, sometimes termed Identity Manager, or by using Windows PowerShell.

To perform a full synchronization using Synchronization Service Manager, perform the following steps:

1. Open Synchronization Service Manager located in the C:\Program Files\Windows Azure Active Directory Sync\SYNCBUS\Synchronization Service\UIShell folder as miisclient.exe.

2. Click the Management Agents tab.

3. On the Management Agents tab, click Active Directory Connector as shown in Figure 4-33.

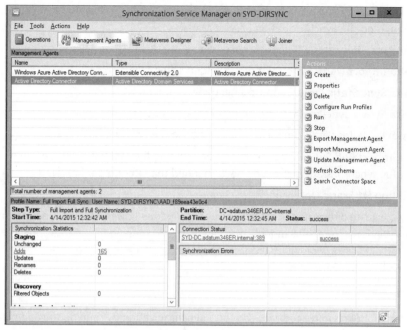

FIGURE 4-33 Synchronization Service Manager

4. On the Actions pane, click Run.

5. In the Run Management Agent dialog box, select Full Sync as shown in Figure 4-34.

FIGURE 4-34 Full Sync

Rather than performing a Full Sync, you can trigger one of the following types of synchronization using the Synchronization Service Manager:

- **Full Sync** Performs a full synchronization
- **Delta Import Delta Sync** Imports changed schema and objects
- **Delta Sync Stage Only** Imports changed schema only
- **Delta Sync** Synchronizes only objects changed since the last Sync
- **Export** Writes data from the Azure instance to the on-premises instance
- **Full Import Full Sync** This is suitable for initiating the first full synchronization or the first full synchronization after you have changed the filtering parameters
- **Full Import Stage Only** Imports schema

To manually force directory synchronization using Windows PowerShell, you'll need to import the DirSync Windows PowerShell module. You can do this by running the ImportModules.ps1 script, located in the %programfiles%\Windows Azure Active Directory Sync\DirSync folder and then running the command:

```
Import-Module DirSync
```

Once that module is imported, you can force synchronization by running the command:

```
Start-OnlineCoexsitenceSync
```

EXAM TIP

Remember what the default synchronization period is and what steps you need to take to alter it.

Thought experiment

Deleted user account recovery at Fabrikam

In this thought experiment, apply what you learned about this objective. You can find answers to these questions in the "Answers" section at the end of this chapter.

Some important user accounts were deleted and required recovery at Fabrikam. Consequently, Fabrikam wants to develop appropriate procedures and understand how to recover accidentally deleted accounts without requiring the accounts to be recreated. With this information in mind, answer the following questions:

1. What feature can you enable on the on-premises Active Directory instance that will allow you to recover an accidentally deleted account without having to recreate it with a new GUID?

2. How long after objects are deleted from the Azure Active Directory instance used to support Office 365 are they recoverable?

Objective summary

- When you configure DirSync, the source of authority for objects created in the on-premises Active Directory environment remains the on-premises Active Directory environment.

- When you create new users in the on-premises Active Directory environment and they are within the filtering scope of DirSync, accounts for these users will be created in the Azure Active Directory instance that supports the Office 365 tenancy the next time synchronization occurs.

- When a new user account is created in the on-premises Active Directory environment and then synchronizes to the Azure Active Directory instance that supports the Office 365 tenancy, the account is not assigned an Office 365 license.

- Modifications made to user accounts and groups using the on-premises tools will only apply to the counterpart objects in the Azure Active Directory instance that supports the Office 365 tenancy after synchronization occurs.

- Users and groups that are deleted from the on-premises Active Directory instance will not be deleted from the Azure Active Directory instance that supports the Office 365 tenancy until synchronization occurs.

- Objects that are accidentally deleted from the on-premises Active Directory can be recovered from the on-premises Active Directory Recycle Bin if it is enabled.

- You can force synchronization using the Synchronization Service Manager tool or Windows PowerShell.

Objective review

Answer the following questions to test your knowledge of the information in this objective. You can find the answers to these questions and explanations of why each answer choice is correct or incorrect in the "Answers" section at the end of the chapter.

1. You have configured DirSync to replicate all of the users in your on-premises Active Directory to Office 365. Which of the following tools can you use to change a user's password to ensure that it is the same in both Office 365 and in the on-premises Active Directory environment? (Choose all that apply.)

   A. Active Directory Domains And Trusts

   B. Active Directory Administrative Center

   C. Office 365 Admin Center

   D. DirSync

2. What is the default DirSync synchronization period?

   A. 180 minutes

   B. 300 minutes

   C. 120 minutes

   D. 90 minutes

3. Which file do you need to modify to alter the default DirSync synchronization period?

   A. Microsoft.Online.DirSync.Scheduler.exe.txt

   B. Azure.DirSync.Scheduler.exe.Config

   C. Azure.DirSync.Scheduler.exe.txt

   D. Microsoft.Online.DirSync.Scheduler.exe.Config

4. Which of the following cmdlets, when the DirSync Windows PowerShell module is loaded, allows you to trigger full synchronization?

   A. Enable-MSOnlinePasswordSync

   B. Enable-DirLogSync

   C. Start-OnlineCoexistenceSync

   D. Enable-OnlinePasswordWriteBack

Answers

This section contains the solutions to the thought experiments and answers to the objective review questions in this chapter.

Objective 4.1: Thought experiment

1. DirSync only supports synchronization from a single forest. Adatum has three forests.

2. ADModify.NET can be used to bulk modify the attributes of selected user accounts at Adatum.

Objective 4.1: Review

1. **Correct answer:** B

   A. **Incorrect:** You cannot use the Active Directory Sites And Services console to add a UPN suffix to an existing domain name.

   B. **Correct:** You can use Active Directory Domains And Trusts to add a UPN suffix to an existing domain.

   C. **Incorrect:** You cannot use Active Directory Users And Computers to add a UPN suffix to an existing domain.

   D. **Incorrect:** You cannot use Office 365 Admin Center to add a UPN suffix to an existing domain.

2. **Correct answer:** B

   A. **Incorrect:** Adatum.info is a routable domain name as it uses a recognized top level domain name suffix.

   B. **Correct:** Adatum.internal is not a routable domain name as it does not use a recognized top level domain name suffix.

   C. **Incorrect:** Adatum.net is a routable domain name as it uses a recognized top level domain name suffix.

   D. **Incorrect:** Adatum.com is a routable domain name as it uses a recognized top level domain name suffix.

3. **Correct answers:** B and D

   A. **Incorrect:** You cannot use DirSync to synchronize user objects from multiple forests to a single Azure Active Directory instance that supports an Office 365 tenancy.

   B. **Correct:** You can use Azure Active Directory Connect to synchronize user objects from multiple forests to a single Azure Active Directory instance that supports an Office 365 tenancy.

**C.	Incorrect:** You cannot use Active Directory Domains And Trusts to synchronize user objects from multiple forests to a single Azure Active Directory instance that supports an Office 365 tenancy.

**D.	Correct:** You can use the Azure Active Directory Connector for Forefront Identity Manager to synchronize user objects from multiple forests to a single Azure Active Directory instance that supports an Office 365 tenancy.

4.	**Correct answer:** B

**A.	Incorrect:** Synchronization Service Manager cannot scan Active Directory to locate attributes associated with user objects that will cause problems when you attempt to use DirSync to synchronize those objects.

**B.	Correct:** IdFix can scan Active Directory to locate attributes associated with user objects that will cause problems when you attempt to use DirSync to synchronize those objects.

**C.	Incorrect:** ADModify.NET cannot scan Active Directory to locate attributes associated with user objects that will cause problems when you attempt to use DirSync to synchronize those objects.

**D.	Incorrect:** ADSIEdit cannot scan Active Directory to locate attributes associated with user objects that will cause problems when you attempt to use DirSync to synchronize those objects.

Objective 4.2: Thought experiment

1.	You could configure attribute-based filtering, using the Department attribute, to block replication of accounts associated with the Research Department.

2.	.NET Framework 3.5 SP1 must be installed on the computer before you can install DirSync.

Objective 4.2: Review

1.	**Correct answer:** A

**A.	Correct:** A forest needs to only be at the Windows Server 2003 forest functional level to support DirSync.

**B.	Incorrect:** A forest needs to only be at the Windows Server 2003 forest functional level to support DirSync.

**C.	Incorrect:** A forest needs to only be at the Windows Server 2003 forest functional level to support DirSync.

**D.	Incorrect:** A forest needs to only be at the Windows Server 2003 forest functional level to support DirSync.

2. **Correct answer:** B

    A. **Incorrect:** Members of the Schema Admins group don't have the required permissions to run DirSync Configuration.

    B. **Correct:** The user account that is used to run DirSync configuration must be a member of the Enterprise Admins security group.

    C. **Incorrect:** Members of the Domain Admins group don't have the required permissions to run DirSync Configuration.

    D. **Incorrect:** Members of the Account Operators group don't have the required permissions to run DirSync Configuration.

3. **Correct answer:** C

    A. **Incorrect:** You use Synchronization Service Manager to configure DirSync filtering.

    B. **Incorrect:** You use Synchronization Service Manager to configure DirSync filtering.

    C. **Correct:** You use Synchronization Service Manager to configure DirSync filtering.

    D. **Incorrect:** You use Synchronization Service Manager to configure DirSync filtering.

4. **Correct answer:** D

    A. **Incorrect:** 10,000 objects are supported with the SQL Server express instance.
       Incorrect: 20,000 objects are supported with the SQL Server express instance.

    B. **Incorrect:** 25,000 objects are supported with the SQL Server express instance.

    C. **Correct:** If you have more than 50,000 objects that will replicate through DirSync, Microsoft recommends that you deploy a SQL Server instance on a separate computer rather than use the SQL Server Express instance, which will not support a database of the necessary size.

Objective 4.3: Thought experiment

1. Enabling Active Directory Recycle Bin allows you to recover an accidentally deleted account without having to recreate it with a new GUID.

2. Objects are recoverable from the Azure Active Directory Recycle Bin up to a maximum period of 30 days.

Objective 4.3: Review

1. **Correct answer:** B

    A. **Incorrect:** You cannot change user passwords using Active Directory Domains And Trusts.

    B. **Correct:** You must use an on-premises tool to change a user's password. That change will then replicate to Office 365.

    C. **Incorrect:** You must use an on-premises tool to change a user's password. That change will then replicate to Office 365.

    D. **Incorrect:** You can't use DirSync to change a user's password.

2. **Correct answer:** A

    A. **Correct:** The default DirSync synchronization period is 3 hours or 180 minutes.

    B. **Incorrect:** The default DirSync synchronization period is 3 hours or 180 minutes.

    C. **Incorrect:** The default DirSync synchronization period is 3 hours or 180 minutes.

    D. **Incorrect:** The default DirSync synchronization period is 3 hours or 180 minutes.

3. **Correct answer:** D

    A. **Incorrect:** You cannot modify the default synchronization period by altering the file Microsoft.Online.DirSync.Scheduler.exe.txt.

    B. **Incorrect:** You cannot modify the default synchronization period by altering the file Azure.DirSync.Scheduler.exe.Config.

    C. **Incorrect:** You cannot modify the default synchronization period by altering the file Azure.DirSync.Scheduler.exe.txt.

    D. **Correct:** You modify the file Microsoft.Online.DirSync.Scheduler.exe.Config to alter the default synchronization period.

4. **Correct answer:** C

    A. **Incorrect:** The Enable-MSOnlinePasswordSync cmdlet does not allow you to trigger synchronization.

    B. **Incorrect:** The Enable-DirLogSync cmdlet does not allow you to trigger synchronization.

    C. **Correct:** The Start-OnlineCoexistenceSync cmdlet allows you to trigger synchronization.

    D. **Incorrect:** The Enable-OnlinePasswordWriteBack cmdlet does not allow you to trigger synchronization.

CHAPTER 5

Implement and manage federated identities (single sign-on)

You can configure single sign-on for Office 365 by configuring federation between your on-premises Active Directory environment and Office 365 using Active Directory Federation Services (AD FS). To configure single sign-on, it is necessary to first configure an on-premises Active Directory Federation Services deployment, which includes servers hosting the AD FS role and the Web Application Proxy role. It is then necessary to link that on-premises AD FS deployment with Office 365.

Objectives in this chapter:

- Objective 5.1: Plan requirements for Active Directory Federation Services
- Objective 5.2: Install and manage AD FS Servers
- Objective 5.3: Install and manage AD FS Proxy Servers

Objective 5.1: Plan requirements for Active Directory Federation Services

This objective deals with planning the configuration of the infrastructure required for deploying an Active Directory Federation Services (AD FS) instance to support configuring federation with Office 365. To master this objective, you'll need to understand the requirements for certificates used when configuring federation, the namespace, and network configuration requirements. You'll also need to know what steps you need to take to implement multi-factor authentication in an environment where you have configured single sign-on and to know what parts need to be configured to set up access filtering using claims rules.

This objective covers the following topics:

- Certificate requirements
- Namespace requirements
- Network requirements
- Multi-factor authentication
- Access filtering using claims rules

Deploying AD FS topologies

How you deploy AD FS to work with Office 365 depends on the number of users who need to perform single sign-on operations. The most basic form of AD FS deployment is that you place a server on your internal network running Windows Server 2012 R2 with the AD FS role installed and configured. You then place at least one server on your organization's perimeter network that functions as a proxy, relaying traffic between the AD FS server on the internal network and the Office 365 infrastructure.

EXAM TIP

In Windows Server 2012 R2, the AD FS Proxy server role was modified to become the Web Application Proxy server role. Although the 70-346 exam objectives mention AD FS proxy servers, you'll need to remember that this term is only used when AD FS is installed on computers running Windows Server 2008, Windows Server 2008 R2, and Windows Server 2012.

AD FS is a role service that is available with Windows Server. Microsoft has released the following versions of AD FS:

- **AD FS 1.0**   Released with Windows Server 2003 R2
- **AD FS 1.1**   Released with Windows Server 2008 and Windows Server 2008 R2
- **AD FS 2.0**   Released as a separate download for Windows Server 2008 and Windows Server 2008 R2
- **AD FS 2.1**   Released with Windows Server 2012
- **AD FS 3.0**   Released with Windows Server 2012 R2

An internal AD FS deployment is termed a farm. In versions of AD FS prior to 3, released with Windows Server 2012 R2, you could choose to deploy AD FS as a standalone or as a farm. With AD FS 3, you always install AD FS as a farm. The key to understanding AD FS farms is that an AD FS farm can consist of a single server.

Microsoft makes the following recommendations with respect to the number of AD FS servers that you should deploy in an environment:

- **Fewer than 1,000 users**   Deploy a single AD FS server in a farm. Deploy a single Web Application Proxy server on the perimeter network.

- **1,000 to 15,000 users** Deploy two AD FS servers in a farm. Deploy two load-balanced Web Application Proxy servers on the perimeter network.

- **15,000 to 60,000 users** Deploy between three and five AD FS servers in a farm. Deploy two load-balanced Web Application Proxy servers on the perimeter network.

> **MORE INFO AD FS DEPLOYMENT TOPOLOGIES**
>
> You can learn more about AD FS deployment topologies at *https://technet.microsoft.com/en-us/library/dn554241.aspx.*

Using certificates

Certificates verify the identity of each element of an AD FS deployment. Certificates are also used to secure communication across computers hosting the AD FS Federation Server roles, computers hosting the Web Application Proxy role, as well as the Office 365 servers.

The Service Communications Certificate is the certificate that you install for the purpose of service identification and secure communication. This certificate is a server authentication certificate, occasionally called a Secure Sockets Layer (SSL) certificate or web server certificate.

Federation server certificate requirements

Computers that host the federation server role have different certificate requirements depending on whether they are running AD FS 3.0 on Windows Server 2012 R2 or have a previous version of AD FS running on an earlier version of Windows Server.

If the AD FS Federation Server is running the Windows Server 2012 R2 operating system, it requires a Service Communications Certificate as shown in Figure 5-1. The Service Communications Certificate is a server authentication certificate, also known more colloquially as an SSL certificate.

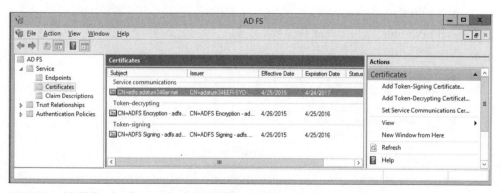

FIGURE 5-1 AD FS Service Communications Certificate

The Service Communications Certificate must have the following properties:

- The certificate's Subject Name and Subject Alternative Name must include the federation service name. For example, adfs.adatum346ER.net.
- The certificate's Subject Alternative Name must contain the value enterpriseregistration and the UPN suffix of the organization. For example, enterpriseregistration.adatum346ER.net.
- Certificate cannot be a wildcard certificate.
- It is necessary to have both the certificate and the private key when running the Active Directory Federation Services Configuration Wizard.
- Certificate must be issued by a trusted third-party certification authority (CA).

Depending on which CA you request the certificate from, there are a variety of methods that will work. Publicly trusted CAs have web forms that enable you to submit a certificate request. You need to obtain the certificate from a public CA as Microsoft Office 365 servers cannot be authenticated by an internal CA.

EXAM TIP

Although you cannot use a certificate generated from an internal Enterprise CA to connect to Office 365, you can perform many of the steps required to configure AD FS using this certificate. For the purposes of exam preparation, this may present a reasonable alternative for those not wishing to go to the expense of purchasing a domain name and a certificate to study for a single objective domain on a certification exam.

For the purpose of demonstrating what is required to request a certificate from a CA, the certificate request process is demonstrated using an internal Enterprise CA. An Enterprise CA is used because each public CA has a separate process for requesting certificates. To request a certificate that has the appropriate properties from an Enterprise CA using the Certificates console, perform the following steps:

1. Sign in to the computer that will host the AD FS role using an account that has local administrator privileges.
2. Right-click the Start hint and click Run.
3. In the Run dialog box, type **mmc.exe** as shown in Figure 5-2 and click OK.

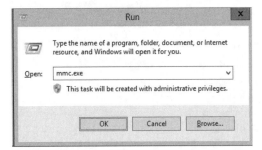

FIGURE 5-2 Run dialog box

4. On the File menu of the Console1 – [Console Root] dialog box, click Add/Remove Snap-in.

5. On the Add Or Remove Snap-ins dialog box, click Certificates as shown in Figure 5-3 and then click Add.

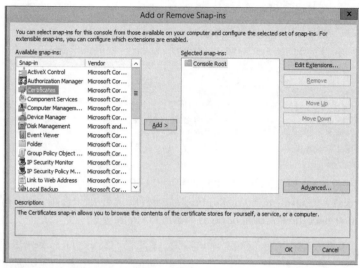

FIGURE 5-3 Certificates snap-in

6. In the Certificates Snap-in dialog box, shown in Figure 5-4, click Computer Account and then click Next.

FIGURE 5-4 Computer account

7. On the Select Computer page, ensure that Local Computer is selected as shown in Figure 5-5 and then click Finish.

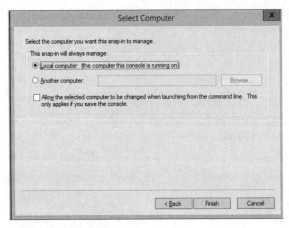

FIGURE 5-5 Select Computer

8. Click OK to close the Add or Remove Snap-ins dialog box.

9. On the Console1 – [Console Root] dialog box, expand the Certificates (Local Computer) node and then select the Personal node as shown in Figure 5-6.

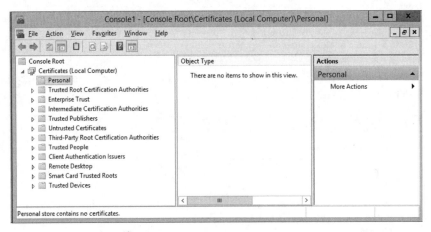

FIGURE 5-6 Personal certificates store

10. On the Action menu, click All Tasks and then click Request New Certificate.

11. On the Before You Begin page of the Certificate Enrollment Wizard, click Next.

12. In the Select Certificate Enrollment Policy dialog box, ensure that Active Directory Enrollment Policy is selected as shown in Figure 5-7 and click Next.

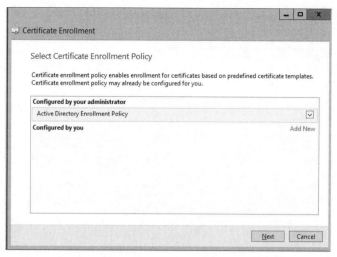

FIGURE 5-7 Enrollment Policy

13. On the Request Certificate page, select Web Server as shown in Figure 5-8 and then click More Information Is Required To Enroll For This Certificate, Click Here To Configure Settings. If the Web Server certificate template is not available, you must ensure that the computer account of the AD FS server is configured with enrollment permissions on the certificate template. You can do this using the Certificate Templates console on an Enterprise CA.

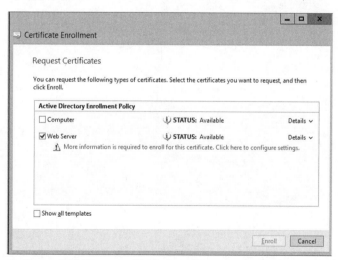

FIGURE 5-8 Web Server certificate enrollment

14. In the Certificate Properties dialog box, set the Subject Name Type to Common Name, enter the fully qualified domain name of the Federation Service name (which is separate from the fully qualified domain name of the AD FS server), and then click Add. Figure 5-9 shows this as adfs.adatum345er.net.

FIGURE 5-9 Common Name setting

15. Under Alternative Name, set the Type to DNS, then enter the value enterpriseregistration with the UPN suffix of the organization and then click Add. Figure 5-10 shows this as enterpriseregistration.adatum346er.net.

FIGURE 5-10 Alternative name

16. Click OK to close the Certificate Properties dialog box.
17. In the Certificate Enrollment dialog box, shown in Figure 5-11, click Enroll.

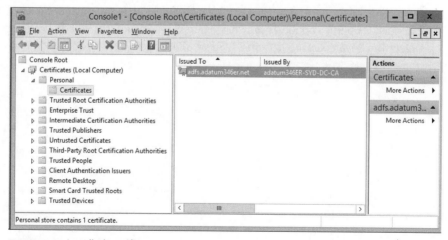

FIGURE 5-11 Web Server certificate

18. On the Certificate Installation Results page, click Finish.

Once you have received the certificate from a CA and installed it on the computer that hosts the AD FS role, you should export the certificate as well as the private key so that you can use the certificate when configuring the Web Application Proxy server or when adding additional AD FS servers to the farm.

To export the private key, perform the following steps:

1. In the Console1 – Console Root console with the Certificates (Local Computer) snap-in added, navigate to the Personal\Certificates node and select the certificate. Figure 5-12 shows the adfs.adatum346er.net certificate selected.

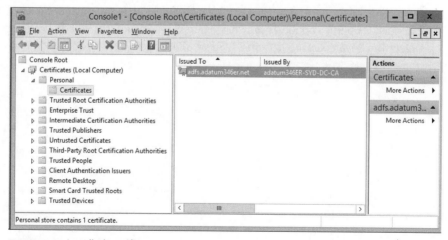

FIGURE 5-12 Installed certificate

2. On the Action menu, click All Tasks and then click Export.

3. On the Welcome To The Certificate Export Wizard page of the Certificate Export Wizard, click Next.

4. On the Export Private Key page, select Yes, Export The Private Key as shown in Figure 5-13. If this option is not available, you need to update the Certificate Template on the Enterprise CA so that you are able to export private keys and then request a new certificate.

FIGURE 5-13 Export Private Key

5. On the Export File Format page of the Certificate Export Wizard, ensure that you select the Include All Certificates In The Certificate Path If Possible option and the Export All Extended Properties option as shown in Figure 5-14. Ensure that you do not select the Delete The Private Key If The Export Is Successful Option. Click Next.

FIGURE 5-14 Export file format

6. On the Security page of the Certificate Export Wizard, select the Password option and then provide a password to protect the certificate as shown in Figure 5-15. Click Next.

FIGURE 5-15 Export security

7. On the File To Export page of the Certificate Export Wizard, select a location to save the exported certificate as shown in Figure 5-16 and then click Next.

FIGURE 5-16 File to Export

8. On the Completing The Certificate Export Wizard page, click Finish.

If the AD FS Federation Server is running a version of AD FS prior to AD FS 3.0, the Service Communications Certificate requirements differ from what is required if the AD FS server is running AD FS 3.0. These requirements are as follows:

- The certificate requires the Subject Name to be a short name, rather than a fully qualified domain name.

- This certificate must be trusted by Microsoft cloud services as well as AD FS clients. This means that it needs to be issued by a trusted third-party CA.

- The certificate cannot be a wildcard certificate.

The AD FS server needs a token-signing certificate. The token-signing certificate is an X.509 certificate. This certificate is used to sign the tokens issued by the federation server that the cloud service accepts and validates. The default is that you use the self-signed token-signing certificate that is generated by AD FS for this task rather than generating a certificate from a CA. The advantage of using a self-signed token-signing certificate is that AD FS automatically manages the certificate, meaning that this specific certificate will require no intervention on the part of the AD FS administrator in the future.

Adhering to Web Application Proxy certificate requirements

The computer that hosts the Web Application Proxy, the AD FS Proxy in previous versions of Windows Server, requires a server authentication certificate that has the same subject name as the server authentication certificate installed on the computer that hosts the AD FS role. This certificate must be imported into the Personal Certificates store of the computer that hosts the Web Application Proxy role. If you are using a computer that has an operating system running Windows Server 2008, Windows Server 2008 R2, or Windows Server 2012 that is functioning as a federation proxy server, this server authentication certificate must be installed on the default website of the computer that hosts the federation proxy server role.

> **MORE INFO** **AD FS CERTIFICATE REQUIREMENTS**
>
> You can learn more about AD FS Certificate Requirements at *https://technet.microsoft.com/en-au/library/dn151311.aspx.*

Using namespaces

The name of the AD FS service must be resolvable through external DNS. For example, if the name of your AD FS service is adfs.adatum346er.net, clients must be able to resolve this name using a DNS server. This means that the name must be configured as a host record in the appropriate publicly accessible DNS zone. Microsoft recommends using a host (A) record for the AD FS service rather than using a CNAME that points to another record. This is because in some circumstances, using a CNAME record rather than a HOST record can cause authentication issues as Kerberos tickets may be issued to the incorrect name.

Kerberos is used to identify the AD FS service on the internal network. This occurs through the service's Service Principal Name (SPN). The AD FS SPN is set automatically when running the AD FS Configuration Wizard.

Meeting network requirements

To ensure that you can configure federation between your on-premises Active Directory instance and Office 365, you need to ensure that the following network requirements are met:

- TCP/IP connectivity must exist between the Internet and the Web Application Proxy servers on the perimeter network. This enables communication between Microsoft Office 365 servers and the computers hosting the Web Application Proxy role.

- For external clients, the fully qualified domain name of the AD FS service must resolve to the public IP address of the Web Application Proxy server. For example, if the AD FS service name is adfs.adatum346er.net, then this address must resolve to the public IP address of the Web Application Proxy server. If you've configured load balancing for the Web Application Proxy servers, then this address will need to resolve to the public IP address of the load balancer.

> **MORE INFO** **NETWORK REQUIREMENTS**
>
> You can learn more about network requirements at *https://technet.microsoft.com/en-au/library/dn151311.aspx#BKMK_3.*

Configuring multi-factor authentication

You can configure AD FS on Windows Server 2012 R2 to support multi-factor authentication by downloading and installing the Azure Multi-Factor Authentication Server. This server can be downloaded from the Microsoft Azure portal and installed either on a server with the AD FS role installed on it or on a separate computer that is a member of the same domain.

When installed, you can configure the multi-factor authentication server to enable users to select their multi-factor authentication method. You can use the following methods for multi-factor authentication:

- Phone Call
- Text Message
- Mobile App
- OATH Token

You can also configure a specific number of security questions as a fallback option. Figure 5-17 shows the Phone Call, Text Message, and Mobile App methods selected.

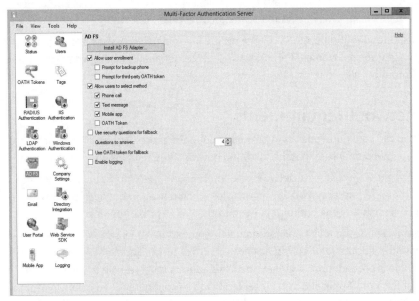

FIGURE 5-17 Multi-Factor Authentication Server

When configured, users will be required to use two forms of authentication when accessing Office 365 resources using single sign-on.

> **MORE INFO MFA AND AD FS**
>
> You can learn more about integrating Multi-Factor Authentication with Windows Server 2012 R2 AD FS and Office 365 at *https://msdn.microsoft.com/en-us/library/azure/dn807157.aspx*.

Accessing filtering using claims rules

By configuring the claim rules after you've configured federation between your on-premises Active Directory environment and Office 365, you can block access to Office 365 depending on the properties of the account making the claim. For example, you could block access to Office 365 for users when they are located on networks outside the organization, but allow the same users access to Office 365 when they are using a computer located on an organizational network. You can do this by editing the Claim Rules for Active Directory using the AD FS console as shown in Figure 5-18.

FIGURE 5-18 Claim Rules

> **MORE INFO** **ACCESS FILTERING USING CLAIM RULES**
>
> You can learn more about access filtering using claim rules at *https://technet.microsoft.com/en-us/library/hh526961%28v=ws.10%29.aspx*.

> ### *Thought experiment*
>
> ### Multi-factor authentication at Margie's Travel
>
> In this thought experiment, apply what you learned about this objective. You can find answers to these questions in the "Answers" section at the end of this chapter.
>
> You are the systems administrator at Margie's Travel. You want to configure multi-factor authentication for your AD FS 3.0 single sign-on solution for Office 365. With this information in mind, answer the following questions:
>
> 1. What do you need to download and install to support multi-factor authentication for Office 365 single sign-on?
>
> 2. What secondary authentication methods are supported for Office 365 multi-factor authentication when single sign-on is configured using AD FS?

Objective summary

- An AD FS 3.0 farm consists of one or more servers running AD FS.
- The Web Application Proxy role in Windows Server 2012 R2 functions as an AD FS proxy.
- The Service Communications Certificate's Subject Name and Subject Alternative Name must include the federation service name.
- The Service Communications Certificate's Subject Alternative Name must contain the value enterpriseregistration and the UPN suffix of the organization.
- The Service Communications Certificate cannot be a wildcard certificate.
- The Service Communications Certificate must be stored in the local computer account's Personal Certificate store.
- The Service Communications Certificate must be issued by a trusted third-party CA.
- The name of the AD FS service must be resolvable through public DNS to the IP address of the Web Application Proxy server.
- Multi-factor authentication can be configured for AD FS by installing the Azure Multi-Factor Authentication Server and connecting it to the on-premises AD FS farm.
- You can filter access to Office 365 by configuring claim rules once you have established federation.

Objective review

Answer the following questions to test your knowledge of the information in this objective. You can find the answers to these questions and explanations of why each answer choice is correct or incorrect in the "Answers" section at the end of the chapter.

1. The AD FS service is going to be configured with the name ADFS.tailspintoys.com. Which of the following names must be present in the Service Communications Certificate's list of Subject Alternative Names? (Choose two.)

    A. Enterpriseregistration.tailspintoys.com

    B. Singlesignon.tailspintoys.com

    C. Office365.tailspintoys.com

    D. Adfs.tailspintoys.com

2. The AD FS service is going to be configured with the name ADFS.tailspintoys.com. Which of the following IP addresses must this name be resolvable to for hosts on the Internet?

    A. The IP address of the organization's DNS server.

    B. The IP address of the AD FS server.

    C. The public IP address of the Web Application Proxy server.

    D. The IP address of the Office 365 server.

3. There will be three servers in the AD FS farm at Tailspin Toys. The primary AD FS server will have the name adfs1.tailspintoys.com. The second server in the farm will have the name adfs2.tailspintoys.com. The third server in the farm will have the name adfs3.tailspintoys.com. The Web Application Proxy server will have the name wap1.tailspintoys.com. The AD FS service will have the name adfssvc.tailspintoys.com. What should the Service Communication Certificate's Subject Name be?

    A. Adfs2.tailspintoys.com

    B. Wap1.tailspintoys.com

    C. Adfs1.tailspintoys.com

    D. Adfssvc.tailspintoys.com

4. Which computer account certificate store should the Service Communications Certificate be located in for a computer that will function as an AD FS server?

    A. Enterprise Trust

    B. Personal

    C. Trusted Publishers

    D. Trusted Root Certification Authorities

Objective 5.2: Install and manage AD FS servers

This objective deals with installing and managing an Active Directory Federation Services server farm. To master this objective you'll need to understand the requirements of configuring the AD FS service account, configuring a farm, adding servers to a farm, converting an Office 365 domain from standard to federated, and managing the certificate life cycle.

This objective covers the following topics:

- Create AD FS service accounts
- Configure farm or stand-alone settings
- Add additional servers
- Convert from standard to federated domain
- Manage certificate life cycle

Creating AD FS service accounts

AD FS requires a dedicated service account. You create this service account before configuring the first AD FS server in a farm. When you add the first server to the farm, or add additional servers, you provide the credentials of this service account.

EXAM TIP

Remember that you will need to provide the same service account credentials each time you add a new server running the AD FS role to an existing AD FS farm.

This account should be configured with the following properties:

- The password should be configured not to expire, as shown in Figure 5-19.

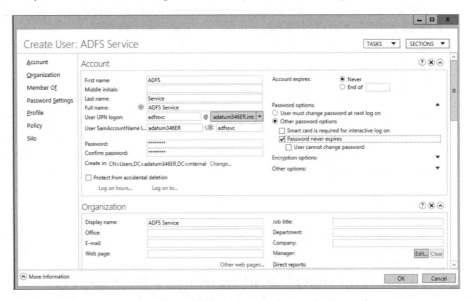

FIGURE 5-19 Service account configured with the Password Never Expires option

- Ensure that the account has the Log On As A Service right on computers hosting the AD FS role. You can configure this through group policy as shown in Figure 5-20.

FIGURE 5-20 Service account configured with the Log On As A Service right

- Ensure that the account has the Log On As A Batch Job on computers hosting the AD FS role. You can configure this right through group policy as shown in Figure 5-21.

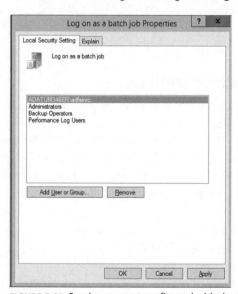

FIGURE 5-21 Service account configured with the Log On As A Batch Job right

When you run the AD FS Configuration Wizard and specify the service account, as shown in Figure 5-22, the AD FS configuration process will automatically configure the appropriate Service Principle Names (SPN).

You can use the setspn.exe command line tool if you want to register the SPN manually. To do this, you use the command with the following format:

```
Setspn.exe -a host/<server name> <service account>
```

For example, to configure the SPN for the server adfs.adatum346er.net for the service account adfssvc, issue the following command using an account that has domain administrator privileges:

```
Setspn.exe -a host/adfs.adatum346er.net adfssvc
```

> **MORE INFO AD FS SERVICE ACCOUNT**
>
> You can learn more about configuring a service account for AD FS at *https://technet.microsoft. com/en-us/library/dd807078.aspx.*

With AD FS in Windows Server 2012 R2, you have the option of using a group Managed Service Account (gMSA). Group Managed Service Accounts have their passwords managed by Active Directory. This makes them more secure than a manually created account configured such that the password never expires. Group Managed Service Accounts require that at least one domain controller in the domain is running Windows Server 2012 or later.

> **MORE INFO GROUP MANAGED SERVICE ACCOUNTS**
>
> You can learn more about group Managed Service Accounts at *https://technet.microsoft.com/ en-us/library/jj128431.aspx.*

Configuring farm or stand-alone settings

In versions of AD FS prior to 3.0, which is included with Windows Server 2012 R2, you were asked during deployment to choose whether you wanted to configure the AD FS deployment as a farm or in a stand-alone configuration. The drawback of choosing the stand-alone configuration was that you were tied to that decision and couldn't convert the deployment to a farm if your requirements changed. As it was possible to deploy a single-server farm, most advice was to deploy versions prior to 3.0 in the farm configuration as it would give you the flexibility to expand the deployment at a later point in time.

With AD FS 3.0 on Windows Server 2012 R2, there is no longer the option to deploy a stand-alone server and you always deploy AD FS as part of a farm. The only choice that an administrator is presented with is whether you will be deploying the AD FS server as the first server in a new farm or as an additional server in an existing farm. Figure 5-22 shows the Active Directory Federation Services Configuration Wizard that displays this option.

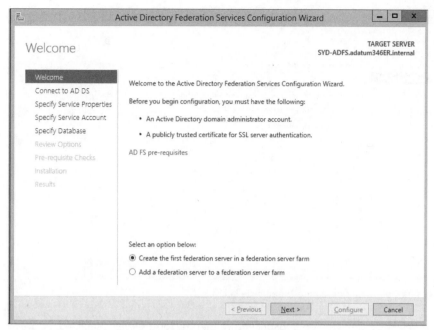

FIGURE 5-22 Create a new farm or add a server to an existing farm

MORE INFO ADDING AD FS SERVER

You can learn more about adding the first federation server in a farm at *https://technet. microsoft.com/en-us/library/dn486807.aspx*.

Installing and configuring AD FS

The AD FS role must be installed on a computer that is joined to a domain. The AD FS role can be installed on a computer that hosts the domain controller role. There are two steps to installing the role: the first is to install the role and the second is to configure the role. Prior to installing and configuring the role, you should create and configure a service account. You also need to have acquired the appropriate server authentication certificate.

To install the role on a computer running the Windows Server 2012 R2 operating system, perform the following steps:

1. In the Server Manager console, select the Dashboard node and then select Add Roles and Features.

2. On the Before You Begin page of the Add Roles And Features Wizard, click Next.

3. On the Installation Type page, select Role-Based Or Feature-Based Installation as shown in Figure 5-23, and then click Next.

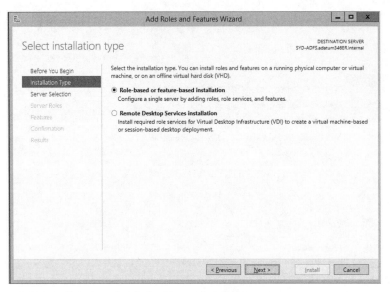

FIGURE 5-23 Role-based or feature-based installation

4. On the Select Destination Server page, ensure that the local server is selected. Figure 5-24 shows the server SYD-ADFS.adatum346er.internal selected. Click Next.

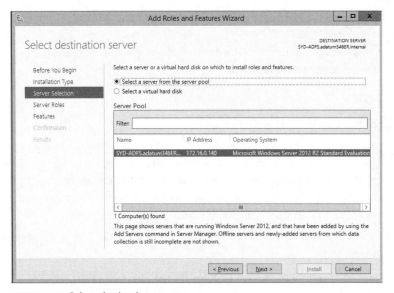

FIGURE 5-24 Select destination server

5. On the Select Server Roles page, select Active Directory Federation Services as shown in Figure 5-25 and then click Next.

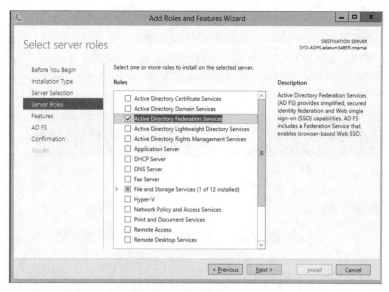

FIGURE 5-25 Select Active Directory Federation Services

6. On the Select Features page, click Next.

7. On the Active Directory Federation Services (AD FS) page, review the information as shown in Figure 5-26 and then click Next.

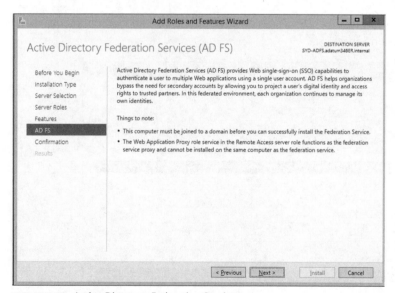

FIGURE 5-26 Active Directory Federation Services

8. On the Confirmation page, select the Restart The Destination Server Automatically If Required check box and then click Install.

9. Click Close to close the Add Roles And Features Wizard.

To configure the first server in a farm, perform the following steps:

1. On the Server Manager console, select the AD FS node.

2. With the AD FS node of the Server Manager console selected, click the text that says More next to Configuration Required For Active Directory Federation Services, as shown in Figure 5-27.

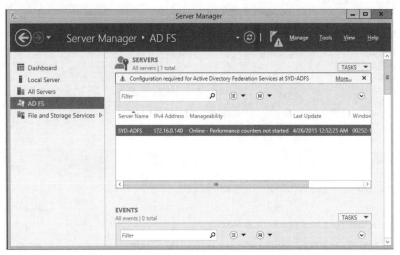

FIGURE 5-27 Server Manager console

3. In the All Servers Task Details dialog box, shown in Figure 5-28, click Configure The Federation Service.

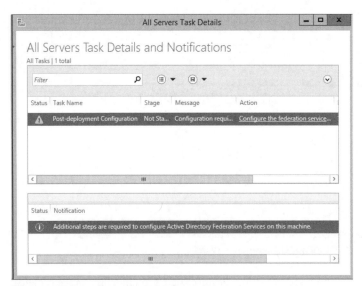

FIGURE 5-28 Post-deployment Configuration

4. On the Welcome page of the Active Directory Federation Services Configuration Wizard, ensure that Create The First Federation Server In A Federation Server Farm is selected as shown in Figure 5-29 and then click Next.

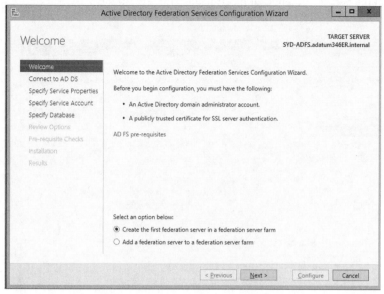

FIGURE 5-29 Create the first federation server in a server farm

5. On the Connect To AD DS page, shown in Figure 5-30, provide the credentials of a user account that has domain administrator permissions, and then click Next.

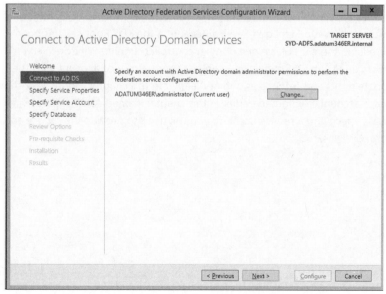

FIGURE 5-30 Provide domain administrator credentials

6. On the Specify Service Properties page, select the Server Authentication certificate that will be used to identify the ADFS service. You should also provide a display name as shown in Figure 5-31. The Federation Service Name will be taken from the Subject Name of the Server Authentication certificate, also termed the SSL Certificate. Click Next.

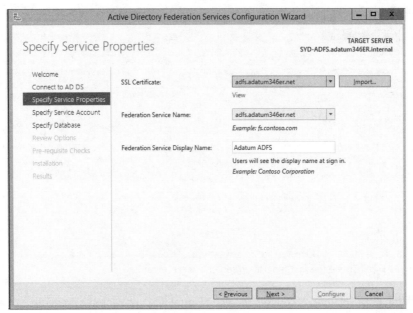

FIGURE 5-31 Specify Service Properties

7. On the Specify Service Account name page, you can have the AD FS Configuration Wizard create a group Managed Service Account if the KDS Root Key has been configured and there is at least one domain controller running Windows Server 2012 in the domain. As an alternative, you can configure a service account with the appropriate rights and settings as outlined earlier in this chapter. Figure 5-32 shows the service account, configured earlier in this chapter, named ADATUM346ER\adfssvc. If manually specifying a service account, you will need to provide the service account password. Click Next.

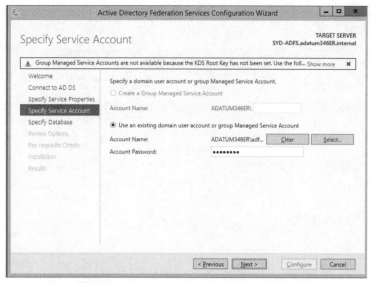

FIGURE 5-32 Specify Service Properties

8. On the Specify Database page, choose between an existing SQL Server instance or having AD FS create a Windows Internal Database instance. Microsoft recommends using a SQL Server instance if the AD FS server experiences performance problems when using the Windows Internal Database. It is possible to migrate from the Windows Internal Database to a separate SQL Server instance using SQL Server Management Studio. Figure 5-33 shows the Specify Configuration Database page.

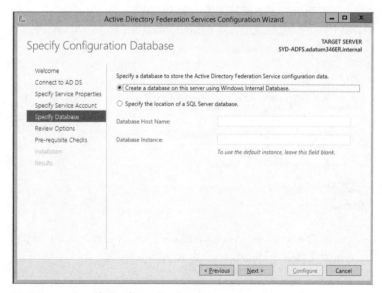

FIGURE 5-33 Specify Configuration Database

9. On the Review Options page, shown in 5-34, review the configuration options and then click Next.

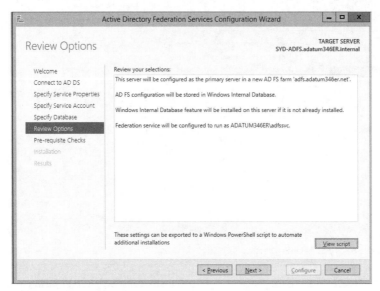

FIGURE 5-34 Review Options

10. You also have the option on this page of clicking View Script. This will provide you with a PowerShell script to add additional servers with the AD FS role to the farm. Figure 5-35 shows an example of this script.

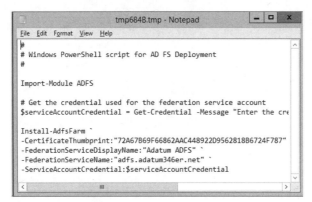

FIGURE 5-35 Installation script

11. On the Pre-requisite Checks page, ensure that all pre-requisite checks are passed successfully, as shown in Figure 5-36, and then click Configure.

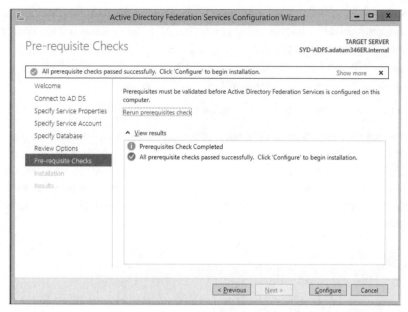

FIGURE 5-36 Pre-requisite checks

12. Click Close to complete the Active Directory Federation Services Configuration Wizard.

> **MORE INFO INSTALLING THE FIRST AD FS SERVER**
>
> You can learn more about installing the first AD FS server at *http://blogs.technet.com/b/ rmilne/archive/2014/04/28/how-to-install-adfs-2012-r2-for-office-365.aspx*.

Adding additional servers

You can add additional AD FS servers to the farm as required. Microsoft recommends that if your organization needs to support more than 1,000 federated users, you should deploy two dedicated federation servers. For each additional 15,000 users, Microsoft recommends adding an additional federation server.

When you deploy AD FS using the Windows Internal Database, the first server deployed in the farm has read and write access to that database. Additional AD FS servers deployed to the farm store read-only copies using their own Windows Internal Database instance. If the first server deployed in the farm fails, one of the other servers in the farm can be promoted so that it has read and write access to the database.

If you deploy AD FS using a SQL Server instance, all servers in the farm have read and write access to the database. The drawback of doing this is that it requires that the SQL Server is licensed appropriately.

To prepare a server to become an additional AD FS server in the farm, which includes importing the appropriate certificate and assigning the AD FS service account the appropriate rights, perform the following steps:

1. Install the Active Directory Federation Services binaries using the method outlined earlier or by issuing the following Windows PowerShell command:

    ```
    Install-WindowsFeature -IncludeManagementTools ADFS-Federation
    ```

2. Ensure that the AD FS Service Communications Certificate is installed in the Personal Certificate store of the computer account. You can do this by copying the exported certificate across to the computer that you want to add to the AD FS farm and then double-clicking it to run the Certificate Import Wizard. On the Welcome To The Certificate Import Wizard page of the Certificate Import Wizard, click Local Machine as shown in Figure 5-37 and then click Next.

FIGURE 5-37 Import the Certificate to the Local Machine certificate store

3. On the File To Import page of the Certificate Import Wizard, enter the name of the file you want to import as shown in Figure 5-38 and then click Next.

FIGURE 5-38 File to import

4. On the Private Key Protection page of the Certificate Import Wizard, provide the password for the private key, ensure that the key is marked as exportable and that you want to include all extended properties as shown in Figure 5-39, then click Next.

FIGURE 5-39 Private key protection

5. On the Certificate Store page, click Place All Certificates In The Following Store and then click Browse.

6. In the Select Certificate Store dialog box, select Personal, as shown in Figure 5-40, and then click OK.

FIGURE 5-40 Select Certificate Store

7. Verify that the Certificate Store page of the Certificate Import Wizard matches Figure 5-41 and then click Next.

FIGURE 5-41 Certificate Store

8. On the Completing the Certificate Import Wizard page, click Finish.

9. Right-click the Start hint and then click Run.

10. In the Run dialog box, type gpedit.msc as shown in Figure 5-42 and then click OK.

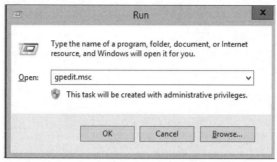

FIGURE 5-42 Open the Local Group Policy Editor

11. In the Local Group Policy Editor, navigate to the Computer Configuration\Windows Settings\Security Settings\Local Policies\User Rights Assignment node as shown in Figure 5-43.

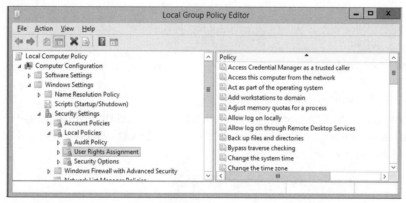

FIGURE 5-43 Local Group Policy Editor

12. In the Policy pane, double-click Log On As A Batch Job.

13. In the Log On As A Batch Job Properties dialog box, click Add User Or Group and then add the service account used for the AD FS service. Click OK. Figure 5-44 shows the ADFSSVC account added.

FIGURE 5-44 Log on as a batch job.

14. In the Policy pane, double-click Log On As A Service

15. In the Log On As A Service Properties dialog box, click Add User Or Group and then add the service account used for the AD FS service. Click OK. Figure 5-45 shows the ADFSSVC account added.

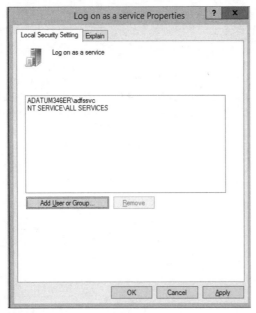

FIGURE 5-45 Log on as a service

16. Close the Local Group Policy Editor.

17. Open a Windows PowerShell window and issue the following command:

```
Gpupdate /force
```

Once the AD FS Service Communications Certificate has been installed and the appropriate rights have been assigned to the service account, you can add the additional AD FS server to the farm by performing the following steps:

1. Click the AD FS node of the Server Manager console.

2. Next to the Configuration Required For Active Directory Federation Services notification, shown in Figure 5-46, click More.

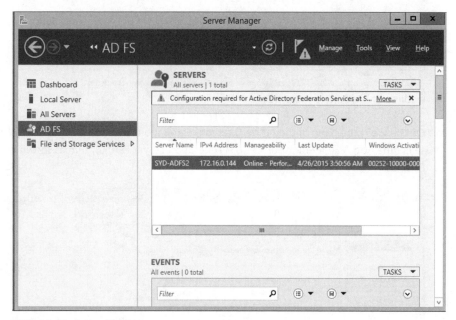

FIGURE 5-46 Server Manager

3. In the All Servers Task Details dialog box, shown in Figure 5-47, click Configure The Federation Service.

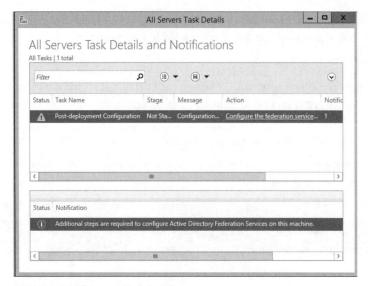

FIGURE 5-47 All Servers Task Details

4. On the Welcome page of the Active Directory Federation Services Configuration Wizard, select the Add A Federation Server To A Federation Server Farm option as shown in Figure 5-48 and then click Next.

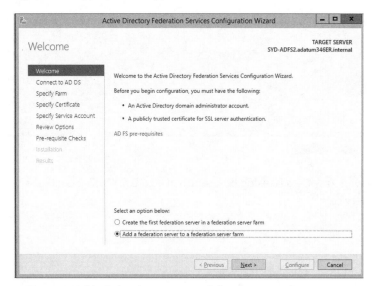

FIGURE 5-48 Add a federation server to a federation server farm

5. On the Connect To Active Directory Domain Services page of the Active Directory Federation Services Configuration Wizard, specify a user account that has Domain Administrator Permissions as shown in Figure 5-49, and then click Next.

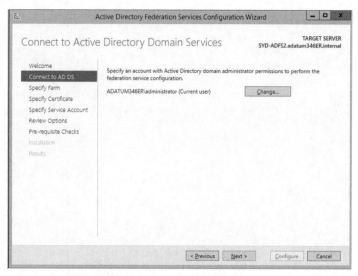

FIGURE 5-49 Domain Administrator Permissions

6. On the Specify Farm page, select the Specify The Primary Federation Server In An Existing Farm Using Windows Internal Database and specify the FQDN of the Primary Federation Server. The Primary Federation Server is the first AD FS server deployed in the farm. If you are using an SQL Server instance to support AD FS, you should instead specify the address of the SQL Server instance. Figure 5-50 shows the Primary Federation Server set to SYD-ADFS.adatum346ER.internal. Click Next.

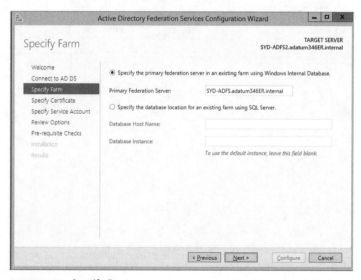

FIGURE 5-50 Specify Farm

7. On the Specify SSL Certificate page of the Active Directory Federation Services Configuration Wizard, specify the SSL Certificate as shown in Figure 5-51.

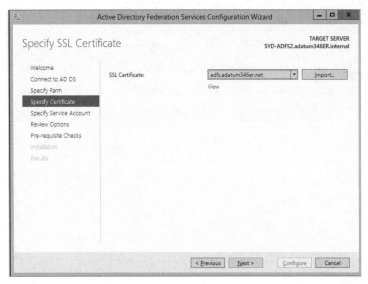

FIGURE 5-51 Specify SSL Certificate

8. On the Specify Service Account page of the Active Directory Federation Services Configuration Wizard, specify the same service account that you configured when configuring the first Federation Server. If you are using an account you created your-self for this purpose, rather than a group Managed Service Account, you will need to specify the password as shown in Figure 5-52. Click Next.

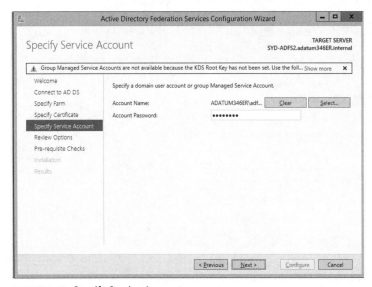

FIGURE 5-52 Specify Service Account

9. On the Review Options page of the Active Directory Federation Services Configuration Wizard, review the options and then click Next.

10. On the Pre-requisite Checks page of the Active Directory Federation Services Configuration Wizard, verify that the pre-requisite checks have completed successfully as shown in Figure 5-53 and then click Configure.

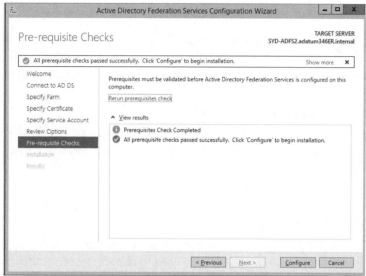

FIGURE 5-53 Service Account

11. On the Results page of the same Wizard, click Close.

> **MORE INFO ADDING ADDITIONAL AD FS SERVERS**
>
> You can learn more about adding AD FS servers to an existing farm at *https://technet. microsoft.com/en-us/library/e340cf8f-acf3-4cba-8135-a9353b85e714#BKMK_2*.

Converting from standard to federated domain

You convert an Office 365 domain from standard to federated using cmdlets found in the Azure Active Directory module for Windows PowerShell. You can only perform the conversion once your AD FS deployment is functioning correctly and you have deployed your Web Application Proxy server on the perimeter network to allow Office 365 to communicate with your internal AD FS deployment. You will learn more about deploying the Web Application Proxy server in the next lesson.

To convert from a standard to a federated domain, you first establish a connection from your Azure Active Directory PowerShell session to Office 365 using the Connect-MsolService cmdlet. Once you have presented your credentials, you provide information about the AD FS deployment by using the Set-MsolADFSContext cmdlet and specifying one of the AD FS servers. For example, to provide information about the server SYD-ADFS.adatum346er.net, use the following command:

```
Set-MsolADFSContext -Computer SYD-ADFS.adatum346er.net
```

Once the connection to Office 365 has been established and the AD FS context has been set, you can convert a domain to a federated one by running the command:

```
Convert-MsolDomainToFederated -DomainName Adatum346er.net
```

You can verify that the domain is now federated by using the Get-MsolDomain cmdlet. If you have been successful, the output of this cmdlet will identify the Authentication for the domain as Federated. Domains that have not been converted will be listed as Managed.

> **MORE INFO CONVERTING TO FEDERATED DOMAIN**
>
> You can learn more about converting an Office 365 domain to a Federated domain at *http://blogs.technet.com/b/rmilne/archive/2014/04/30/how-to-install-adfs-2012-r2-for-office-365-part-3.aspx.*

Managing certificate life cycle

You need to ensure that the AD FS Service Communications Certificates installed on your federation server remain valid. This means that you need to replace the certificates on each AD FS server in the farm before they expire. If you have configured the AD FS server to manage the token-signing certificates, these will automatically be replaced. If you have configured manual management of the token-signing certificates, a configuration which Microsoft doesn't recommend, you'll have to replace these certificates before they expire.

You can replace the Service Communications Certificate, which is the server authentication certificate, also known as an SSL or web server certificate you specified when deploying AD FS, by performing the following steps:

1. Ensure that you have installed the new Service Communications Certificate in the Personal Store of each AD FS server in the AD FS farm.

2. Click AD FS Management on the Tools menu of the Server Manager console.

3. In the AD FS console, click the Certificates node under the Service node and then select the Service Communications certificate as shown in Figure 5-54.

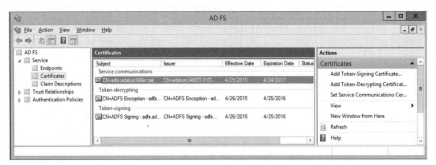

FIGURE 5-54 AD FS console

4. In the Actions pane, click Set Service Communications Certificate.

5. In the Windows Security dialog box, shown in Figure 5-55, confirm the correct Service Communications Certificate to use with AD FS by clicking OK. You may be prompted with a warning about the private key being required on each AD FS server in the farm.

FIGURE 5-55 Select Service Communications Certificate

EXAM TIP

Remember which console you use to update the Service Communications Certificate. Also remember that the token-signing and token-decrypting certificates are managed by AD FS and do not require manual replacement.

Thought experiment

In this thought experiment, apply what you learned about this objective. You can find answers to these questions in the "Answers" section at the end of this chapter.

You want to ensure that the password used with the AD FS service account password is changed on a regular basis, but you want to minimize the amount of direct intervention needed to perform this task. Rather than have the AD FS Configuration Wizard configure the Service Principal Name (SPN), you want to perform this task manually. With this information in mind, answer the following questions:

1. What service account option should you use?

2. Which utility can you use to set the SPN for the AD FS service account manually?

Objective summary

- AD FS 3.0 can use group Managed Service Accounts.
- If configuring a service account manually, ensure that the password is set not to expire and that the account has been granted the Log On As A Service and the Log On As A Batch Job rights.
- The AD FS Configuration Wizard sets the SPN for the service account automatically during setup. You can do this manually with the Setspn.exe command.
- When adding additional servers, you will need to import the Service Communications Certificate, including the private key, to the Private Certificate store of each additional AD FS server in the farm.
- You must use the same Service Account when adding potential AD FS servers to a farm. This account must be granted the Log On As A Service and the Log On As A Batch Job rights on each potential AD FS server.
- To specify the AD FS server prior to converting a standard Office 365 domain to a federated domain, use the Set-MsolADFSContext cmdlet.
- To convert a standard Office 365 domain to a federated Office 365 domain, use the Convert-MsolDomainToFederated cmdlet.

Objective review

Answer the following questions to test your knowledge of the information in this objective. You can find the answers to these questions and explanations of why each answer choice is correct or incorrect in the "Answers" section at the end of the chapter.

1. Which local rights must be assigned to a custom account that will function as the AD FS service account?

   A. Allow log on locally

   B. Allow log on through remote desktop services

   C. Log on as a batch job

   D. Log on as a service

2. When performing initial AD FS configuration, you need to provide the credentials of an account that has certain privileges. Which of the following privileges must the account have?

   A. Domain administrator

   B. Enterprise administrator

   C. Schema administrator

   D. Backup operator

3. You are in the process of installing AD FS on a computer running Windows Server 2012 R2. Under which conditions can you use a group Managed Service Account for the AD FS service account?

   A. The KDS Root Key has been configured.

   B. KMS has been deployed in your environment.

   C. You have at least one domain controller running Windows Server 2012 or later.

   D. DNSSEC has been configured.

4. You want to ensure that each of the five AD FS servers in your farm have write access to the AD FS database. Which of the following must you do to accomplish this goal?

   A. Configure AD FS to use the Windows Internal Database.

   B. Configure AD FS to use a SQL Server database.

   C. Configure AD FS to use a group Managed Service Account.

   D. Configure AD FS to use a wildcard Service Communications Certificate.

Objective 5.3: Install and manage AD FS Proxy servers

This objective deals with installing and managing AD FS Proxy servers. Very important to remember is that from Windows Server 2012 R2 onward, the role service known as AD FS Proxy Server has been renamed Web Application Server. To master this objective you'll need to understand what steps you need to take to set up perimeter network name resolution, what roles and features need to be deployed to install the Web Application Proxy, the properties of the certificate to install on the Web Application Proxy, and how to configure custom settings for the proxy login page.

> **This objective covers the following topics:**
> - Set up perimeter network name resolution
> - Install required Windows roles and features
> - Set up certificates
> - Configure AD FS Web Application Proxy
> - Set custom proxy forms login page

Setting up perimeter network name resolution

Microsoft recommends that for external name resolution you configure an A record that maps the public name of the AD FS service to the public IP address of the Web Application Proxy server on the perimeter network.

The needs of the Web Application Proxy server itself are a little different. The computer that will function as the proxy server itself needs to be able to resolve the address of the

AD FS servers. You can perform this operation by configuring DNS if you are using a split DNS. An alternative is to configure the hosts file on each computer, mapping the name of the AD FS service to the IP addresses of each member of the AD FS server farm.

EXAM TIP

Remember that the name resolution requirement for the Web Application Proxy server is different from the name resolution requirement for the Office 365 servers. One requires resolution of the AD FS service name to the Web Application Proxy server, while the other requires name resolution to the AD FS servers on the internal network.

Setting up certificates

You need to install the AD FS Service Communications Certificate on each Web Application Proxy server. This certificate needs to be placed in the Personal Certificate Store as shown in Figure 5-56.

FIGURE 5-56 Import Service Communications Certificate

Installing required Windows roles and features

Installing the Web Application Proxy role involves installing the Remote Access role rather than the AD FS role. To install the Web Application Proxy role, perform the following steps:

1. In the Dashboard node of the Server Manager console, click Add Roles And Features

2. On the Before You Begin page of the Add Roles And Features Wizard, click Next.

3. On the Installation Type page, click Role-Based Or Feature Based Installation and then click Next.

4. On the Select Destination Server page, ensure that the server that you want to host the Web Application Proxy server role is selected. Figure 5-57 shows the server SYD-WEBAP selected. Click Next.

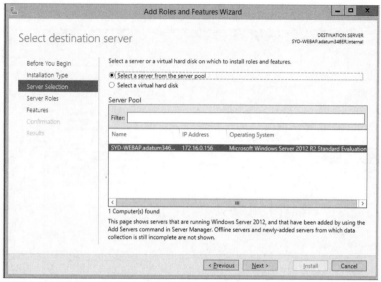

FIGURE 5-57 Select server from pool

5. On the Select Server Roles page, ensure that Remote Access is selected as shown in Figure 5-58 and then click Next.

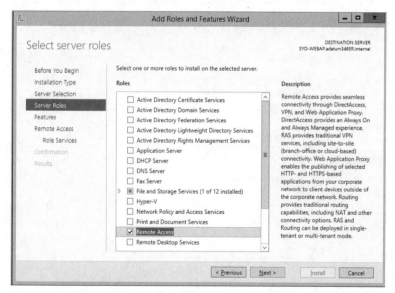

FIGURE 5-58 Remote Access

6. On the Features page, click Next.

7. On the Remote Access page, click Next.

8. On the Select Role Services page, select Web Application Proxy as shown in Figure 5-59 and then click Next.

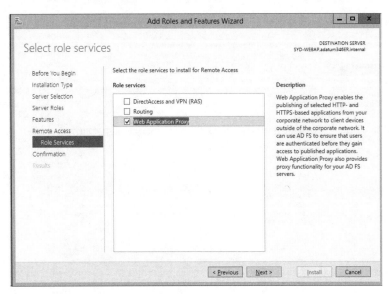

FIGURE 5-59 Select Web Application Proxy

9. On the Confirm Installation Selections page, shown in Figure 5-60, click Install.

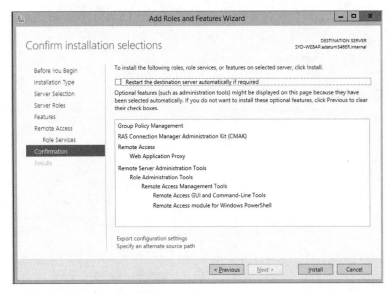

FIGURE 5-60 Confirmation Page

MORE INFO **AD FS PROXY DEPLOYMENT**

You can learn more about configuring the Web Application Proxy role at *http://blogs.tech-net.com/b/rmilne/archive/2014/04/28/how-to-install-adfs-2012-r2-for-office-365_1320_part-2.aspx*.

Configuring AD FS Web Application Proxy

Once you install the Web Application Proxy role, you can configure it by performing the following steps:

1. Click the Remote Access node of the Server Manager console and then click More next to Configuration Required For Web Application Proxy as shown in Figure 5-61.

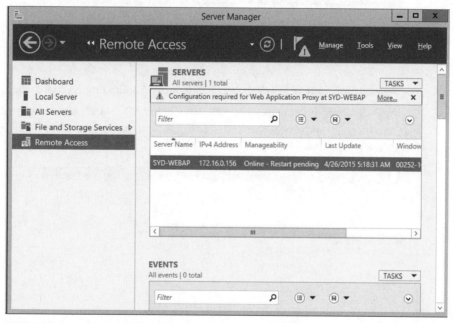

FIGURE 5-61 Configure Web Application Proxy

2. On the All Servers Task Details And Notifications page of the All Servers Task Details console, shown in Figure 5-62, click Open The Web Application Proxy Wizard.

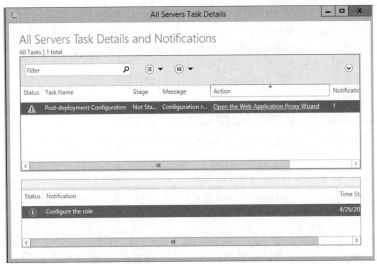

FIGURE 5-62 All Servers Task Details

3. On the Welcome page of the Web Application Proxy Configuration Wizard, click Next.

4. On the Federation Server page, enter the name of the AD FS and provide the credentials of an account with Local Administrator rights on those servers as shown in Figure 5-63. Click Next.

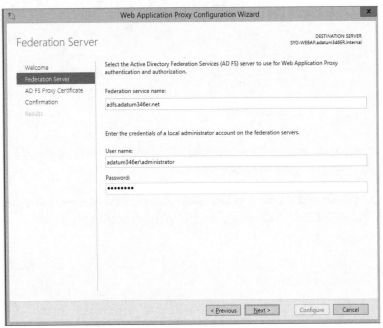

FIGURE 5-63 Federation Server

5. On the AD FS Proxy Certificate page, select the AD FS Service Communications Certificate, which you have already installed in the Personal Certificate Store of the Web Application Proxy server's computer account, as shown in Figure 5-64 and click Next.

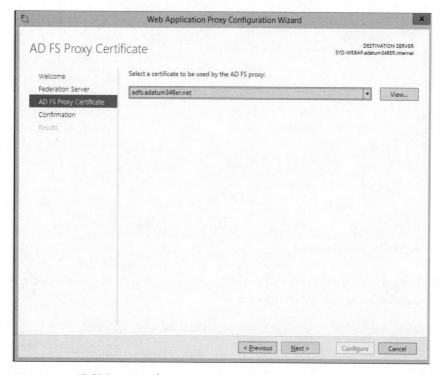

FIGURE 5-64 AD FS Proxy Certificate

6. On the Confirmation page, shown in Figure 5-65, review the information and then click Configure.

FIGURE 5-65 Confirmation

7. On the Results page, verify that the Web Application Proxy was configured successfully as shown in Figure 5-66 and click Close.

FIGURE 5-66 Confirmation

To confirm that the Web Application Proxy server is functioning correctly, open the Remote Access Management Console and then select the Operations Status node as shown in Figure 5-67.

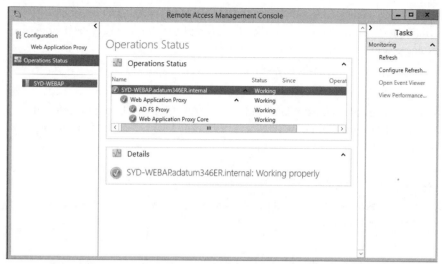

FIGURE 5-67 Verify Web Application Proxy server operation

MORE INFO **CONFIGURE WEB APPLICATION PROXY**

You can learn more about configuring the Web Application Proxy at *https://technet.microsoft. com/en-au/library/dn528859.aspx.*

Setting custom proxy forms login page

You can customize the proxy form login so that it better represents your organization's needs. You do this by using a specific set of Windows PowerShell commands.

To set the company name, use the Set-AdfsGlobalWebContent cmdlet with the CompanyName parameter. For example, to set the company name to "Adatum Hovercraft," use the following PowerShell command:

```
Set-AdfsGlobalWebContent -CompanyName "Adatum Hovercraft"
```

You can change the company logo displayed on the sign-in page with an image file in PNG format that has a resolution of 260 pixels by 35 and which is no greater than 10 KB in size using the Set-AdfsWebTheme cmdlet with the Logo parameter. For example, to set the company logo to a file named c:\logos\logo.png, issue the following command:

```
Set-AdfsWebTheme -TargetName default -Logo @{path="c:\logos\logo.png"}
```

To change the large illustrative graphic on the left, you use the Set-AdfsWebTheme cmdlet with the –Illustration parameter. The file for the illustration should be 1420 pixels by 1080 pixels in PNG format and should be no larger than 200 KB. For example, to set the illustration to the file illustration.png in the folder c:\illustrations, issue the following command:

```
Set-AdfsWebTheme -Targetname default -Illustration @{Path="c:\illustrations\
illustration.png}
```

You can add a sign-in page description using the Set-AdfsGlobalWebContent cmdlet with the SignInPageDescriptionText parameter. For example, to add the text "Welcome to the Adatum single sign-on page," issue the command:

```
Set-AdfsGlobalWebContent -SignInPageDescriptionText "Welcome to the Adatum single
sign-on page"
```

You can use the HelpDeskLink parameter with the Set-AdfsGlobalWebContent cmdlet to configure a help desk link, the HomeLink parameter to specify a home link, and the PrivacyLink parameter to add a privacy link.

> **MORE INFO** **CUSTOM PROXY FORMS**
>
> You can learn more about customizing the AD FS sign-in pages at *https://technet.microsoft.com/en-au/library/dn280950.aspx.*

Thought experiment

Proxy forms login page at Tailspin Toys

In this thought experiment, apply what you learned about this objective. You can find answers to these questions in the "Answers" section at the end of this chapter.

You are interested in changing the default proxy forms login page for the Tailspin Toys AD FS deployment used to support Office 365. You want to change the logo to a file named c:\images\newlogo.png, you want to change the illustration to a file named c:\images\newillustration.png, and you want to change the company name to Tailspin Toys. With this information in mind, answer the following questions:

1. What Windows PowerShell command should you use to change the logo?

2. What Windows PowerShell command should you use to change the illustration?

3. What Windows PowerShell command should you use to change the company name?

Objective summary

- The computer that hosts the Web Application Proxy server role on the perimeter network must be able to resolve the IP address of the AD FS service to an AD FS server on the internal network.
- The AD FS Service Communications Certificate must be installed in the computer account's Personal Certificate Store.
- The Web Application Proxy role service is part of the Remote Access role.
- Configuring the Web Application Proxy role service requires that you specify the federation service name and enter the credentials of an account that has local administrator privileges on the AD FS servers.

Objective review

Answer the following questions to test your knowledge of the information in this objective. You can find the answers to these questions and explanations of why each answer choice is correct or incorrect in the "Answers" section at the end of the chapter.

1. Which of the following Windows Server 2012 R2 roles hosts the Web Application Proxy role service?

   A. Remote Access

   B. Active Directory Federation Services

   C. Network Policy And Access Services

   D. Remote Desktop Services

2. You are configuring a computer on the perimeter network to host the Web Application Proxy role. The AD FS service name is adfs.fabrikam.com. A single AD FS server is deployed on the private network. When the computer on the perimeter network performs a DNS lookup on adfs.fabrikam.com, which IP address should it receive?

   A. The IP address of the Office 365 server.

   B. The public IP address of the Web Application Proxy server.

   C. The private IP address of the Web Application Proxy server.

   D. The private IP address of the AD FS server.

3. The Web Application Proxy server that you are deploying on the perimeter network has the name wap-syd.adatum.com. The AD FS server on the internal network has the name adfs-svr1.adatum.com. The AD FS service has the name adfs.adatum.com. What should be the subject name of the certificate installed on wap-syd.adatum.com to support Office 365 federation?

   A. Enterpriseregistration.adatum.com

   B. Adfs.adatum.com

   C. Wap-syd.adatum.com

   D. Adfs-svr1.adatum.com

Answers

This section contains the solutions to the thought experiments and answers to the objective review questions in this chapter.

Objective 5.1: Thought experiment

1. You can configure multi-factor authentication for Office 365 single sign-on by downloading and installing the Azure Multi-Factor Authentication Server.

2. You can configure the following secondary authentication methods: Phone Call, Text Message, Mobile App, and OATH Token.

Objective 5.1: Review

1. **Correct answers:** A and D

   A. **Correct:** The Service Communications Certificate's Subject Alternative Name must contain the value enterpriseregistration and the UPN suffix of the organization.

   B. **Incorrect:** The Service Communications Certificate's Subject Alternative Name does not need to contain the name Singlesignon.

   C. **Incorrect:** Service Communications Certificate's Subject Alternative Name does not need to contain the name Office365.

   D. **Correct:** The Service Communications Certificate's Subject Alternative Name must include the federation service name.

2. **Correct answer:** C

   A. **Incorrect:** Incorrect: The name of the AD FS service must resolve to the public IP address of the Web Application Proxy server, not the IP address of the organization's DNS server.

   B. **Incorrect:** The name of the AD FS service must resolve to the public IP address of the Web Application Proxy server, not the IP address of the AD FS server.

   C. **Correct:** The name of the AD FS service must resolve to the public IP address of the Web Application Proxy server.

   D. **Incorrect:** The name of the AD FS service must resolve to the public IP address of the Web Application Proxy server, not the IP address of the Office 365 server.

3. **Correct answer:** D

   A. **Incorrect:** The subject name of the Service Communications Certificate should be the AD FS service name, not Adfs2.tailspintoys.com.

   B. **Incorrect:** The subject name of the Service Communications Certificate should be the AD FS service name, not Wap1.tailspintoys.com

   C. **Incorrect:** The subject name of the Service Communications Certificate should be the AD FS service name, not Adfs1.tailspintoys.com

   D. **Correct:** The subject name of the Service Communications Certificate should be the AD FS service name which is Adfssvc.tailspintoys.com.

4. **Correct answer:** B

   A. **Incorrect:** The Service Communications Certificate must be located in the Personal certificate store, not the Enterprise Trust store, of a computer that will function as an AD FS server.

   B. **Correct:** The Service Communications Certificate must be located in the Personal certificate store of a computer that will function as an AD FS server.

   C. **Incorrect:** The Service Communications Certificate must be located in the Personal certificate store, not the Trusted Publishers store, of a computer that will function as an AD FS server.

   D. **Incorrect:** The Service Communications Certificate must be located in the Personal certificate store, not the Trusted Root Certification Authorities store, of a computer that will function as an AD FS server.

Objective 5.2: Thought experiment

1. You should configure a group Managed Service Account to ensure that passwords are managed by Active Directory and don't have to be changed manually.

2. You use the setspn.exe utility to configure the SPN for the AD FS service account manually.

Objective 5.2: Review

1. **Correct answers:** C and D

   A. **Incorrect:** The Allow log on locally right is not required. The AD FS service account must have the Log On As A Batch Job and the Log On As A Service rights on each server that will function as an AD FS server.

   B. **Incorrect:** The Allow log on through remote desktop services right is not required. The AD FS service account must have the Log On As A Batch Job and the Log On As A Service rights on each server that will function as an AD FS server.

   C. **Correct:** The AD FS service account must have the Log On As A Batch Job and the Log On As A Service rights on each server that will function as an AD FS server.

D. Correct: The AD FS service account must have the Log On As A Batch Job and the Log On As A Service rights on each server that will function as an AD FS server.

2. **Correct answer:** A

   A. Correct: When configuring AD FS you need to provide the credentials of an account that has domain administrator privileges.

   B. Incorrect: When configuring AD FS you need to provide the credentials of an account that has domain administrator rather than enterprise administrator privileges.

   C. Incorrect: When configuring AD FS you need to provide the credentials of an account that has domain administrator rather than schema administrator privileges.

   D. Incorrect: When configuring AD FS you need to provide the credentials of an account that has domain administrator rather than backup operator privileges.

3. **Correct answers:** A and C

   A. Correct: To use a group Managed Service Account for the AD FS service account, both the KDS Root Key must be configured and at least one domain controller in the domain must be running Windows Server 2012 or later.

   B. Incorrect: You don't have to have deployed KMS to use a group Managed Service Account.

   C. Correct: To use a group Managed Service Account for the AD FS service account, both the KDS Root Key must be configured and at least one domain controller in the domain must be running Windows Server 2012 or later.

   D. Incorrect: You don't have to have configured DNSSEC to use a group Managed Service Account.

4. **Correct answer:** B

   A. Incorrect: When AD FS uses a Windows Internal Database, only one AD FS server in the farm has write access.

   B. Correct: When AD FS uses SQL Server for the AD FS database, all servers in the farm have write access.

   C. Incorrect: Using a group Managed Service Account doesn't change whether multiple servers in the farm have write access to the AD FS database.

   D. Incorrect: AD FS cannot use a wildcard Service Communications Certificate.

Objective 5.3: Thought experiment

1. You should use the command:

```
Set-AdfsWebTheme -TargetName default -Logo @{path="c:\images\logo.png"}
```

2. You should use the command:

```
Set-AdfsWebTheme -TargetName default -Illustration @{path="c:\Contoso\
illustration.png"}
```

3. You should use the command:

```
Set-AdfsGlobalWebContent -CompanyName "Contoso Corp"
```

Objective 5.3: Review

1. **Correct answer:** A

   A. **Correct:** The Web Application Proxy role service is part of the Remote Access role.

   B. **Incorrect:** The Web Application Proxy role service is part of the Remote Access role and not the Active Directory Federation Services role.

   C. **Incorrect:** The Web Application Proxy role service is part of the Remote Access role and not the Network Policy and Access Services role.

   D. **Incorrect:** The Web Application Proxy role service is part of the Remote Access role and not the Remote Desktop Services role.

2. **Correct answer:** D

   A. **Incorrect:** The potential Web Application Proxy server must receive the private IP address of the AD FS server, not the IP address of the Office 365 server, so that it can function as a proxy for AD FS traffic from the Internet.

   B. **Incorrect:** The potential Web Application Proxy server must receive the private IP address of the AD FS server, not the public IP address of the Web Application Proxy server, so that it can function as a proxy for AD FS traffic from the Internet.

   C. **Incorrect:** The potential Web Application Proxy server must receive the private IP address of the AD FS server, not the private IP address of the Web Application Proxy server, so that it can function as a proxy for AD FS traffic from the Internet.

   D. **Correct:** The potential Web Application Proxy server must receive the private IP address of the AD FS server, so that it can function as a proxy for AD FS traffic from the Internet.

3. **Correct answer:** B

A. **Incorrect:** The certificate installed on the Web Application Proxy server must have the AD FS service name as the certificate subject name and not enterpriseregistration.adatum.com.

B. **Correct:** The certificate installed on the Web Application Proxy server must have the AD FS service name as the certificate subject name.

C. **Incorrect:** The certificate installed on the Web Application Proxy server must have the AD FS service name as the certificate subject name and not wap-syd.adatum.com.

D. **Incorrect:** The certificate installed on the Web Application Proxy server must have the AD FS service name as the certificate subject name and not adfs-svr1.adatum.com

CHAPTER 6

Monitor and troubleshoot Office 365 availability and usage

Office 365 provides a large number of reports that allow organizations to determine exactly how subscribed users are using the service. There are many ways that you can monitor Office 365, from using the built-in reporting functionality to deploying a special Office 365 Management Pack for System Center 2012 R2 Operations Manager. Finally, Microsoft provides a number of different tools that you can use to troubleshoot Office 365 should it, or specific Office 365 functionality, become unavailable.

Objectives in this chapter:

- Objective 6.1: Analyze reports
- Objective 6.2: Monitor service health
- Objective 6.3: Isolate service interruption

Objective 6.1: Analyze reports

This objective deals with several of the reports that are available through the Office 365 Admin Center. To master this objective, you'll need to understand the types of reports that are available and the information these reports display.

> **This objective covers the following topics:**
> - Mail reports
> - Usage reports
> - Auditing reports
> - Protection reports

Office 365 reports

Office 365 offers a large number of reports that tenant administrators can use to learn how an organization consumes Office 365 services. It's possible to view these reports either through the web console, or to export the data from these reports into a format that can be displayed in Microsoft Excel. Office 365 also supports the creation of custom reports through the Office 365 web services.

> **MORE INFO OFFICE 365 REPORTS**
>
> You can learn more about Office 365 reports at *https://support.office.com/en-us/article/ View-and-download-reports-about-service-usage-in-Office-365-30e5558f-d3c0-4a3b- a0d5-58fc7750c0ad?omkt=en-us&ui=en-US&rs=en-US&ad=US.*

Mail reports

The following mail reports are available through the Office 365 Admin Center:

- **Active and inactive mailboxes**   Shows the number of active and inactive mailboxes over time. A mailbox is listed as inactive if the user associated with it has not connected to it for more than 30 days.

- **New and deleted mailboxes**   Lists the number of mailboxes that have been created and the number that have been deleted.

- **New and deleted groups**   Shows the number of groups created and deleted for the Office 365 subscription.

- **Mailbox usage**   Shows the total number of mailboxes associated with the Office 365 subscription, the number of mailboxes that are exceeding their storage quota, and the number of mailboxes using less than 25 percent of their storage limit. Figure 6-1 shows this report.

- **Types of mailbox connections**   Lists the number of mailboxes accessed by each of the following protocols: MAPI, Outlook on the web, Exchange ActiveSync, EWS, IMAP, and POP3.

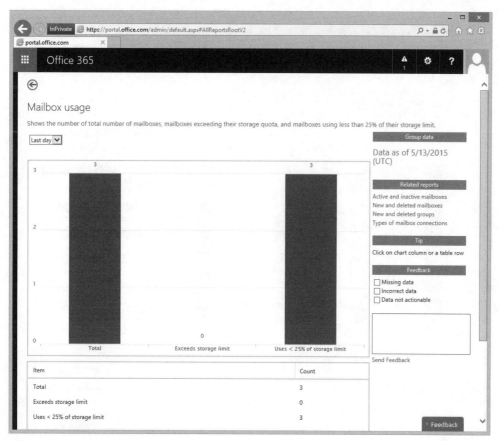

FIGURE 6-1 Mailbox usage report

Usage reports

The following usage reports are available through the Office 365 Admin Center:

- **Browser used** Shows information about the different web browsers used to access Office 365 by users.

- **Operating system used** Shows information about the different operating systems used to access Office 365 by users.

- **Licensing vs. Active Usage** Provides information on how Office 365 services are used in comparison to what the subscription level provides. Figure 6-2 shows this report.

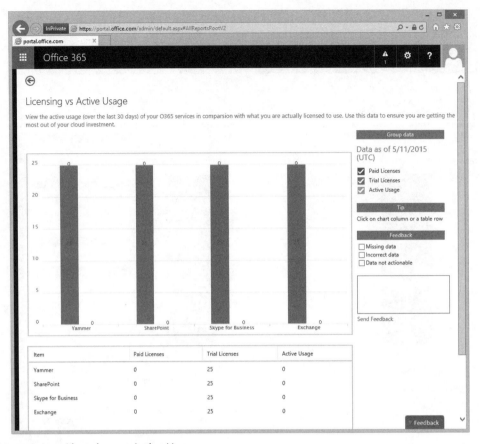

FIGURE 6-2 Licensing vs. Active Usage

Skype for Business

The following Skype for Business (formerly known as Lync) reports are available through the Office 365 Admin Center:

- **Active users**   Number of users who took part in at least one peer-to-peer session in the reporting period.
- **Peer-to-peer sessions**   Total number of peer-to-peer sessions, including instant messaging, audio, video, application sharing, and file transfers during the specified time period.
- **Conferences**   Total number of conferences during the specified reporting period.
- **Audio minutes and video minutes**   Total number of minutes that were spent in either audio or video peer-to-peer sessions during the reporting period.
- **Client devices**   Tracks the number of unique users per type of device accessing Skype for Business.

- **Client devices per user** Allows you to track the number of peer-to-peer sessions that a specific user engaged in during the last three months.
- **User activities** Allows you to view the types of activities, including peer-to-peer sessions, instant messaging, audio, video, application sharing, file transfers, and conferences an individual user participated in during the reporting period.

SharePoint

The following SharePoint reports are available through the Office 365 Admin Center:

- **Tenant storage metrics** Shows the storage space used by the entirety of the Office 365 subscription.
- **Team sites deployed** Shows the number of active and inactive team sites deployed across the Office 365 subscription. Figure 6-3 shows this report.
- **Team site storage** Displays the storage space used for team sites across the entire Office 365 subscription.

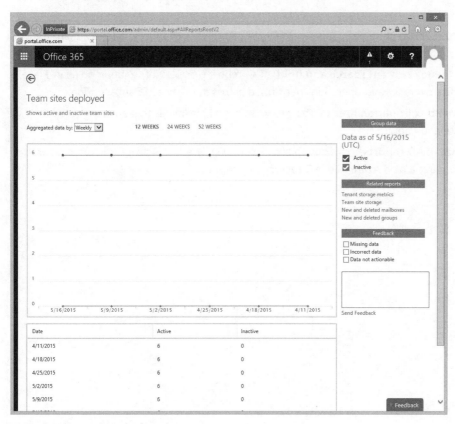

FIGURE 6-3 Team sites deployed

OneDrive for Business

The following OneDrive for Business reports are available through the Office 365 Admin Center:

- **OneDrive for Business sites deployed**   This report shows the number of OneDrive for Business sites deployed within the reporting period.

- **OneDrive for Business storage**   This report shows the storage space consumed by OneDrive for Business sites. This report can also be configured to show the amount of storage space consumed by team sites as well as the entire Office 365 subscription.

Auditing reports

The following auditing reports are available through the Office 365 Admin Center:

- **Mailbox access by non-owners**   You can use this report to search for mailboxes accessed by people other than their owners. One reason to use this report would be to check whether users with Administrative privileges have accessed certain Office 365 mailboxes.

- **Role group changes**   This report allows you to view changes made to administrator role groups. This report is shown in Figure 6-4.

- **Mailbox content search and hold**   This report provides information on all In-Place eDiscovery & Hold operations performed across the Office 365 subscription.

- **Mailbox litigation holds**   This report shows all mailboxes that are configured for litigation hold.

- **Azure AD reports**   This option allows you to view Azure Active Directory reports. It requires a paid Azure Active Directory subscription.

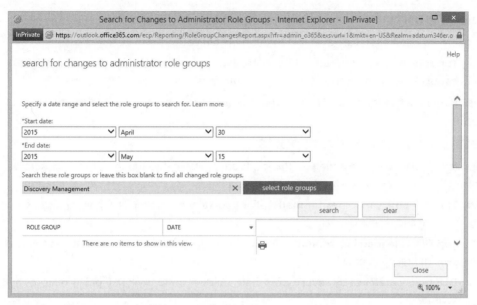

FIGURE 6-4 Changes to Administrator Role Groups

Protection reports

The following protection reports are available through the Office 365 Admin Center:

- **Top senders and recipients** This report allows you to view the top mail senders, the top mail recipients, the top spam recipients, and the top malware recipients across the Office 365 subscription.

- **Top malware for mail** This report shows the amount of malware received through email for the reporting period.

- **Malware detections** This report shows the amount of malware sent and received through the Office 365 subscription for the reporting period.

- **Spam detections** This report shows the amount of spam on the basis of the content being filtered or the original sending host being blocked.

- **Sent and received mail** This report shows the amount of sent and received mail categorized by good mail, malware, spam, and messages dealt with by rules.

Rules reports

The following rules reports are available through the Office 365 Admin Center:

- **Top rule matches for mail**   This report allows you to view the number of messages based on sent and received transport rule matches.
- **Rule matches for mail**   This report shows all rule matches for received and sent email.

Data Loss Prevention reports

The following Data Loss Prevention (DLP) reports are available through the Office 365 Admin Center:

- **Top DLP policy matches for mail**   Allows you to view the top DLP policy matches for sent and received email.
- **Top DLP rule matches for mail**   Allows you to view the top DLP rule matches for sent and received email.
- **DLP policy matches by severity for mail**   Allows you to track DLP policy matches by severity.
- **DLP policy matches, overrides, and false positives for mail**   Allows you to view DLP matches, overrides, and false positives for incoming and outgoing messages.

EXAM TIP

The best way to learn about the reports available in Office 365 is to access them through your organization's subscription or to create your own trial subscription and to investigate them there.

Thought experiment

Skype for Business at Contoso

In this thought experiment, apply what you've learned about this objective. You can find the answers to these questions in the "Answers" section at the end of the chapter.

Contoso has recently started using Skype for Business as part of its Office 365 deployment, replacing a third-party product that had similar functionality. As part of assessing the success of the adoption, management wants data on how the Skype for Business functionality available through Office 365 is being utilized. With this information in mind, answer the following questions:

1. Which report would you access to find out about the number of Skype for Business conferences held?

2. Which report would you access to determine the number of users leveraging Skype for Business?

Objective summary

- Mail reports allow you to view how Office 365 mailboxes are used.
- Usage reports allow you to view information about browsers, operating systems, and license consumption.
- Skype for Business reports allow you to see how Skype for Business is being used in the organization.
- SharePoint reports allow you to see how SharePoint is being used with the Office 365 subscription.
- OneDrive for Business allows you to view the OneDrive for Business storage statistics.
- Auditing reports allow you to view information about auditing of mailboxes, and mailbox litigation holds.
- Protection reports allow you to view statistics about malware and spam.
- Rules reports allow you to view how transport rules are being used.
- Data Loss Prevention reports allow you to view how Data Loss Prevention rules and policies are being applied to message traffic.

Objective review

Answer the following questions to test your knowledge of the information in this objective. You can find the answers to these questions and explanations of why each answer choice is correct or incorrect in the "Answers" section at the end of the chapter.

1. Which of the following Office 365 reports could you use to determine the number of users in your organization accessing their Office 365 mailbox using the IMAP protocol?

    A. Active and inactive mailboxes

    B. New and deleted mailboxes

    C. Mailbox usage

    D. Types of mailbox connections

2. You want to determine the number of Office 365 mailboxes associated with your organization's subscription that haven't been accessed for 30 or more days. Which of the following reports would provide you with that information?

    A. New and deleted mailboxes

    B. Mailbox usage

    C. Active and inactive mailboxes

    D. Types of mailbox connections

3. Which of the following Office 365 reports can you use to determine whether administrators have accessed the Office 365 mailboxes of other users?

   A. Role group changes

   B. Mailbox content search and hold

   C. Mailbox access by non-owners

   D. Mailbox litigation holds

4. Which of the following Office 365 reports would you run to determine which Office
   365 mailboxes are subject to litigation hold?

   A. Mailbox content search and hold

   B. Mailbox litigation holds

   C. Role group changes

   D. Mailbox access by non-owners

Objective 6.2: Monitor service health

This objective deals with determining whether a specific element of Office 365 is not functioning properly or is undergoing maintenance. To master this objective you'll need to understand what you can learn by accessing the service health dashboard, what you can learn using
the Office 365 Management Pack for System Center 2012 R2 Operations Manager, as well as
what you can learn about the messaging environment using Windows PowerShell.

> **This objective covers the following topics:**
> - Service Health Dashboard
> - RSS feed
> - Office 365 Management Pack
> - Windows PowerShell cmdlets

Service Health Dashboard

The Service Health Dashboard allows you to view the health of all of the services related
to your organization's Office 365 subscription. For example, the screen shot of the Service
Health Dashboard shown in Figure 6-5 shows that the Exchange and SharePoint services are
in a Service Degraded state and that the Office 365 Portal is in a Service Restored state. It
also shows that the Identity Service, Office Subscription, Rights Management Service, Skype
for Business (formerly known as Lync) and Yammer Enterprise services are all experiencing
no issues.

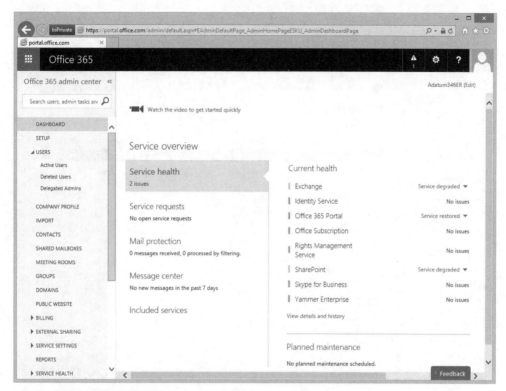

FIGURE 6-5 Service Health Dashboard

Details and History

By clicking View Details and History, you can view the status history for the past seven days, as shown in Figure 6-6.

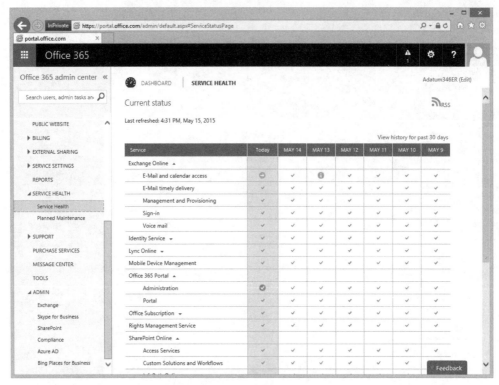

FIGURE 6-6 Service health over the previous seven days

Figure 6-7 provides a guide to the different status icons used with the Service Health Dashboard.

FIGURE 6-7 Service health status icons

These icons have the following meanings:

- **Normal service** This icon indicates that the service has suffered no issues in the reporting time period.

- **Investigating** This icon indicates that Microsoft is investigating a potential issue and that more information will be forthcoming.

- **Service interruption** This icon indicates that the service is not functioning.

- **Service degradation** This icon indicates that the service is slow and occasionally unresponsive for brief periods.

- **Restoring service**   This icon indicates that the service is in the process of being fixed.

- **Extended recovery**   This icon indicates that while steps have been completed to resolve the incident, an extended amount of time might be required before operations return to normal.

- **Service restored**   This icon indicates that an incident was active in the last 24 hours but that service has been restored.

- **Additional information**   This icon indicates that the incident was active in the previous 48 hours and that you should check the Today column to determine if the incident has been resolved.

- **PIR published**   The Post Incident Report (PIR) is a report published about the service incident that provides additional data about the status.

You can also view the history for the previous 30 days by clicking the View History For Past 30 Days item. Figure 6-8 shows part of the 30-day history for the Adatum 346 ER subscription.

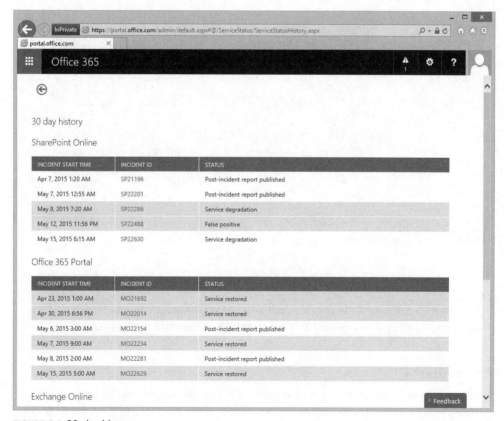

FIGURE 6-8 30-day history

Planned maintenance

The Planned Maintenance page, shown in Figure 6-9, provides details of upcoming planned maintenance events, as well as recent planned maintenance events.

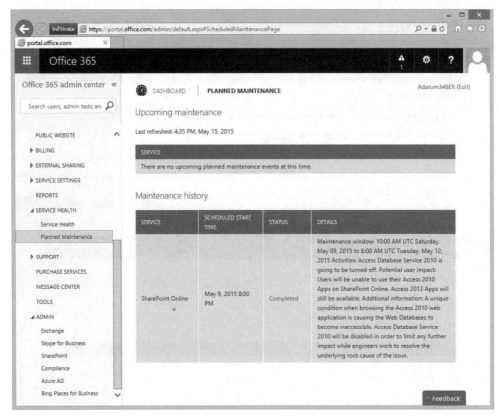

FIGURE 6-9 Planned maintenance

> **MORE INFO SERVICE HEALTH DASHBOARD**
>
> You can learn more about the Service Health dashboard at *https://support.office.com/en-us/article/View-the-status-of-your-services-932ad3ad-533c-418a-b938-6e44e8bc33b0*.

RSS feed

In the Service Health Dashboard, you can click the RSS icon to access an RSS feed. This will provide you with notifications, using the RSS protocol, when a new event is added or an existing event is modified. You can use Outlook to subscribe to RSS feeds.

Office 365 Management Pack

The Office 365 Management Pack for System Center Operations Manager allows you to monitor the status of one or more Office 365 subscriptions from your on-premises Operations Manager deployment. System Center Operations Manager is the Microsoft monitoring solution. Management Packs are add-on components that allow you to monitor specific products. Management Packs are available not only for Office 365, but for almost all Microsoft products like Exchange Server and SQL Server, as well as for a large number of third-party products.

Installing the Office 365 Management Pack

To install the Office 365 Management Pack for System Center Operations Manager, perform the following steps:

1. Download the Office 365 Management Pack from *https://www.microsoft.com/en-us/download/details.aspx?id=43708* to the desktop of the Operations Manager server.

2. Double-click the System Center Management Pack for Office 365 MSI installer file.

3. On the License Agreement page, click I Accept, and then click Next.

4. In the Select Installation Folder dialog box, shown in Figure 6-10, accept the default location, and then click Next, click Install, and click Close.

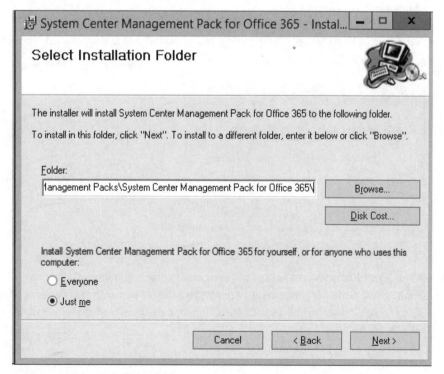

FIGURE 6-10 Select installation folder

5. Open the Operations Manager console and then select the Administration workspace.

6. Select the Management Packs node as shown in Figure 6-11 and then click Import Management Packs from the Tasks pane.

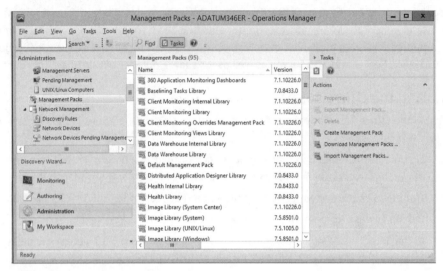

FIGURE 6-11 Management Packs

7. In the Import Management Packs dialog box, click Add and then click Add From Disk.

8. In the Online Catalog Connection dialog box, shown in Figure 6-12, click Yes.

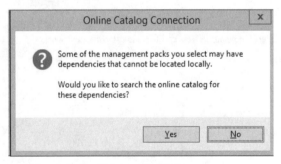

FIGURE 6-12 Online Catalog Connection

9. In the Select Management Packs To Import dialog box, navigate to C:\Program Files (x86)\System Center Management Packs\System Center Management Pack for Office 365\ and select Microsoft.SystemCenter.O365.mpb as shown in Figure 6-13 and then click Open.

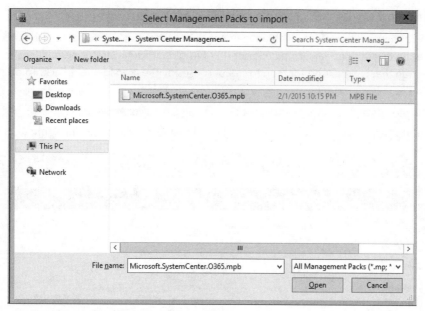

FIGURE 6-13 Select Management Packs To Import

10. On the Import Management Packs dialog box, ensure that Microsoft Office 365 is selected, as shown in Figure 6-14, and then click Install. When the import completes, click Close.

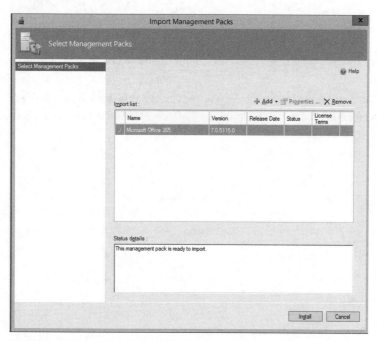

FIGURE 6-14 Import Management Packs

Configuring Office 365 for use with the Management Pack

Prior to configuring the Office 365 Management Pack to monitor a specific subscription, you need to create a special Office 365 user that has global administrator permissions to the subscription that can be used for monitoring purposes by the Management Pack. To do this, perform the following steps.

1. In the Office 365 Admin Center, click Users and then click Active Users.

2. In the Select a View drop-down list, select Global Admins as shown in Figure 6-15.

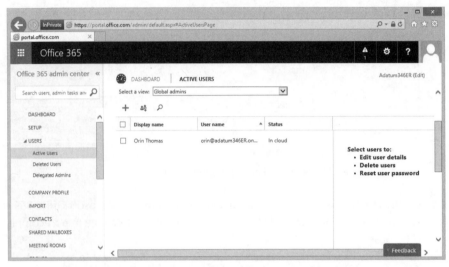

FIGURE 6-15 Global Admins

3. In the list of Global Admins, click the Plus icon to open the Create New User Account dialog box.

4. In the Create New User Account dialog box, provide a name and password. The creation of an account named adatum346ERmonitor@adatum346er.onmicrosoft.com is shown in Figure 6-16. Click Create.

Create new user account ×

First name   Last name

Adatum   Monitoring

* Display name

Adatum Monitoring

* User name

adatum346ERmonitor   @   adatum346ER.onmic ⌄

Auto-generated password | **Type password**

••••••••

strong

••••••••

☐ Make this person change their password the next time they
sign in.

* Email password to the following recipients

orin@adatum346er.onmicrosoft.com

Select licenses for this user:

Office 365 Enterprise E3 license will be assigned to this user.

Create   Cancel

FIGURE 6-16 Create new user

5. Once the account is created, select the All Users view, select the account, and click Edit.

6. Click Settings. Under Assign role, click Yes and then set the Global Administrator role as shown in Figure 6-17 and click Save.

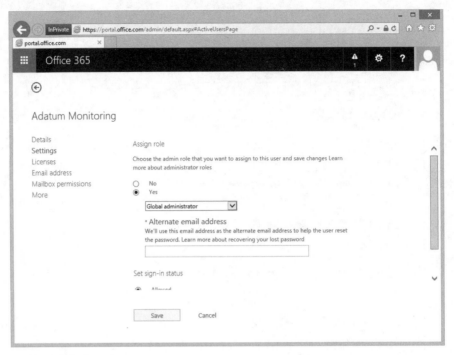

FIGURE 6-17 Assign role

Configuring the Management Pack

To configure the Office 365 Management Pack to work with your Office 365 subscription, perform the following steps:

1. In the Administration node of the Operations Manager console, click the Office 365 node as shown in Figure 6-18.

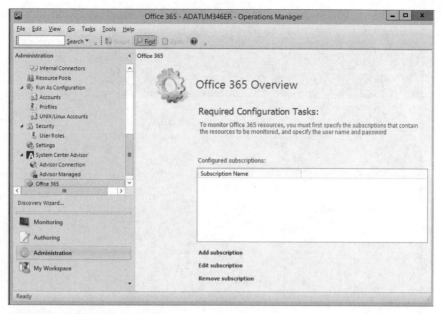

FIGURE 6-18 Office 365 node

2. On the Office 365 Overview page, click Add Subscription. This opens the Add Subscription Wizard.

3. On the Subscription Details page, specify a subscription name and the password for that account. This will be the name of the account you set up to monitor the subscription. Figure 6-19 shows this information provided for the Adatum346ER subscription.

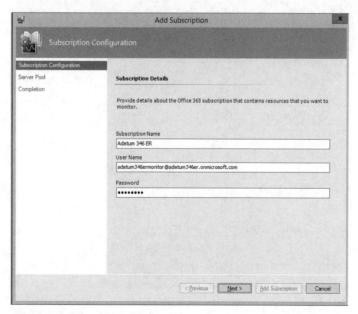

FIGURE 6-19 Subscription Configuration

4. On the Server Pool page, accept the default as shown in Figure 6-20 and click Add Subscription.

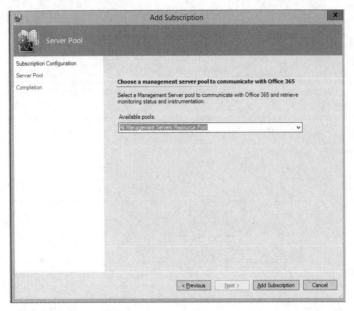

FIGURE 6-20 Server Pool

5. Verify that you get the message that the Office 365 Subscription is ready for monitoring, as shown in Figure 6-21, and click Finish.

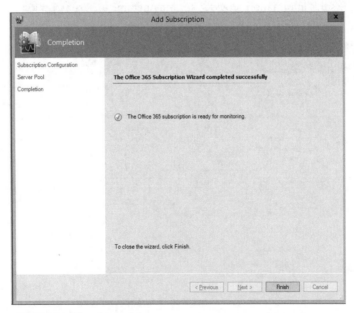

FIGURE 6-21 Wizard complete

Office 365 Monitoring Dashboard

Once you have installed the Office 365 Management Pack, you can access the Monitoring Dashboard through the Monitoring node of the Operations Manager console. This dashboard is shown in Figure 6-22 and includes the following sections:

- Subscription Health
- Service Status
- Active Incidents
- Resolved Incidents
- Message Center

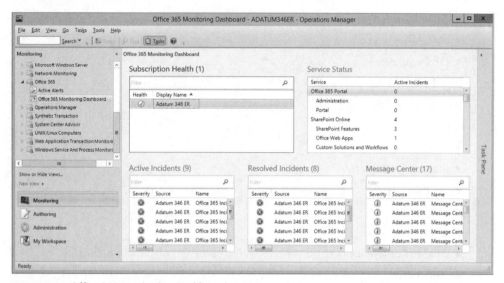

FIGURE 6-22 Office 365 Monitoring Dashboard

SUBSCRIPTION HEALTH

The Subscription Health area provides you with information about each of the monitored Office 365 subscriptions. The Office 365 Management Pack can be used to monitor the status of multiple Office 365 subscriptions. A healthy state indicates that a connection has been successfully made from the Operations Manager instance to a specific Office 365 subscription. A critical state indicates that a connection cannot be made from the Operations Manager instance to the Office 365 subscription.

SERVICE STATUS

The Service Status area displays a tree of services and features for the subscription selected in the Subscription Health area. This area lists the Service as well as any active incidents related to that service. For example, for the Adatum346ER subscription, data for the following services and features is displayed:

- Office 365 Portal
  - Administration
  - Portal
- SharePoint Online
  - SharePoint Features
  - Office Web Apps
  - Custom Solutions and Workflows
  - Provisioning
  - Search and Delve
  - Tenant Admin
  - Access Services
  - SP Designer
  - InfoPath Online
  - Project Online
- Lync Online
  - Audio and Video
  - Instant Messaging
  - Sign-In
  - Presence
  - All Features
  - Dial-In Conferencing
  - Federation
  - Online Meetings
  - Mobility
  - Management and Provisioning
- Identity Service
  - Administration
  - Sign-In
- Rights Management Service
  - RMS Available
- Mobile Device Management
- Office Subscription
  - Network Availability
  - Office Professional Plus Download
  - Licensing and Renewal

- Exchange Online
  - Voice Mail
  - Email timely delivery
  - Sign-in
- Yammer Enterprise
  - Yammer Components

ACTIVE INCIDENTS

The Active Incidents area displays a list of alerts for currently active Office 365 incidents for the subscription selected in the Subscription Health area. Each alert contains information about the list of affected services, features, and the status of those features. Figure 6-23 shows the properties of an alert.

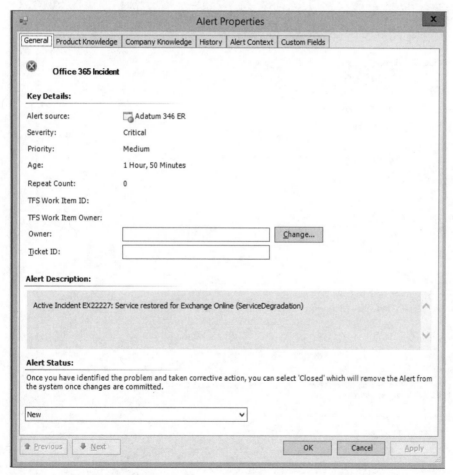

FIGURE 6-23 Alert Properties

Alerts can have one of the following states:

- Information Unavailable
- Investigating
- Service Interruption
- Service Degradation
- Restoring Service
- Extended Recovery

RESOLVED INCIDENTS

The Resolved Incidents section shows a list of resolved alerts for the currently selected subscription. Figure 6-24 shows the properties of a resolved alert.

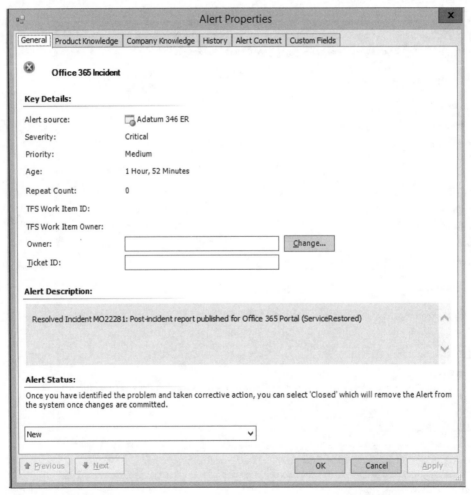

FIGURE 6-24 Resolved Incident

Message Center

The Message Center provides a list of information messages related to the Office 365 subscription. Each alert in the Message Center will provide an external link to an article or blog post with details. Figure 6-25 shows the properties of a message from the Message Center.

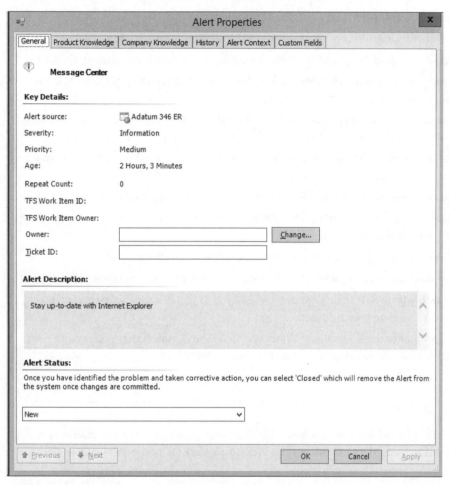

FIGURE 6-25 Message

> **MORE INFO** **OFFICE 365 MANAGEMENT PACK**
>
> You can learn more about the Office 365 Management Pack for System Center Operations Manager at *http://blogs.office.com/2014/07/29/new-office-365-admin-tools/*.

Windows PowerShell cmdlets

There are a number of auditing and reporting related Windows PowerShell cmdlets that you can use with the messaging element of your organization's Office 365 subscription.

Windows PowerShell cmdlets related to message auditing include:

- **Search-AdminAuditLog** Search the administrator audit log.
- **Write-AdminAuditLog** Add entries to the administrator audit log.
- **Get-AdminAuditLogConfig** View the configuration of the administrator audit log.
- **New-AdminAuditLogSearch** Search the administrator audit log, outputting the results as email to specified recipients.
- **Get-MailboxAuditBypassAssociation** View mailboxes that are configured to bypass mailbox audit logging.
- **Set-MailboxAuditBypassAssociation** Configure one or more mailboxes so that they bypass mailbox audit logging.
- **Search-MailboxAuditLog** Examine the contents of the mailbox audit log.
- **New-MailboxAuditLogSearch** Search the mailbox audit log, outputting the results as email to specified recipients.

Windows PowerShell cmdlets related to message tracking include:

- **Get-MessageTrackingReport** Provides data from a specific message tracking report.
- **Search-MessageTrackingReport** Allows you to locate a specific message tracking report based on search criteria.

More comprehensive coverage of Windows PowerShell cmdlets that you can use with Office 365 is provided in Chapter 3, "Manage Cloud Identities."

EXAM TIP

Remember that you need to configure an account with global administrator privileges in Office 365 to be used for the Office 365 Management Pack for System Center Operations Manager.

> ### *Thought experiment*
>
> #### Auditing Office 365 with Windows PowerShell at Adatum
>
> In this thought experiment, apply what you've learned about this objective. You can find the answers to these questions in the "Answers" section at the end of the chapter.
>
> You are in the process of investigating the Windows PowerShell auditing functionality that is available for use with your organization's Office 365 messaging deployment. You are interested in configuring a bypass of audit logging for certain Office 365 mailboxes. You are also interested in performing regular searches of the admin audit log for suspicious activity. With this information in mind, answer the following questions:
>
> 1. Which Windows PowerShell cmdlet would you use to bypass audit logging on specific mailboxes?
>
> 2. Which Windows PowerShell cmdlet would you use to search the administrator audit log, sending the results to your manager?

Objective summary

- The Service Health Dashboard is available from the Office 365 Admin Center and allows you to determine the status of the various elements of Office 365, including fault history and planned maintenance.
- The Office 365 Management Pack for System Center 2012 R2 Operations Manager allows you to monitor the status of multiple Office 365 subscriptions from your on-premises System Center 2012 R2 Operations Manager deployment.
- You can use certain Windows PowerShell cmdlets to review the configuration of your Office 365 and on-premises messaging environment.

Objective review

Answer the following questions to test your knowledge of the information in this objective. You can find the answers to these questions and explanations of why each answer choice is correct or incorrect in the "Answers" section at the end of the chapter.

1. You are in the process of configuring your organization's Office 365 subscription so that you can monitor it using the Office 365 Management Pack for System Center 2012 R2 Operations Manager. You are in the process of creating an Office 365 user account to be used by the Management Pack. Which of the following roles would you assign the account?

A. Billing administrator

B. Global administrator

C. Service administrator

D. User management administrator

2. You want to be notified each time there is a change to service status of your organization's Office 365 deployment. Which of the following should you configure to accomplish this goal?

A. Skype for Business

B. RSS feed

C. SharePoint

D. OneDrive for Business

3. Which section of the Office 365 Monitoring Dashboard, available when the Office 365 Management Pack is installed in an Operations Manager instance, would you consult to determine whether a particular incident had been resolved?

A. Subscription Health

B. Message Center

C. Service Status

D. Resolved Incidents

Objective 6.3: Isolate service interruption

This objective deals with tools and methods that you can use to troubleshoot issues when Office 365 or your hybrid deployment isn't functioning as expected. To master this objective you'll need to understand the different tools available from Microsoft for resolving issues, including creating a service request, the Microsoft Remote Connectivity Analyzer, the Microsoft Connectivity Analyzer Tool, the Transport Reliability IP Probe, and the Hybrid Free/Busy Troubleshooter.

This objective covers the following topics:

- Create a service request
- Microsoft Remote Connectivity Analyzer
- Microsoft Connectivity Analyzer Tool
- Transport Reliability IP Probe
- Hybrid free/busy troubleshooter

Create a service request

Service requests allow tenant administrators to contact Microsoft to resolve problems. You can create a service request online through the Office 365 Admin Center or by telephone. To create a service request online, perform the following steps:

1. Sign in to the Office 365 Admin Center with an account that has tenant administrator privileges.

2. In the left pane, click Support. Under Support, click Service Requests.

3. On the Service Requests page, shown in Figure 6-26, click the Plus item to create a new Service Request.

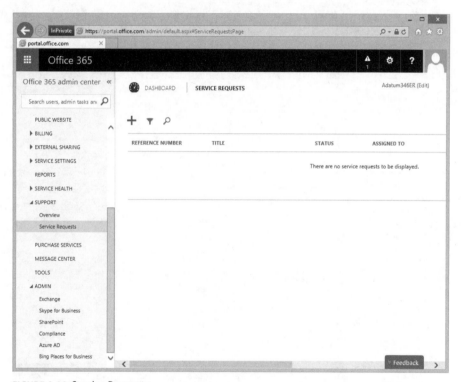

FIGURE 6-26 Service Requests

4. On the Create a Service Request page, shown in Figure 6-27, select a category of Service Request. You can choose from the following:

   - Billing

   - Mail

   - Online collaboration

   - Sites and document sharing

   - Office client subscription

- Visio Pro
- Project Pro
- Yammer Enterprise
- Identity management
- User and domain management
- Delve
- Mobile Device management

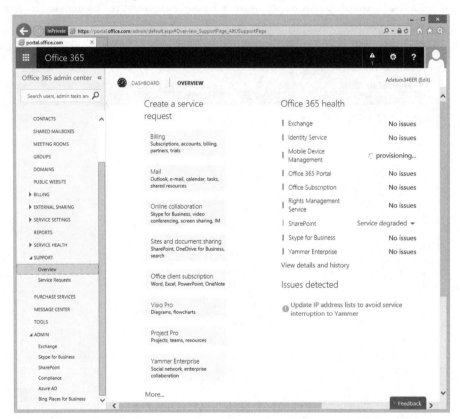

FIGURE 6-27 Service Request Overview

5. Once you've selected an issue, you'll be presented with the New Service Request page, shown in Figure 6-28. Here you'll be asked to:

- Identify the issue
- Review suggestions
- Add details
- Confirm and submit

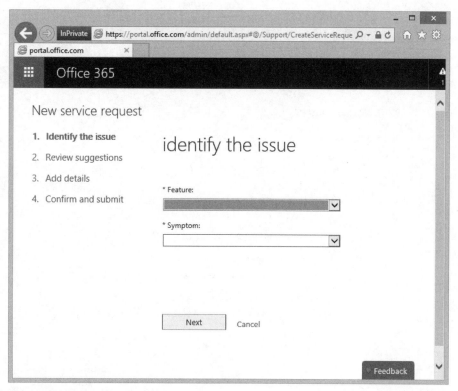

FIGURE 6-28 Identify the issue

6. The features that you can select from the drop-down list will depend on the category of problem that you have selected. The symptoms that you can select will depend on the feature that you choose. Make your selections and click Next.

7. When you have selected a Feature and a Symptom, you'll need to provide an issue summary and issue details, and then click Next. Figure 6-29 shows an issue related to mailbox recovery with a summary and a description.

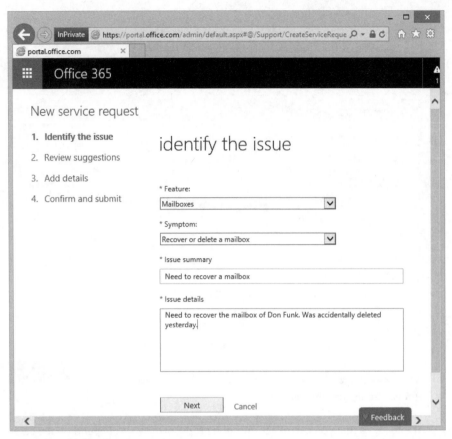

FIGURE 6-29 Mailbox issue

8. On the Review Suggestions page, you will be presented with some suggestions that may assist you in resolving the problem without having to lodge a service request. Figure 6-30 shows suggestions related to the recovery of deleted mailboxes.

FIGURE 6-30 Review suggestions

9. On the Add Details page, shown in Figure 6-31, provide more information about the disruption causing the service request. The content of this page will vary depending on the type of issue you are attempting to get resolved. You can add up to five screen shots or additional documents on this page, as long as each document is less than 5 MB in size.

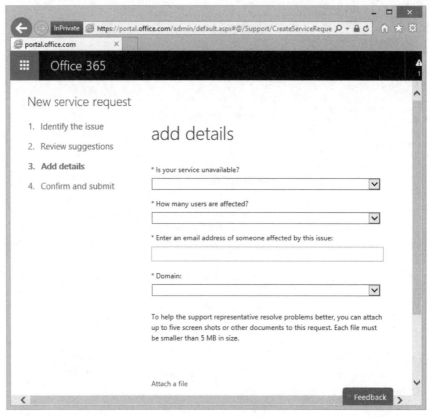

FIGURE 6-31 Add details

10. Once you have added the appropriate details, you can confirm and submit the request. Response times will depend on the severity of the issue and the type of subscription that your organization has to Office 365.

> **MORE INFO CREATING SERVICE REQUESTS**
>
> You can learn more about creating service requests for Office 365 support at *http://blogs. technet.com/b/praveenkumar/archive/2013/07/18/how-to-create-service-requests-to-contact-office-365-support.aspx.*

Microsoft Remote Connectivity Analyzer

The Microsoft Remote Connectivity Analyzer is a web application that you can access at *https://testconnectivity.microsoft.com/.* The Microsoft Remote Connectivity Analyzer allows you to perform remote tests that run from Microsoft's servers on the Internet. You can use the Microsoft Remote Connectivity Analyzer to diagnose common connectivity problems for Office 365, on-premises Exchange, Lync/OCS Server, the Outlook client and Internet email.

The Microsoft Remote Connectivity Analyzer supports the following tests for an on-premises Exchange deployment, as long as that deployment is running Exchange 2007 or later as shown in Figure 6-32:

- Microsoft Exchange ActiveSync Connectivity Tests
  - **Exchange ActiveSync**   Checks that clients on the Internet can connect to an on-premises Exchange deployment using ActiveSync.
  - **Exchange ActiveSync Autodiscover**   Checks that clients on the Internet can be automatically configured with an on-premises Exchange deployment's settings.
- Microsoft Exchange Web Services Connectivity Tests
  - **Synchronization, Notification, Availability, and Automatic Replies**   Checks the functionality of many on-premises Exchange Web Services tasks.
  - **Service Account Access (Developers)**   Checks that a specified service account is able to access a nominated on-premises mailbox and to perform operations such as the creation and deletion of mailbox items. Also checks Exchange impersonation functionality.
- Microsoft Office Outlook Connectivity Tests
  - **Outlook Connectivity**   Checks that an Outlook client on the Internet is able to connect to the on-premises Exchange deployment.
  - **Outlook Autodiscover**   Checks that an Outlook client on the Internet can be configured with on-premises Exchange settings through Autodiscover.
- Internet Email Tests
  - **Inbound SMTP Email**   Checks that inbound SMTP email can be successfully sent to the on-premises Exchange deployment.
  - **Outbound SMTP Email**   Checks outbound SMTP configuration to ensure that Reverse DNS, Sender ID, and RBL (Realtime Blackhole List) checks are passed.
  - **POP Email**   Checks that a client can access an on-premises Exchange mailbox using the POP3 protocol.
  - **IMAP Email**   Checks that a client can access an on-premises Exchange mailbox using the IMAP4 protocol.

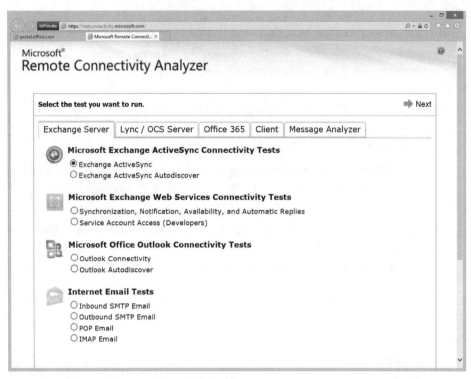

FIGURE 6-32 Microsoft Remote Connectivity Analyzer

Use this tool if you suspect that the on-premises component of a hybrid deployment is causing problems.

If you suspect that there is a problem with the messaging elements of Office 365, you can use the Office 365 tab of the Microsoft Remote Connectivity Analyzer to test Office functionality. These tests allow you to check basic Office 365 messaging functionality, including allowing you to assess whether or not the DNS configuration for Office 365 messaging elements is configured correctly. The following tests are available for an Office 365 deployment as shown in Figure 6-33:

- Office 365 General Tests

  - **Office 365 Exchange Domain Name Server (DNS) Connectivity Test**   Checks the external domain name settings, including checking whether there are issues for mail delivery and any client connectivity issues related to DNS.

  - **Office 365 Lync Domain Name Server (DNS) Connectivity Test**   Checks the external domain name settings related to Lync for a custom Office 365 domain user.

  - **Office 365 Single Sign-On Test**   This test allows you to verify that it is possible to sign on to Office 365 using on-premises credentials. This test also performs basic validation of the Active Directory Federation Services configuration.

- Microsoft Exchange ActiveSync Connectivity Tests
  - **Exchange ActiveSync**   This test checks whether a mobile device can connect to Office 365 messaging resources using Exchange ActiveSync.
  - **Exchange ActiveSync Autodiscover**   This test checks whether a device uses Exchange ActiveSync to successfully obtain configuration settings from the Autodiscover service hosted through Office 365.
- Microsoft Exchange Web Services Connectivity Tests
  - **Synchronization, Notification, Availability, and Automatic Replies**   Checks the availability and functionality of Exchange Web Services resources in the Office 365 deployment.
  - **Service Account Access (Developers)**   Checks the ability for a service account to access an Office 365 mailbox, create and delete items in the mailbox, and access the mailbox through Exchange Impersonation.
- Microsoft Office Outlook Connectivity Tests
  - **Outlook Connectivity**   Checks client connectivity to Office 365 using both RPC over HTTP and MAPI over HTTP.
  - **Outlook Autodiscover**   Checks the provisioning of Office 365 settings to outlook through the Autodiscover service.
- Internet Email Tests
  - **Inbound SMTP Email**   Checks that inbound SMTP email can be sent to the Office 365 domain.
  - **Outbound SMTP Email**   Checks that the Office 365 mail domain is correctly configured for Reverse DNS, Sender ID, and RBL (Realtime Blackhole List) checks.
  - **POP Email**   Performs a POP3 client email check against an Office 365 mailbox.
  - **IMAP Email**   Performs an IMAP4 client email check against an Office 365 mailbox.
- Mail Flow Configuration
  - **Verify Service Delivery Test**   Checks delivery from Office 365 by sending service-generated messages to a specified IP address.
  - **Verify MX Record and Outbound Connector Test**   Verifies MX record configuration and that Office 365 is configured to enable mail delivery on the basis of this record.
  - **Free/Busy Test**   Checks that an Office 365 mailbox is able to access free/busy information of an on-premises mailbox. Also checks that an on-premises mailbox is able to access the free/busy information of an Office 365 mailbox.

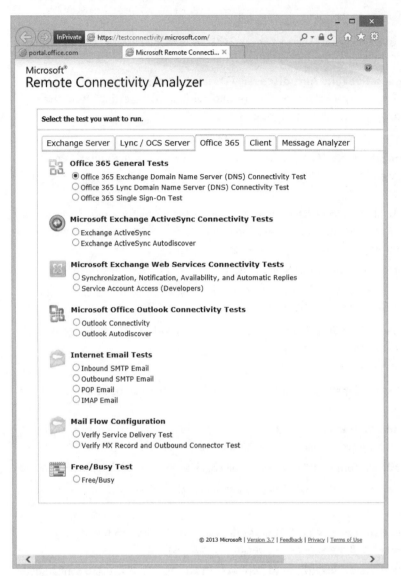

FIGURE 6-33 Office 365 tab

When you perform the test, the Microsoft Remote Connectivity Analyzer will provide details about the parts of the test that were performed successfully, any steps that failed, and possible resolution methods. Figure 6-34 shows the results of the Office 365 Exchange Domain Name Server (DNS) Connectivity test.

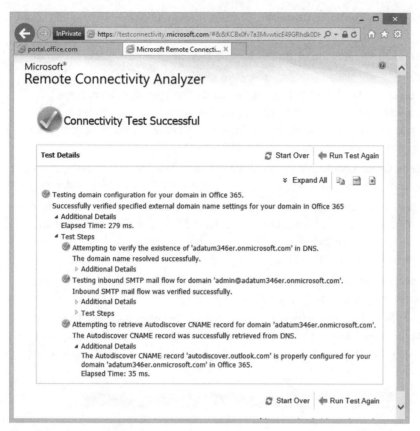

FIGURE 6-34 Successful test

> **MORE INFO** Microsoft Remote Connectivity Analyzer
>
> You can learn more about the Microsoft Remote Connectivity Analyzer at *https://technet. microsoft.com/en-US/library/ff701693%28v=exchg.150%29.aspx*.

Microsoft Connectivity Analyzer

The Microsoft Connectivity Analyzer is a companion tool for the Remote Connectivity Analyzer. The main difference between these tools is that you run the Microsoft Remote Connectivity Analyzer from a website on the Internet, whereas you run the Microsoft Connectivity Analyzer from your local on-premises infrastructure. Rather than run from a webpage, you download and install the tool from the Remote Connectivity Analyzer website.

The Microsoft Connectivity Analyzer allows you to perform connectivity tests against your on-premises messaging deployment as well as against Office 365. You can use the Microsoft Connectivity Analyzer, shown in Figure 6-35, to perform the following diagnostic tests:

- **I Can't Log On With Office Outlook**   This test checks Outlook Anywhere (RPC over HTTP) functionality.

- **I Can't Send Or Receive Email On My Mobile Device**   This test checks Exchange ActiveSync functionality.

- **I Can't Log On To Lync On My Mobile Device Or The Lync Windows Store App**   This check verifies that DNS records have been correctly configured in your on-premises environment. It also checks the Autodiscover web service to verify that authentication and certificates are configured correctly.

- **I Can't Send Or Receive Email From Outlook (Office 365 Only)**   This test verifies the incoming and outgoing SMTP configuration. The test will also check DNS configuration.

- **I Can't View The Free/Busy Information Of Another User**   This test will perform a check to see if an Office 365 mailbox can access the free/busy information of an on-premises mailbox, or that an on-premises mailbox is able to access the free/busy information of an Office 365 mailbox.

- **I Am Experiencing Other Problems With Outlook (English Only)**   This test checks for Outlook configuration problems.

- **I Can't Set Up Federation With Office 365, Azure, Or Other Services That Use Azure Active Directory**   This test checks the prerequisites for setting up federation between an on-premises Active Directory deployment, Office 365, and Azure Active Directory.

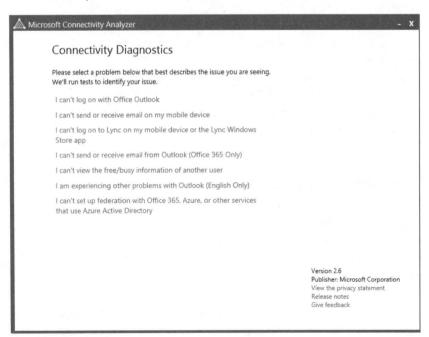

FIGURE 6-35 Connectivity Diagnostics

Transport Reliability IP Probe

The Transport Reliability IP Probe (TRIPP) is a tool that allows you to validate the following:

- The path between a computer and a specific Lync, now termed Skype for Business, online hosting location
- The availability of specific ports
- Routing to the Lync/Skype for Business datacenter
- Voice over IP quality
- Network speed

TRIPP performs the following tests:

- **Speed** This test will determine download and upload speed, data quality, and TCP efficiency. The test uses TCP port 443. Speeds below 1 Mbps will lead to problems with audio and video quality.

- **Rout** This test determines route quality by measuring packet loss, latency, round trip time, and ISP peering points and test uses ICMP.

- **VoIP** This test determines VoIP quality by assessing UDP loss and jitter. It uses UDP ports 50021 and 50022 It checks whether the round trip response time is consistent. Inconsistent round trip times may lead to choppy or jittery connections. In general, if there is more than a 5ms variance in round trip time, VoIP will be jittery. If greater than 2 percent packet loss is experienced, then the audio and video quality will be degraded.

- **Firewall** This test checks the following ports:

  - TCP port 443 for Client Signaling plus AppShare
  - TCP port 5061 for Federation Signaling
  - UDP port 3478 for Media Access
  - UDP ports in range 50,000 through 59,999 for Audio/Video transport tests

Hybrid Free/Busy Troubleshooter

The Hybrid Free/Busy Troubleshooter is a tool that you can access at *http://aka.ms/hybrid-freebusy*. It allows you to troubleshoot free/busy calendar issues when you have Office 365 deployed in a hybrid configuration with an on-premises Exchange deployment. The Hybrid Free/Busy Troubleshooter tool is designed to be used with Office 365 Tenant Administrator privileges.

Accessing the Hybrid Free/Busy Troubleshooter tool gives you the following options, shown in Figure 6-36:

- My Cloud User Cannot See Free/Busy For An On-Premises User
- My On-Premises User Cannot See Free/Busy For A Cloud User
- I Want To See Some Common Tools For Troubleshooting Free/Busy Issues

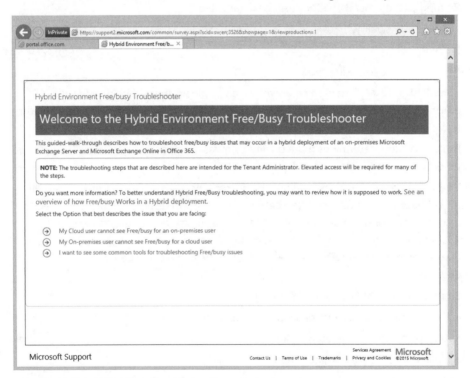

FIGURE 6-36 Hybrid Free/Busy Troubleshooter

Accessing the last of these options will link you to the Remote Connectivity Analyzer tool, advice on how to troubleshoot free and busy issues for Outlook 2007 and Outlook 2010 clients, as well as a video providing troubleshooting tips.

You can use the Hybrid Free/Busy Troubleshooter tool to troubleshoot free and busy issues for on-premises deployments of Exchange when your on-premises deployment uses Exchange Server 2010 or Exchange Server 2013 as shown in Figure 6-37.

FIGURE 6-37 Exchange 2010/2013 free/busy workflow

You can also use the Hybrid Environment Free/Busy Troubleshooter to assist in resolving issues if your organization's on-premises deployment is running Exchange 2007 as shown in Figure 6-38.

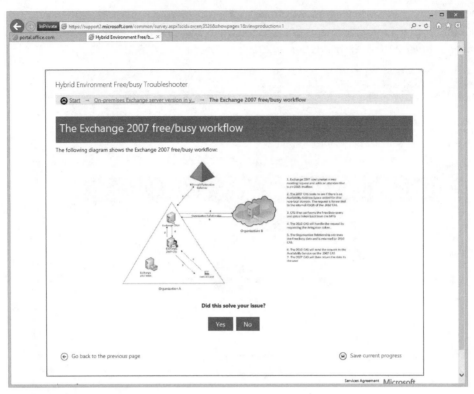

FIGURE 6-38 Exchange 2007 Free/Busy Workflow

The Hybrid Environment Free/Busy Troubleshooter can also be used to troubleshoot problems if your organization has Exchange 2003 as shown in Figure 6-39. It is reasonable to assume that when Exchange 2003 reaches the end of extended support, the Hybrid Environment Free/Busy Troubleshooter will no longer support this scenario. It is also reasonable to assume that when Exchange 2016 is released, the Hybrid Environment Free/Busy Troubleshooter will be updated to support scenarios involving the product.

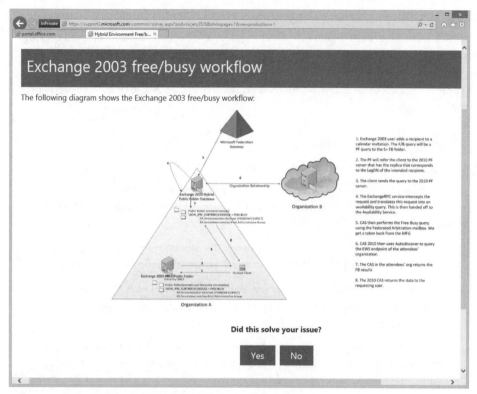

FIGURE 6-39 Exchange 2003 Free/Busy Workflow

MORE INFO **HYBRID FREE/BUSY TROUBLESHOOTER**

You can learn more about the Hybrid Free/Busy Troubleshooter at *http://blogs.techn et.com/b/exchange/archive/2013/06/03/the-hybrid-free-busy-troubleshooter-now-avail-able.aspx*.

EXAM TIP

Remember which tools you can use to diagnose specific problems. For example, when you might want to use the Transport Reliability IP Probe or when you might want to use the Microsoft Connectivity Analyzer.

Microsoft Online Services Diagnostics and Logging Support Toolkit

The 70-346 exam objectives mention the Microsoft Online Services Diagnostics and Logging Support Toolkit. This toolkit is no longer available from Microsoft and no information has been provided about a replacement. You can learn more about Office 365 troubleshooting tools at *http://social.technet.microsoft.com/wiki/contents/articles/24620.office-365-trouble-shooting-tools.aspx*.

Thought experiment
Office 365 diagnostics at Fabrikam

In this thought experiment, apply what you've learned about this objective. You can find the answers to these questions in the "Answers" section at the end of the chapter.

You are in the process of preparing to diagnose the functionality of your organization's Office 365 deployment. With this in mind, answer the following questions:

1. Which tool should you use to diagnose the functionality of your Office 365 deployment from the Internet when it comes to the automatic configuration of Outlook clients?

2. Which tool should you use to diagnose the functionality of your Office 365 deployment from your organization's on-premises network when it comes to the automatic configuration of Outlook clients?

Objective summary

- You can create a service request from the Office 365 Admin Center if you are having problems with Office 365. This involves specifying the type of problem you are having and providing supporting documentation.

- The Microsoft Remote Connectivity Analyzer is a website that allows you to run diagnostic tests against your on-premises Exchange or Office 365 messaging deployment from a location on the Internet.

- The Microsoft Connectivity Analyzer is a downloadable tool that you can use to run diagnostic tests against your on-premises Exchange or Office 365 messaging deployment from a computer on the organizational network.

- The Transport Reliability IP Probe is a set of diagnostic tools that you can use to verify the functionality of Skype for Business.

- The Hybrid Free/Busy Troubleshooter is a webbased tool that allows you to resolve free/busy calendar issues between on-premises mailboxes and those hosted in Office 365.

Objective review

Answer the following questions to test your knowledge of the information in this objective. You can find the answers to these questions and explanations of why each answer choice is correct or incorrect in the "Answers" section at the end of the chapter.

1. Which Microsoft Remote Connectivity Analyzer test should you run to verify that mobile devices are being correctly configured to access Office 365 mailboxes using ActiveSync?

   A. Exchange ActiveSync Autodiscover

   B. Exchange ActiveSync

   C. Outlook Connectivity

   D. Outlook Autodiscover

2. Which Microsoft Remote Connectivity Analyzer test should you run to verify that Outlook clients on the Internet are able to interact properly with Office 365 mailboxes?

   A. Outlook Autodiscover

   B. Exchange ActiveSync

   C. Outlook Connectivity

   D. Exchange ActiveSync Autodiscover

3. Which Microsoft Connectivity Analyzer test should you run to check incoming and outgoing SMTP configuration of your organization's Office 365 deployment?

   A. I can't log on with Office Outlook.

   B. I can't send or receive email on my mobile device.

   C. I can't send or receive email from Outlook (Office 365 Only).

   D. I can't log on to Lync/Skype for Business on my mobile device or the Lync/Skype for Business Windows Store app.

4. Which Microsoft Connectivity Analyzer test should you run to verify that a user is able to interact with their Office 365 mailbox using Outlook?

   A. I can't send or receive email from Outlook (Office 365 Only).

   B. I can't log on to Lync/Skype for Business on my mobile device or the Lync/Skype for Business Windows Store app.

   C. I can't send or receive email on my mobile device.

   D. I can't log on with Office Outlook.

Answers

This section contains the solutions to the thought experiments and answers to the objective review questions in this chapter.

Objective 6.1: Thought experiment

1. The Conferences report would provide information about the number of Skype for Business conferences held.

2. You would use the Active Users report to determine the number of users leveraging Skype for Business.

Objective 6.1: Review

1. **Correct answer:** D

   A. **Incorrect:** This report shows the number of active and inactive mailboxes over time.

   B. **Incorrect:** This report lists the number of mailboxes that have been created and the number that have been deleted.

   C. **Incorrect:** This report shows the total number of mailboxes associated with the Office 365 subscription, the number of mailboxes that are exceeding their storage quota, and the number of mailboxes using less than 25% of their storage limit.

   D. **Correct:** This report lists the number of mailboxes accessed by each of the following protocols: MAPI, Outlook on the web, Exchange ActiveSync, EWS, IMAP, and POP3.

2. **Correct answer:** C

   A. **Incorrect:** This report lists the number of mailboxes that have been created and the number that have been deleted.

   B. **Incorrect:** This report shows the total number of mailboxes associated with the Office 365 subscription, the number of mailboxes that are exceeding their storage quota, and the number of mailboxes using less than 25% of their storage limit.

   C. **Correct:** This report shows the number of active and inactive mailboxes over time. A mailbox is listed as inactive if the user associated with it has not connected for more than 30 days.

   D. **Incorrect:** This report lists the number of mailboxes accessed by each of the following protocols: MAPI, Outlook on the web, Exchange ActiveSync, EWS, IMAP, and POP3.

3. **Correct answer:** C

   A. **Incorrect:** This report allows you to view changes made to administrator role groups.

   B. **Incorrect:** This report provides information on all In-Place eDiscovery & Hold operations performed across the Office 365 subscription.

   C. **Correct:** You can use this report to search for mailboxes accessed by people other than their owners. One reason to use this report would be to check whether users with administrative privileges have accessed certain Office 365 mailboxes.

   D. **Incorrect:** This report shows all mailboxes that are configured for litigation hold.

4. **Correct answer:** B

   A. **Incorrect:** This report provides information on all In-Place eDiscovery & Hold operations performed across the Office 365 subscription.

   B. **Correct:** This report shows all mailboxes that are configured for litigation hold.

   C. **Incorrect:** This report allows you to view changes made to administrator role groups.

   D. **Incorrect:** You can use this report to search for mailboxes accessed by people other than their owners. One reason to use this report would be to check whether users with administrative privileges have accessed certain Office 365 mailboxes.

Objective 6.2: Thought experiment

1. You would use the Set-MailboxAuditBypassAssociation cmdlet to configure an audit logging bypass on a specific mailbox.

2. You would use the New-AdminAuditLogSearch cmdlet to search the administrator audit log, outputting the results as email to forward to your manager.

Objective 6.2: Review

1. **Correct answer:** B

   A. **Incorrect:** You should not assign the billing administrator role. The Office 365 user account used by the Management Pack must be assigned the global administrator role.

   B. **Correct:** The Office 365 user account used by the Management Pack must be assigned the global administrator role.

   C. **Incorrect:** You should not assign the service administrator role. The Office 365 user account used by the Management Pack must be assigned the global administrator role.

   D. **Incorrect:** You should not assign the user management administrator role. The Office 365 user account used by the Management Pack must be assigned the global administrator role.

2. **Correct answer:** B

   A. **Incorrect:** You cannot configure Skype for Business to inform you of changes in service status for your organization's Office 365 deployment.

   B. **Correct:** You can configure an RSS feed to notify you if there is a change in service status of your organization's Office 365 deployment.

   C. **Incorrect:** You cannot configure SharePoint to inform you of changes in service status for your organization's Office 365 deployment.

   D. **Incorrect:** You cannot configure OneDrive for Business to inform you of changes in service status for your organization's Office 365 deployment.

3. **Correct answer:** D

   A. **Incorrect:** You would consult the Resolved Incidents section of the Office 365 Monitoring Dashboard in Operations Manager rather than the Subscription Health section to determine if a particular incident had been resolved.

   B. **Incorrect:** You would consult the Resolved Incidents section of the Office 365 Monitoring Dashboard in Operations Manager rather than the Message Center section to determine if a particular incident had been resolved.

   C. **Incorrect:** You would consult the Resolved Incidents section of the Office 365 Monitoring Dashboard in Operations Manager rather than the Service Status section to determine if a particular incident had been resolved.

   D. **Correct:** You would consult the Resolved Incidents section of the Office 365 Monitoring Dashboard in Operations Manager to determine if a particular incident had been resolved.

Objective 6.3: Thought experiment

1. You should use the Microsoft Remote Connectivity Analyzer to check the functionality of your Office 365 deployment from the Internet.

2. You should use the Microsoft Connectivity Analyzer to perform Office 365 diagnostics from an on-premises environment.

Objective 6.3: Review

1. **Correct answer:** A

   A. **Correct:** The Exchange ActiveSync Autodiscover test checks whether a device will be properly configured through ActiveSync.

   B. **Incorrect:** The Exchange ActiveSync test only checks whether a device can connect to an Office 365 messaging resource, not that it is being correctly configured.

   C. **Incorrect:** The Outlook Connectivity test checks Outlook connectivity, not mobile device automatic configuration.

   D. **Incorrect:** The Outlook Autodiscover test checks whether Outlook will automatically be configured.

2. **Correct answer:** C

   A. **Incorrect:** The Outlook Autodiscover test checks whether Outlook will automatically be configured.

   B. **Incorrect:** The Exchange ActiveSync test only checks whether a mobile device can connect to an Office 365 messaging resource using ActiveSync. This test does not check Outlook.

   C. **Correct:** The Outlook Connectivity test checks Outlook connectivity and whether Outlook can connect to a mailbox resource.

   D. **Incorrect:** The Exchange ActiveSync Autodiscover test checks whether a device will be properly configured through ActiveSync.

3. **Correct answer:** C

   A. **Incorrect:** This test checks Outlook Anywhere (RPC over HTTP) functionality.

   B. **Incorrect:** This test checks Exchange ActiveSync functionality.

   C. **Correct:** This test verifies the incoming and outgoing SMTP configuration. The test will also check DNS configuration.

   D. **Incorrect:** This check verifies that DNS records have been correctly configured in your on-premises environment. It also checks the Autodiscover web service to verify that authentication and certificates are configured correctly.

4. **Correct Answer:** D

   A. **Incorrect:** This test verifies the incoming and outgoing SMTP configuration. The test will also check DNS configuration.

   B. **Incorrect:** This check verifies that DNS records have been correctly configured in your on-premises environment. It also checks the Autodiscover web service to verify that authentication and certificates are configured correctly.

   C. **Incorrect:** This test checks Exchange ActiveSync functionality.

   D. **Correct:** This test checks Outlook Anywhere (RPC over HTTP) functionality.

Index

billing administrator 75
delegated administrator 77
edit 14
global administrator 75
Global Administrator 258–260
password administrator role 77
service administrator 76
user management administrator 76
Personal Certificates 194, 226, 231
phone call authentication 104
pilot project
connecting existing email accounts for 36–37
creating test plan/use case for 35–36
designation of pilot users for 32
identifying workloads that don't require migration 32–33
planning 31–41
service descriptions 38–39
pilot users 32
connecting existing email accounts for 36
platform-as-a-service. *See* PaaS
POP email 277, 279
port 80 62
port 443 62
ports
firewall 60–61, 62
Post Incident Report 253
Power BI for Office 365 39
Primary Federation Server 219
primary name server 29
PrivacyLink parameter 234
private key
exporting 191–194
Project Online 38
project portfolio management 38
Project Professional software 39
Project Pro for Office 365 39
Protect Document menu 69
protected documents
recovery of 72
protection reports 247
Protect-RMSFile cmdlet 72
Prove You're Not A Robot page 8
Proxy Certificate 231
proxy form login customization 233–234
proxy servers
authentication 62
configuration 60

Proxy servers, AD FS
configuration of 229–233
installing and managing 225–234
installing required Windows roles and features 226–229
perimeter network name resolution 225–226
setting custom proxy forms login page 233–234
setting up certificates 226

R

Recycle Bin 115–116, 173
Redo-MsolProvisionContact cmdlet 124
Redo-MsolProvisionGroup cmdlet 120
Redo-MsolProvisionUser cmdlet 119
region
tenant 10
Remote Access role 226–229
remote tests 276–281
Remove-MsolAdministrativeUnit cmdlet 125
Remove-MsolAdministrativeUnitMember cmdlet 125
Remove-MsolContact cmdlet 124
Remove-MsolDomain cmdlet 121
Remove-MsolFederatedDomain cmdlet 122
Remove-MsolGroup cmdlet 120
Remove-MsolGroupMember cmdlet 120
Remove-MsolRoleMember cmdlet 81, 120
Remove-MsolScopedRoleMember cmdlet 125
Remove-MsolServicePrincipalCredential cmdlet 121
Remove-MsolUser cmdlet 103, 116, 118
reports
Azure Active Directory 246
Office 365 241–250
auditing reports 246
Data Loss Protection reports 248
mail reports 242
OneDrive for Business reports 246
protection reports 247
rules reports 248
SharePoint reports 245
Skype for Business reports 244–245
usage reports 243–244
Post Incident Report 253
Resolved Incidents 266
Restore-MsolUser cmdlet 119
Restrict Access menu 70
rights management 64–74
Azure Rights Management 64–73
Office integration with 68–71

About the author

ORIN THOMAS is an MVP, a Microsoft Regional Director, an MCT and has a string of Microsoft MCSE and MCITP certifications. He has written more than 30 books for Microsoft Press on topics including Windows Server, Windows Client, Azure, System Center, Exchange Server, Security, and SQL Server. He is an author at PluralSight and is a contributing editor at *Windows IT Pro* magazine. He has been working in IT since the early 1990's and regularly speaks at conferences in Australia and around the world. Orin founded and runs the Melbourne System Center, Security, and Infrastructure Group and is completing a Doctorate in Information Technology at Charles Sturt University. You can follow him on twitter at *http://twitter.com/orinthomas*.